SOL'S STORY

A triumph of the human spirit.

RICHARD CHARDKOFF

Dedication

This book is in memory of Sol's immediate family, his mother and father, Froim and Chaya, and his sisters, Frania and Tobcia, whose lives were taken in the Holocaust.

It is also a testament to Sol's refusal to die.

Acknowledgements

I am indebted to several people for their contributions to the book. The research grant provided by the University of Louisiana at Monroe enabled me to go to Poland and Germany and track, document, and verify Sol's extraordinary odyssey of survival through Eastern Europe. My typists, Jo Ann Lewis and Karen Darling, never faltered. Karen, especially, was always there to not only type, but offer suggestions for improvement. My daughter, Deena helped walk the book through the publication stage and provided valuable guidance and insight.

Finally, my wife, Joan, made the book possible. She read the early drafts of the manuscript, assisted with the writing and did much of the rewriting and proof-reading. She was involved in every phase of the book's evolution, from conception to the finished product. Her research, organizational, and writing skills, suggestions for improvement, and valuable insights helped guide the book to completion. Her extraordinary involvement made the book a reality.

To all, I extend my heartfelt thanks.

SOL'S STORY

A triumph of the human spirit.

RICHARD CHARDKOFF

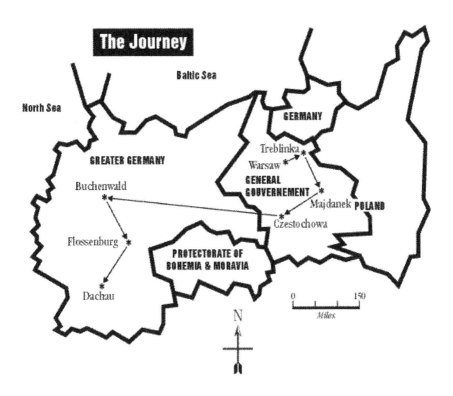

Prologue

Sol's Story

I first met Sol Rosenberg and his lovely wife, Tola, more than 25 years ago when I moved to the small southern town of Monroe, Louisiana. I had been hired as a professor at The University of Louisiana at Monroe. I forget the exact occasion when I met Sol, but I do remember he had an outgoing personality and greeted my wife and me warmly. He had many friends and was known and respected within the entire community.

In his late forties, Sol was still an extremely good-looking man. Five foot six and stocky, he was muscular and full of strength and vitality. He had sparkling blue eyes and a full head of reddish-brown hair, which I could only envy. He seemed to take pride in his appearance and was always very sharply dressed.

By any measure, Sol was extremely successful. He had arrived in the United States as a poor immigrant with a weak grasp of English. After arriving in New Orleans, he settled in Monroe. He first found work in a local furniture store loading and unloading furniture onto vans. Later, he took a job in a scrap iron yard, again involving heavy labor. After several years he had learned enough to branch out and begin his own pipe and steel business. It was not long before it became a thriving multi-state enterprise, which supported him and his five children in more than adequate style.

I suppose, however, the main reason I was so impressed by Sol is that I was told both he and Tola had survived the concentration camps. Yet neither seemed bitter; on the contrary, both seemed to thoroughly enjoy life. People talked about what Sol and Tola had experienced in hushed tones, but no one seemed to know the details. For my part, in spite of my curiosity, I did not raise the subject.

Then, on April 28, 1995, there was a memorial service at the Temple to commemorate the Holocaust, or "Yom Ha Sho-ah," and to honor both the dead and the survivors of that tragedy. The Mayor of Monroe was present and proclaimed a Day of Remembrance. Sol Rosenberg was to be the main speaker. I sat transfixed for almost an hour, as Sol described the horrifying details of his life in the death camps more than fifty years before. Sol admitted that even though they were not visible, he still carried the emotional scars which time could not heal. As I strained to listen from the back of the packed hall, Sol's voice was low and his European accent thick. Even though I could not comprehend all Sol said, I heard enough to know that his very brief account could not begin to adequately describe the horror of his experiences. I knew that I wanted to learn more.

Yet, even after his speech at the Temple, Sol was still not ready to say any more about his past. I am not really certain why he finally changed his mind after so many years. However, I suspect he realized he wasn't getting any younger. He wanted his children and their children to know what he had survived. Perhaps, also, he was affected by "revisionist" historians who denied the very existence of events Sol and Tola had endured. Finally, the movie "Schindler's List," and especially Stephen Spielberg's Shoah Foundation, helped raise public consciousness about the Holocaust. Sol participated in Spielberg's Survivors of the Shoah Visual History Foundation project, recording his story on tape to add to the many others. In a locally televised interview, recorded when Spielberg's representatives came to Monroe, Sol said that he felt he had a responsibility to those who had died to make sure the truth was told by someone who had lived through these horrific events.

Sol first spoke to me about helping him tell his story in the fall of 1995. I imagine this was because I was a history professor as well as a friend. Initially I was hesitant. I told Sol that my only writing experience was with scholarly articles. I didn't feel confident I could do justice to Sol's story, but Sol insisted. Countless hours of interviews followed. The more I listened to Sol, the more fascinated, perhaps even obsessed, I became. Sol's repressed thoughts came back to him in piecemeal fashion. After years of trying to block these traumatic memories, Sol found it difficult to reconstruct the details of what happened within a chronological framework. Everything he did remember was disjointed and out of sequence. He alternated from vague impressions to total recall. Gradually, over many months, we put together an entire mosaic from the broken fragments of his memories. Once Sol surprised even himself, blurting out his thoughts in German, a language he hadn't used in fifty years. Tola, on the other hand, just listened. Apparently, even after all these years, she found the memories just too painful.

The result is the story of a young boy cruelly uprooted from a normal life. Nothing could have prepared him for the unimaginable horror he was to go through. The war destroyed life as he had known it forever. For almost six years, he endured physical pain, starvation, misery, and terror. Yet, despite everything, Sol was determined to survive and to outlast his enemies. He was able to escape the slaughter that befell most of his family and friends, as well as millions of others. Sol's story is an inspirational account of the triumph of the human spirit. Though defenseless, Sol resisted the Nazi genocide machine with determination and resourcefulness. He somehow managed to survive the war with both his dignity and sense of humanity intact.

This account is a tribute not only to Sol Rosenberg, but to all the other innocent victims of war. I only hope that I have done justice both to Sol and his story, which definitely deserves to be told.

Chapter I

The Early Years

Sol's parents lived in the unsettled times that followed World War I. On Sol's mother's side, the family was well-established and rather wealthy. Sol's grandfather, Dr. Jacob Deurschmann, was a quiet, dignified, and well-respected veterinarian in Breslau, Germany. His professional expertise was well known. Due to his reputation, he was invited to Warsaw by a member of the Polish cavalry to examine one of their prized horses that had been crippled in a riding accident. Dr. Deurschmann traveled to Warsaw, examined the horse, and recommended surgery to save the horse's life. The Polish veterinarians agreed and asked him to perform the operation, an intricate and delicate task they were anxious to avoid, due to the high risk that would be involved. The surgery was successful and while waiting for the horse to recover, Dr. Deurschmann had an opportunity to explore Warsaw.

Always energetic and adventurous, he spent several days walking the streets and getting to know the various neighborhoods. During this time, he decided to move his family to the Polish capital, where he thought he would have more professional opportunities. Upon his return to Breslau, Dr. Deurschmann told his wife of his decision. After much discussion she agreed. Before very long he sold his home and business, and moved his family

to Warsaw's Jewish Quarter. There he set about building a
successful veterinary practice. In the following years, he and
Sol's grandmother, Rahula, had four children, two daughters and
two sons. Sol's mother, Chaya, was the youngest child. Like her
brothers and sister, she was attractive, with a fair complexion and
striking red hair.

Even as a teenager, Chaya had a strong personality and an
optimistic outlook. She was very driven in everything she did,
whether household chores or schoolwork, and her parents were
proud of her and her accomplishments. Many of the characteristics
that would help her family through the dark days of occupation
became evident during her teenage years: inner strength, determination, and selflessness. Nourished by her parents, who had a deep
sense of family, Chaya and her siblings were very close.

Sol's father, Froim, and his family were natives of
Warsaw; but they were still considered relative newcomers,
having been in the city for only three generations. His ancestors
on his father's side could also be traced back to Germany. In the
late nineteenth century, his great-grandfather had moved to
Warsaw in search of better economic opportunities. There, he
established a small bakery. Under his son, Sol's grandfather, the
bakery underwent considerable expansion. By the time Sol was
born, the family-owned business, known as the Rosenberg
Bakery, had become one of the most successful bakeries in the
city. It served residents throughout the community through daily
deliveries in a horse-drawn wagon.

As a child, Froim helped in the family bakery. He decided
early in life that he, too, would become a baker. As the youngest
of ten children, Froim did not receive an inheritance, but his
parents did help him start his own business. He met and married
Sol's mother when they were both only teenagers. Shortly after
their marriage, Froim and Chaya opened a bakery in a family-
owned complex on Grujecka Street. The complex included not
only baking facilities, but an attached store, a comfortable and

spacious upstairs apartment, and a stable, complete with stalls for the horses, a pony, and a delivery wagon. Next door to the stable, Sol's grandfather maintained a blacksmith shop and feed supply store for horses. The businesses were family owned, and many of the workers were family members. This created a good working environment and loyal employees. Through long hours and hard work, the Rosenbergs achieved financial success. Within a few years, as their business grew, Froim and Chaya were able to save enough money to buy the property outright.

During these relatively happy times, the Rosenbergs began their family. Sol's older sister, Frania, was born late in 1924. Sol was born on November 18, 1926, when Frania was two years old. Then, in 1928, when Sol was two years old, Tobcia, his younger sister, was born. As a child, Sol was captivated by his mother's beauty. He would repeatedly ask his father, "How were you so lucky to find such a beautiful woman as Mamala to marry?"

Frania, Sol's older sister, grew to become quite statuesque. As a teenager, she was about five feet six inches tall, and wore her brown hair combed straight back. She was quiet, almost shy, soft-spoken, and attractive. She was popular, and her friends would often visit in the evenings. She enjoyed dressing up; much to the dismay of her mother, she wore lipstick and jewelry, which made her look much older. Indeed, Frania had to hide her lipstick from Chaya, who remained adamant—no lipstick or makeup until Frania was older. Frania was very close to Sol, not only in age, but in outlook. She was very proud of him, introduced him to all her friends, and included him in her activities. She faithfully attended Sol's soccer games, where she would loudly yell her support.

As Frania became a teenager, she became obsessed with her weight. Although Sol always thought she was attractive, Frania remained self-conscious about her figure. Concerned, Chaya spoke of the problem to her sister, Sara, who was well-to-do compared with the other members of the family. Sara offered to take Frania to the country in the summer. It was hoped that the fresh air and wholesome food would take Frania's mind off her weight. For several summers, Frania accompanied her aunt to the country, where she enjoyed herself. Under the watchful eye of her Aunt Sara, she ate three balanced meals a day. However, as soon as Frania returned to the city to start school in the fall, she would once again revert to her old habits and starve herself to lose weight. Instead of eating the lunches that Chaya prepared for her, she would give them to less fortunate strangers whom she saw on the street on her way to school. Although Sol was aware of what she was doing, he kept her secret.

Tobcia, too, was blessed with fine features: large brown eyes, a beautiful smile, and long curly brown hair, which she either combed straight back or parted in the middle. She also looked much older than her years because of her poise and physical grace. When she was not yet twelve, she appeared to be sixteen. Indeed, her looks did not go unnoticed by Sol's friends or by the other boys in the neighborhood. Unlike her older sister, Tobcia had an independent spirit and did not lack self-confidence. This was reflected in her personality, enthusiastic, decisive, and thoroughly captivating. She loved to flirt and attracted many friends of both sexes. Moreover, she was a natural athlete, strong, muscular, and well-coordinated, even at an early age. She used her height and strength to good advantage on the school volley-ball team, where she became one of the best players.

Tobcia also loved to dance. At home in the evenings she would practice her dancing with Sol. On weekends she would persuade Sol to wind up the old hand-cranked Victrola that had been borrowed from an uncle; then the two would dance around the kitchen of their apartment. Sometimes, after the song on the record was over, Tobcia would sit Sol down and sing to him. Sol grew very close to both of his sisters. He was also very protective of them.

Froim and Chaya's economic success allowed them to hire Olesza, a Ukrainian maid, to help with the children and housework. Olesza, in her mid-twenties, lived with the family, sleeping on a small roll-away bed. The family adored her and treated her as one of their own. Froim even hired her boyfriend to work in the bakery. When Sol was a toddler, after Olesza had finished her chores, she often took Sol to Saski Park. There, Olesza would sit on a park bench and chat with the other maids and nannies while keeping an eye on Sol. For his part, Sol soon joined in games with other boys he met in the park.

Although Sol's parents didn't know it, Olesza, who was very devout, sometimes took Sol to services in the neighborhood Catholic church. Since Olesza was far from home and with no family in Poland, the church filled a void in her life and eased her loneliness. But for Sol, the services proved to be an initial exposure to institutionalized anti-Semitism. Sermons blamed the Jews for all the world's ills and reinforced the ever-present anti-Semitism in Polish society. Sol could not understand why Jews were the target. He became very uncomfortable as he sat rigidly in his pew, stone-faced and silent. But even as a young boy, he questioned this deep-seated prejudice. However, he never told Olesza of his discomfort. Nor did he ask her not to take him to church because he sensed how much it meant to her.

When he was six, Sol was enrolled in a neighborhood public school. He looked forward to classes and to being with his new friends. He enjoyed his days and maintained an even balance between his studies and after-school sports. During these early years, Sol developed a passion for soccer. His enthusiasm for the game kept him at school after classes ended so that he could play pick-up games. He quickly mastered the sport and became one of the top players at the school. This boosted his self-confidence and greatly enhanced his popularity.

All three children had been assigned jobs to do before and after school. One of Sol's tasks was to feed and care for the delivery horses at the bakery. Each morning before school, when the first loaves of bread came out of the ovens, Sol brushed, fed, and hitched up the horses for deliveries.

After the delivery wagons left, Sol would spend a few moments with his pet pigeons before hurrying off to school. The pigeons were in a small outer room above the stable. Sol would pull a rope which hung down from the stable ceiling in order to release a ladder. He would then climb up through a trap door to the roof to visit his pigeons. In addition, every day, late in the afternoon following soccer practice, he returned to clean out the cage and feed his pigeons bread which he tore into small pieces and placed on a tray in the cage. When Sol could not be there, the pigeons were fed by one of Froim's employees. There was a total of twelve pigeons—all purchased by Sol's grandfather, Dr. Deurschmann. Sol named all of them; he could identify them individually by their color and markings, and enjoyed watching them. They appeared so gentle and so innocent. His fascination with the birds made it difficult for him to leave them. Many days his father would have to climb the steps to tell Sol it was time to go home for dinner.

These early years for Sol were full of happy memories. His relatives, including a large extended family, were warm and close-knit. Social life centered around community functions. A calendar of engagement parties, weddings, birthdays, and religious festivities enriched their lives and kept them busy. Moreover, his father's business success provided a sense of security.

Then, without warning, in 1935, Sol's parents experienced a severe economic setback as a result of a worldwide depression. They were forced to liquidate all their assets. Although Sol was too young to understand the cause of the sudden reversal in the family's fortunes, he accepted these changes without question. Yet he knew that his sheltered existence was disrupted. He could sense how worried his parents were; they became quiet whenever the children were present, but when they were alone in their bedroom, Sol overheard them speaking in hushed but anxious tones. After his sisters had gone to sleep, in the quiet of the night, he eavesdropped as his parents talked about whether they would be able to pay their bills. They worried about having enough money for the future: money to educate their children, to provide a dowry for their daughters, or even to provide the basic necessities of life. Their anxiety left Sol unsettled; for the first time in his life he felt a sense of insecurity. Sol and his sisters had not previously known adversity. They also missed Olesza, who had been let go. She had been Sol's friend and confidant for as long as Sol could remember. For him and his sisters, she was not an employee, but a member of the family, and her loss was like a death.

The poor economy affected many other Poles, and many of their neighbors were hit by similar reversals. But most of them were used to hardship; they stubbornly refused to give up and prepared to fight to build a better future for their families. Likewise, Froim and Chaya, while down, were not defeated. With the resources they still had available, they purchased a much smaller apartment on the second floor of a five-story complex at 49 Nowalipki Street in the Old Quarter.

Their new neighborhood was much more depressed than their former one. Architecturally, the district was a contrast of different styles, with buildings huddled closely together in congested city blocks. Small industries and many family-owned retail businesses were crowded along crooked streets in the same buildings that housed tenement apartments. Scattered throughout the district were restaurants, cafes, theaters, bakeries, and delicatessens, as well as religious and cultural organizations. Sidewalk stalls were everywhere. Push-carts and salesmen peddling their wares added to the congestion during working hours. Noise filled the streets as buyers and sellers haggled over prices. Their apartment building itself, like hundreds of others in the district, was run-down and in need of repair. Built of brick in the mid-to-late nineteenth century, it was a big comedown from their former home. The new apartment was modest and very confining. It lacked the space, privacy, and amenities of the former, such as a telephone. All family members had to make adjustments to accommodate one another. Furthermore, there were only two bedrooms, one for the parents, and a second of similar size for the three children. Sol and his two sisters eventually managed to carve out their "living space" in their cramped bedroom, but there was very little privacy. The only other room, the kitchen, served as both a living and dining room. In future years, it was here at the dinner table that all major family discussions would take place.

A long, narrow hallway connected the kitchen to the two bedrooms. A bathroom with an old freestanding copper tub was located at the end of the hall. There was no hot water, so the family had to heat the water on the coal-burning stove in the kitchen, and then carry it down the hall to the tub. Also, they had to share the bathroom with the next-door neighbors, each family possessing a key. A schedule was drawn up, and everyone had to knock first to make sure the bathroom was vacant. The whole arrangement was inconvenient, especially as the children got older and had to get in and out of the bathroom quickly in order to get to school on time. Nevertheless, young Sol felt very fortunate, for he knew that many apartments had no bathrooms at all and the tenants had to use a public bathroom on the street below.

Laundry posed another problem. Without Olesza to help, Chaya and the girls shared new responsibilities. Sol's mother had to first heat the water on the stove and then pour it into a wooden vat in the kitchen. She would then dump the clothes in, rub them back and forth over a scrub board, rinse them, and wring them out. If the stains and dirt on the clothes were not removed, the entire process had to be repeated. When Chaya was finished, the clothes were boiled briefly on top of the stove, and wrung out yet again. Finally, the girls helped her carry the laundry up the narrow stairwell to the sixth floor roof where they would hang it on the family clothesline. When the weather was bad, temporary lines had to be strung throughout the small apartment.

Froim, together with his older brother Aaron, purchased a small bakery on Dzielona Street. The new bakery was located in a poorer neighborhood than the previous one. However, milling crowds filled the street daily, and there was a very competitive business atmosphere. Artisans, who engaged in a number of skilled crafts, owned and operated their own small businesses. Jewelers, shoemakers, clothiers, watchmakers, and tailors competed with one another and kept customer traffic flowing. Moreover, although the bakery was over a mile away, it was within walking distance of the apartment. While limited in space, its equipment and ovens were actually more modern than in the larger bakery they had owned previously.

Through hard work and with the help of the whole family, the apartment and business took shape. All of the children were assigned tasks to keep them busy and take their minds off the move. Floors were scrubbed, walls were painted, and electrical and plumbing work completed. Through it all, Chaya maintained an upbeat attitude and never gave in to defeat. She had a deep affection for her children and sensing their concern, she did her best to boost their spirits and praise their work. Froim amazed Sol with his carpentry and electrical skills, as he rewired the ovens and prepared the bakery for its opening. Finally the long awaited day arrived. The neighborhood supported the new business enthusiastically because of the quality of the bread, reasonable prices, and good honest service. However, the family earned less money due to the bakery's location in a more depressed neighborhood and because they no longer had a wagon to help distribute their goods. Also, they had to share their profits with Froim's brother, Aaron.

Yet the Rosenbergs were determined to do whatever it took to make a success of their business. The bakery was open Sunday through Friday. Saturday, the Sabbath, the bakery was closed; while the Rosenbergs did not attend Synagogue regularly, they did use the day to sleep late and rest from their exhausting schedules. The day of rest was welcome, for Sunday was one of their busiest days. However, opening on Sunday violated the

Warsaw blue laws which ordered businesses to close on that day. But Froim and Chaya dealt with that difficulty by giving baked goods as "gifts" to the local police so they would turn a blind eye and permit the bakery to remain open.

The family could not afford a car, so Froim would leave for work every morning at 4:00 A.M. No matter what the season—the oppressive heat of summer or the cold of winter—he would walk to work to begin the many tasks that went into making bread and pastries. Days were long and hard, and the heat from the ovens in such a confined area drained his energy. There was no free time. Chores seemed to be never ending, but Froim was well organized and never complained. He worked briskly with little lost motion. Many years of experience had taught him what to do and when to do it. Froim started each day determined to turn out the best possible product. He took pride in his work, and he prepared his pastries with great care. The bread always tasted as good as it looked. In fact, many people who were just passing by on the street would smell the aroma of freshly baked bread and come in to make a purchase. The bakery was Froim's life, his passion, and it gave him a sense of self-worth.

Before long, Froim's bread began appearing on tables throughout the community. Froim's success as a baker was in large part due to Chaya, who often accompanied him to work. She relieved him of the burden of financial accountability, as she monitored the business as well as household finances. Deliberate, shrewd, and careful, and with a better education than her husband, Chaya made certain money was well-managed and used only for necessities both at home and at work. While Froim baked, Chaya balanced the books, ordered bakery staples, and paid the bills. She even helped make sales, as she was able to win over customers because of her friendly and efficient manner. Meanwhile, Froim was so busy with his work that some evenings he would stay at the bakery all night, cleaning and repairing the ovens. It was hard work, and kept the parents away from the children much of the time.

Not only did Sol see much less of his parents and have to learn to get along without Olesza, he even had to give away his pigeons as there was no longer any place to keep them. As if all these changes were not enough, the move meant that Sol had to change schools and give up all his old friends. Although classified as a public school, the school where he was enrolled in the new neighborhood was administered by the Catholic church. For all practical purposes, it was parochial. Of the more than 1,000 students, only a few were Jews or Protestants. Sol was the only non-Catholic in his class. As part of his daily schedule, he was forced to attend Mass. This was very foreign to him, and he felt quite uncomfortable. He refused to make the sign of the cross and only mouthed the prayers. Nor did Sol like the compulsory school uniform: dark trousers and a blue jacket with a handkerchief in the pocket worn with a white shirt.

Froim and Chaya sensed Sol's unhappiness. After dinner when the table had been cleared, they asked him what was troubling him. Trying to reassure him, Chaya told him to "just do what you feel comfortable with, and never be ashamed of who you are." Sol knew his parents were doing the best they could under the circumstances. He knew they would have moved him to another school if they were doing better economically. In the meantime, Sol, while not enthusiastic, was an obedient student and generally well-behaved. He made the necessary adjustments, started making new friends, and began to apply himself to his studies. He excelled in mathematics, his favorite subject. Knowing that the bakery business meant long hours and low profits, Sol's parents hoped his interest in mathematics would lead Sol to a career as an engineer.

In spite of the family's reduced standard of living, dinner was always a special occasion, for it was the only time during the day they were all together. Froim tried to be home for dinner even on evenings when he had to return to the bakery to finish his chores or prepare for the next day. In spite of all the demands on

Chaya's time, she always prepared special dishes, which all enjoyed. After dinner, Froim and Chaya questioned the children about their school day. When they finished, Froim picked up a newspaper and slowly and deliberately read articles aloud, describing events happening worldwide. He was especially interested in current events in Europe, particularly news from Germany and Austria. Froim wanted the children to be aware of political developments in those countries.

One evening in November 1938, shortly before Sol's twelfth birthday, Froim read the accounts of "Kristillnacht," or the night of the broken glass. Ordered by Hitler himself, Kristallnacht was a convulsion of anti-Jewish violence which resulted in the looting and destruction of Jewish businesses throughout Germany and Austria as well as in the murder of Jews. The Nazis then decreed a number of blatantly anti-Semitic laws designed to bankrupt the Jews and drive them from Germany. The shocking accounts alarmed the children as they sat transfixed, listening gravely to Froim's every word. During the next two weeks, the approach of Sol's twelfth birthday was almost forgotten as the family came to realize the seriousness of the persecution. They discussed the desperate plight of Germany's Jews and their own uncertain fate with mounting concern.

Through these discussions, the children gradually became aware of the growing threat of Nazism to all of Europe. As they learned more about the world, the children grew more anxious about Germany's future designs on Poland. This was especially true in the Spring of 1939. Hitler began to demand diplomatic concessions from Poland, the "repatriation" of the Free City of Danzig to Germany, and transit across Polish territory to East Prussia. Lively and animated conversation always followed Froim's reading of the newspaper articles describing the latest German threats. There were so many questions. The girls took the lead, as Sol's youth and lack of historical knowledge about Poland limited his participation in the discussions. Nevertheless, he listened attentively. The girls wanted to know what the outcome of Nazi behavior in Germany would mean for the German people and themselves. Would Poland be partitioned and absorbed by its neighbors once again if it gave in to German threats? Froim tried to calm and reassure them. Perhaps he did not want to worry the children, or he may have completely misread the situation. It is also possible that Froim simply did not want to believe his own intuition. But on the surface he appeared convinced that Nazi rule was only a temporary evil. He felt it would pass and that in the end there would be continued peace and stability in Europe. As for the security of the Polish nation, Froim did not believe Germany would violate its sovereignty. While Sol did not openly contradict his father partly for fear it would upset his sisters, over time he came to believe that his father was misguided. Instinctively, he knew something wasn't right. He could not understand his father's logic and did not agree with his conclusions. Inwardly, he knew he could neither accept nor accommodate himself to Nazi rule. But, as he became more aware of the worsening conditions in Germany, his immediate concern was for his family's welfare.

Froim made Sol aware of the barriers in place to prevent Jewish advancement. Yet, he told the children of his hope that future elections would end the age-old discrimination against Jews, and prayed that officials sensitive to Jewish problems would be elected. He was hopeful that equality would be enforced by new legislation. Sol saw the discrimination first-hand when his cousins, who wanted to attend medical school, were rejected by Polish medical schools and forced to apply to schools in Austria, Germany, or Italy, where entrance quotas were not as restrictive. The many Jewish theaters, clubs, restaurants, and social organizations in their district were further evidence to Sol that Jews were not welcome in Polish establishments; therefore, they were forced to open associations and clubs of their own.

Because of his long days, usually beginning before dawn, by dinnertime Froim was very tired; he began to doze off shortly after the discussions ended and excused himself. Chaya, who followed the same exhausting schedule, stayed up with the children a bit longer. On school nights, she helped the children make their lunches for the next day, and then she would count out change for each to buy tokens for the streetcar ride to school. She was also the one Sol would go to for an allowance.

After lunch was made, Chaya, by now visibly tired, went to her bedroom. The children helped clear the table, and wash, dry, and put away the cutlery and china, according to their assigned jobs. When they finished, they went to their room, laid out their school notebooks and books for the next day, and finished their homework assignments. Oftentimes, however, they turned from their studies to discuss the newspaper articles Froim had read earlier. They did not understand the reasons for the growing wave of anti-Semitic legislation in Germany and the continuing curbs in place in Poland, but they were all concerned. Their only hope was that the anti-Semitism could be contained in Germany and die there before it spread elsewhere.

When Sol left for school in the morning, he did not use the money that Chaya had given him for the trolleys as intended; instead he would hop aboard the streetcar and jump off when the conductor approached to collect the fares. He then would walk to school or hitch a ride on another trolley for a few blocks before jumping off again. The streetcar money was saved until after school, when Sol would use it to buy ice cream on his way to soccer practice at the Maccabee Club.

Every spring, Froim and Chaya looked forward to Passover; these were the busiest days of the year for the bakery. Froim hired additional help and spent almost every night at the bakery cleaning the ovens and utensils from the day's work and preparing for the increased trade the following day. Normally, enough money would be earned so that Chaya could take the girls shopping. They could only afford to buy the most basic items, but Frania and Tobcia enjoyed the simple pleasure of spending a day going to the stores. This was their once-a-year treat and they always appreciated it. They returned at dinnertime, exhausted yet excited. Loaded down with shopping bags and seemingly all three talking at once, they proudly displayed their purchases to Sol and Froim.

Froim and Chaya had to watch what they spent very carefully. They were frugal whenever possible, but they still managed to save a small amount of money for unforeseen circumstances. One spring evening, Froim called the children into the kitchen. He told them to look closely at the chandelier hanging from the kitchen ceiling. The chandelier had highly polished brass arms with beautifully cut crystal droplets extending down from each cup. It had been in the family for at least two generations. It had hung in the dining room of their former home on Grujecka Street, giving the room an air of elegance. Because it was a family heirloom and very valuable, Froim and Chaya had kept it during their move. It was with great difficulty that they had transferred it to their new apartment. Since they did not have a dining room, living room, or even a spacious entrance hall, Froim had hung it from the kitchen ceiling. Although it overwhelmed the small room, to the Rosenbergs it was a comforting link to the past.

Following their father's instructions, Sol and the girls looked at the chandelier. At first Sol saw nothing unusual, but Froim insisted they look even closer. Barely visible inside the cups of the light bulb holders were twenty-dollar gold pieces; Froim had purchased them at the money exchange and then inserted them in the fixture. The money, Froim told them, was to be used only for an emergency. "I want you to know there is something," Froim said, "in case I am not available and there is an emergency. No one else is to know of this family secret." This was the first and last time that Sol ever heard of a family "savings account."

With a reduced income, the family never took trips and had little opportunity to even go on family outings. Sol rarely saw his parents enjoy themselves. However, Froim did treat himself to one luxury. Once a week, Chaya would pack clean clothes in a small suitcase, and Froim would walk to a Turkish bath several blocks from the apartment. There, he would relax, get a massage, and use the sauna; for just a short while, he could close his eyes and forget the pressures of business and demands of family. Froim often asked Sol to go with him. Sol considered the sauna a special treat. Unfortunately, because of the popularity of the baths, customers were limited to only one hour. Yet, even this brief time was better than none at all.

Another pleasure which Sol looked forward to was when his maternal grandfather came to visit. Dr. Deurshmann, although he had lived in Poland for many years, still retained many German customs. In fact, when he was present, they all spoke German at home. Now phasing out his practice, he had more free time and visited the family often. During these visits, he would wink at Sol and ask him to join him for a walk. Sol accompanied his grandfather to a local tavern. There Dr. Deurshmann ordered his favorite beer, which he always shared with his grandson. Then he would sit back in his chair and question Sol about school, his extracurricular activities, and his friends. Sometimes they talked for the better part of an hour, with Dr. Deurshmann showing genuine interest in all of Sol's activities. Often Sol would ask his grandfather to tell him what his mother had been like when she was a girl. As he listened, Sol tried to imagine how his mother had looked then, and what kinds of mischief she had been involved in. He always wished he had more time with his grandfather. After they finished their beer, they walked back to the apartment. Froim was aware of his father-in-law's slyness, but he had too much respect for him to ever tell Chaya, who would be sure to disapprove.

Sol also accompanied his grandfather around the city as he tended to his work. Dr. Deurshmann made house calls to visit sick horses or to appraise horses that were to be put up for sale. They rode in his grandfather's two-wheeled wagon pulled by one of Dr. Deurschmann's favorite horses. A pony was always tethered to the back of the wagon, and often Sol would ride it. Sometimes Sol would wait for his grandfather in the wagon. Frequently, however, Sol would join him on his consultations. He couldn't help but notice that when they were in the poorer neighborhoods he did not charge for his services. When they finished their visits, they would go to the park where Dr. Deurshmann would sit on a bench and watch Sol play soccer, or go to a tavern to drink beer together.

The two took many such excursions. On one occasion they rode to Bonyfraterskat Street, where they stopped in front of a sanitarium for the mentally retarded. Dr. Deurshmann talked to the inmates who gathered behind the barred windows, waving and yelling unintelligible words. "What are they saying? ," asked Sol.

"They are asking for cigarettes," answered his grandfather. Dr. Deurshmann would always oblige them. The inmates became excited and lowered a long string to the ground. The cigarettes were then tied to the string in a knot and the inmates pulled them up to their second floor window. Minutes later Sol and his grandfather were doused with water. Grandfather Deurshmann laughed heartily. For some unknown reason, he appeared to enjoy the whole exchange. He promised Sol they would return again soon. However, one drenching was enough for Sol. The next time, Sol promised himself, he would watch the second floor window more carefully.

Sol's grandfather was a creative, intelligent man, with a strong sense of family, and Sol admired him tremendously. At the same time, Sol felt very comfortable around him. Dr. Deurshmann seemed to have the wisdom of years without the problems of age. Although his hair was already threaded with gray, he was in excellent health, vibrant, and very active. Sol looked upon him as more of a friend and co-conspirator than a grandfather.

The family was not deeply religious although they did maintain Jewish traditions. They kept the Sabbath and holidays faithfully. Chaya left the bakery early every Friday afternoon to do her shopping for the Sabbath and begin cooking. That evening when the family sat down for dinner, they were greeted with the wonderful scents of a meal that was always special. The kitchen was transformed; the table was covered with a beautiful white tablecloth. On it Chaya placed her best dinnerware and two well-polished brass candlesticks. Froim led the family in prayers and then the Rosenbergs enjoyed a traditional meal of soup, roast chicken, cooked vegetables, and Froim's freshly made breads and dessert pastries. They attended Synagogue sporadically, but always observed the High Holidays on a regular basis. Moreover, Sol was sent to Hebrew School several days a week, where he studied Jewish History and Hebrew, so that he would be able to read the Holy Books.

Like most young boys, Sol's interests lay elsewhere. His passion for sports preoccupied his thoughts. To work off his excess energy, of which there was a great deal, he participated in soccer after school. The Rosenbergs took out a low-cost membership in a nearby athletic club, the Maccabee Club. Sol could hardly wait until after school each day to go there. He was able to develop his athletic ability under the supervision of veteran coaches. Since Sol's parents could not afford special soccer shoes, he was forced to play barefoot. The field was rough, and on many days, practice left his feet bruised and sore. But Sol knew that he had to keep his shoes clean for school, so he never even thought about wearing these shoes for soccer. Nor did he ask his parents to buy him soccer shoes because he knew they would have if they could have afforded it.

Nevertheless, Sol soon became one of the leading players on the club team; secretly he hoped someday to become a professional soccer player. Even though he was only twelve, Sol found he could compete successfully against sixteen- and seventeen-year-olds. Playing right wing, Sol became one of the team's leading scorers. He even attracted the attention of a sports reporter, who featured Sol in several articles for a neighborhood Jewish paper.

The publicity finally caused Froim to take notice. One day, in total contrast to his usual habits, he left the bakery early to watch Sol play in an important game. He was so proud of Sol, that for days afterwards he beamed whenever he talked about his son's exploits. His only regret was that he could not attend more of his games. But the family was always well represented, as Frania and Tobcia and many of their girlfriends always showed up to cheer Sol on.

Sol had a relatively carefree childhood, although there were several unforgettable anti-Semitic incidents which made him aware of the deep divisions in Polish society. Over time he came to realize that because of his religion he would always be treated differently.

In high school, he was captain of the soccer team. One day after practice, he took Helene, a classmate, for a bicycle ride. He stopped at an ice cream parlor and ordered a five-cent dish of ice cream. A fellow student, older and bigger, whom Sol knew as a neighborhood bully, began yelling obscenities at Helene, accusing her of going out with a "dirty Jew." Angry and without thinking, Sol returned the insult, calling the boy a "Polish Pig." Then Sol struck him, breaking the boy's nose.

The next morning at school, Sol was called into the principal's office. There he received a stern lecture from a grim-faced priest. Sol felt very resentful, for he was not permitted to tell his side of the story. Indeed, the scolding was all one-sided, and to Sol's way of thinking, unfair. The priest had decided that Sol was guilty and did not even criticize the boy who had caused the incident. Sol remained silent throughout the reprimand. When he finished, the priest sent Sol home and told him to return the following day with his father.

That night, afraid to tell his father what had happened, Sol confided instead in his mother. The next morning Chaya accompanied Sol to school. The priest ushered them into his office. He made it clear he was not so much interested in which of the boys had started the fight as in the outcome. He told Mrs. Rosenberg that it would cost 25 zloty (U.S. $3.50) to repair the other boy's nose, and that the Rosenbergs would be held responsible. Even though the punishment could have been worse, the money still represented a punitive sum for a family on a tight budget. The Rosenbergs made clear to Sol that they were not happy with his behavior and that such an incident must never happen again. Sol was also suspended from school for three days. During this time, his parents warned him about his behavior and made him stay home. Sol said nothing, but inwardly he rebelled; he was determined to better defend himself in the future if he ever found himself in a similar situation. His solution was to take up boxing.

Fortunately for Sol, the premier boxing program in Poland was housed at the Maccabee Club, which was the home of four national champions: Runstein in the featherweight division, Jacobovitch in lightweight, Rosenblum in middleweight, and Neuding in heavyweight. Sol was amazed by their agility and power. He would watch the champions spar and train; eventually he volunteered to be their water boy. In this way, he was able to pick up techniques and solicit advice. One of the coaches took Sol aside and offered to help him; he worked out a special practice drill for Sol. Training was hard, but over time the instructor taught Sol basic boxing skills. Sol learned to parry, sidestep, thrust, and jab until the moves came effortlessly. By the time he was twelve, Sol was fighting preliminary bouts on the boxing card, and his athletic ability was earning recognition throughout the neighborhood.

Shortly after beginning his boxing lessons, Sol was choosing teammates at his soccer club for an after-school pick-up game. One boy, who was visibly annoyed because Sol did not choose him for his team, shouted *parzhive zhid*, "dirty Jew." Sol thought of him as little more than a foulmouthed coward who was mostly talk. By all accounts he had a brooding and volatile personality and a long history of disciplinary problems with school authorities. Most of the students looked down on him and avoided him whenever possible. But this was one time Sol was not going to let him get away with his insults. Sol exploded. Words followed and another fistfight took place. Sol's boxing lessons were more than adequate; Sol broke the boy's nose. Once more, Sol found himself called into the priest's office. In no uncertain terms, the priest expressed his displeasure with Sol's continued unruly behavior. There was no excuse, he said, for striking a fellow student. Much to his parents' dismay, he was again suspended, this time for two days.

Yet another incident came about because of his friendship with a Catholic girl. A longtime schoolmate, whom Sol had grown to like, hesitantly confided to Sol that they could never be more than friends because he was a Jew. To be closer would be to risk the anger of her parents. This brief encounter left Sol disappointed and frustrated. He didn't want to be considered different and an outsider, but was at a loss as to what to do about it.

Even one of Sol's closest friends from school, a classmate named Staszek, helped teach Sol the meaning of prejudice. The two boys got along well and always did their homework together. However, one afternoon, Staszek told Sol that his grandfather had ordered him not to see Sol any more because Sol's father had killed Jesus. Sol was hurt and confused. He thought for a moment and told Staszek that was impossible because Jesus was much older than his father. Staszek thought this was logical and went home to tell his grandfather that he must be wrong; the grandfather then told him that Sol's ancestors had killed Jesus. He said the Jews were outsiders who had no place in the Polish nation. Staszek was warned to never again have anything to do with Sol. The next day Staszek told Sol of the conversation with his grandfather;

although the two boys remained friends, they had to meet away from the grandfather's house, where Sol would never be welcome.

Incidents such as these caused Sol to be on his guard against the non-Jewish community. He could sense the negative attitude and instinctively he reacted defensively. He could not understand the causes of anti-Semitism, but knew that many students despised him just because of his religion. Prejudice was commonplace; distrust and discrimination were always present. Therefore, Jews were forced to make a life for themselves within their own community.

While Sol struggled with these various anti-Semitic incidents, the situation for all of Poland's Jews continued to deteriorate. By the late 1930's, there was an increasingly open anti-Semitism, fed by high unemployment and the growing influence of anti-Jewish propaganda from Germany. In turn this led to the rise of political extremism and growing social unrest. As existing class and political antagonisms worsened, the status of Poland's large Jewish minority grew increasingly precarious.

Anti-Jewish riots swept the country and calls for expulsion of the Jews increased. Extremist Polish politicians blamed the Jews for the economic calamity that had befallen Poland. Many began to propose legislation curbing Jewish economic opportunity. The government responded by gradually institutionalizing the prejudice. More restrictive quotas were imposed on entrance to secondary schools, universities, and graduate programs. In addition, Jews were dismissed from jobs in both industry and the public sector. Some professions were purged of all Jews. In 1938, government decrees effectively closed the legal profession to all Jews. When massive unemployment affecting every strata of Polish society swept the country in the wake of the Great Depression, the government introduced a system of welfare assistance. Jews were effectively excluded from the rolls. The results were catastrophic. More than one third of Poland's three million Jews found themselves below the poverty line with no social safety net. Confronted by the government's indifferent and hostile economic policy, Poland's Jews grew even more desperate.

Given these circumstances, a number of Jewish organizations tried to take up the slack. They engaged in intense debate to win support among Poland's Jews. Some advocated emigration to escape the distressing situation. Others were vehemently opposed to emigration and urged the people to remain and fight for their rights as Polish citizens. Unfortunately, there was little agreement as to what to do.

Sol saw the flyers posted in the neighborhood announcing the lectures by various groups. One evening he asked his parents for permission to attend one of the lectures given by the Zionist organization Betar. This group advocated both emigration and collective physical resistance against those who persecuted the Jews. Froim reluctantly allowed Sol to go. He viewed these organizations as composed of political radicals who could only worsen the position of the Jews in Polish society. "Be careful whom you associate with," he cautioned Sol, "because no good will come of this."

Sol, though, was curious and wanted to know more about Betar. Despite the lukewarm attitude of his parents, Sol attended several sessions. The meetings were unstructured but informative. Usually there was either a speaker or readings. The audience, a mix of students and workers from the neighborhood, listened attentively. They seemed to share similar interests and common backgrounds. In spite of his youth, Sol was accepted and made to feel comfortable.

While the meetings themselves were rather mild affairs, Sol became fascinated by one particular speaker, a young Pole named Menachim Begin. Begin, who was destined to become the Prime Minister of Israel, made Sol aware of the need to remain vigilant. After reviewing what was happening on the European scene and the rising anti-Jewish sentiment, Begin warned them of the mortal dangers posed by anti-Semitism; he noted the anti-Jewish riots, looting, boycotts, confiscations, exploitation, and discrimination then pervasive in both Germany and Poland. The hour of crisis was fast approaching, he predicted, and the Jews of Poland had no future. Faced with public indifference and a lack of international support, the Jews of Poland should emigrate while there was still time. Begin urged them to go to Palestine.

While many in the audience did not or would not believe Begin, Sol was jolted by his words. It was difficult to assimilate everything he had heard. He had never before heard the threats to his family's safety put in such forceful language. Unlike Sol's father, Begin offered no hopeful middle ground where reason could prevail. The tone and urgency of Begin's pleas alarmed Sol. As he thought about it, Sol agreed that it was possible events in Germany could spill over into Poland and that Jews had to have a country of their own as a refuge.

Sol returned to his apartment after the meetings broke up and discussed these ideas with his parents. They were concerned and somewhat taken aback by what Sol told them, but Froim and Chaya told Sol that hardship had always characterized the life of the Jewish community in Poland. Emigration was not a feasible option. Begin, Froim argued, was little more than a professional socialist whose outlook was colored by his personality and political philosophy.

Froim believed that Zionism's goals were worthy, but felt they were also impractical. It was not possible to return to the Promised Land. Although Jews had suffered abuses in Poland for centuries, he thought the only solution was to work for change at home.

While they did not forbid Sol to attend the Betar sessions, Sol's parents did caution him to maintain an open mind and not to be taken in by everything he heard. However, they saw how eagerly Sol looked forward to the meetings and worried where all this might lead.

Until this point, Sol's life had been fairly uncomplicated. Unpleasant episodes did occur, but they were part of the historic fabric of Polish life. There had been warning signs, but the disparity between Jew and Gentile had existed for centuries. In the past, Sol almost always had agreed with his parents, but now he found himself going through a period of self-examination and doubt. Yet, he kept his own counsel and did not discuss these concerns with his parents. Begin had started him thinking about what might happen in the future. Although he was only twelve, Sol believed that his parents failed to understand the full implications of Nazism for Poland. He therefore took up the cause, and in 1938, Sol joined Betar.

Froim was not pleased, but since he was fairly easy-going, he did not criticize Sol or prevent him from attending the meetings. While grudgingly accepting Sol's decision, Froim did ask Sol to reconsider. However, the more Sol thought about it, the more he became convinced Begin was right. Begin had urged the members not to accept the status quo, not to be second class citizens in their own country, and not to be cowards and run from the Poles. He told them to arm themselves in order to defend themselves. This made a deep impression on Sol. Indeed, he began to carry a pocket knife with him wherever he went. Betar not only reduced his insecurities but increased his pride.

By September 1939, although not yet thirteen, Sol was already five feet six inches tall. He had large blue eyes, curly black hair, a high forehead and handsome face. Years of strenuous physical activity had given him a compact, lean, and muscular physique. His almost daily exercise on the soccer fields and in the boxing ring also gave him excellent stamina. Everyday life in Warsaw had taught him to be independent, extremely self-reliant, and to follow his instincts. When he was not helping his father at the bakery or involved in sports, Sol, full of energy, ran through the streets of Warsaw with his friends.

Sol came to know Warsaw well, not only his own district, but the Gentile neighborhoods as well. When his district later became the site of the Jewish Ghetto, where half a million Jews were to suffer malnutrition, sickness, degradation, and death, it was Sol's physical strength and intimate knowledge of the buildings and streets that helped him to survive the horrendous times that lay ahead.

Chapter II

Invasion and Occupation

On September 1, 1939, after weeks of rising tension, life in Poland began to unravel. German planes raked Warsaw with bombs while the German Army launched its invasion of Poland. On September 3, Great Britain and France declared war on Germany. By September 8, German armored units had reached the outskirts of Warsaw. A little over a week later, on September 17, Soviet forces invaded Eastern Poland.

Sol and his family had been listening to radio news reports of German advances for days. The quick destruction of the famed Polish military completely unnerved them. Froim and Chaya didn't know where to go or what to do. Intense and continual German artillery shelling and air bombardments smashed into the besieged city, striking the Jewish Quarter with particular ferocity. Two weeks into the siege, as the shelling grew increasingly violent, the Rosenbergs began to fear for their lives. Adding to the destruction, incendiary bombs were dropped from low flying German bombers, causing fierce firestorms that led to widespread destruction. Panicked, the Rosenbergs finally decided to pack baskets of food and water and to seek shelter in the basement beneath their apartment building. The basement was dark and damp and already crowded with other tenants from the building. The Rosenbergs slowly made their way past their neighbors, through the dimly-lit cellar. Locating a small unoccupied space, Sol and his family sat down to wait out the attack. The first day, the electricity went off. Except for a few candles, they remained in total darkness. They could hear the explosions up above and shuddered from the force of thuds from artillery shells. Dust and particles from the ceiling of the cellar rained down on them. Moreover, it was almost impossible to sleep on the hard, cold floor. Few people talked; many sobbed. They were too afraid to be of much comfort to one another. For three days and three nights, they waited.

Sol and his family managed relatively well, given the circumstances. Chaya did her best to calm the children. Most of the time they remained still, immersed in their own thoughts. For Sol, the time went by slowly. He sensed panic and fear all around him, as some of his neighbors complained bitterly, while others sobbed, afraid that the apartment building would collapse on them. Sol sat still, but by the third day, his discomfort was acute. His muscles were stiff and sore, his back ached from lying on the concrete floor, and the musty air in the basement was almost impossible to breathe.

Suddenly the bombing stopped. The silence was a welcome, but strange sensation. After a short time, Sol's family joined the others who were climbing the steps to street level. Sol was stunned by what he saw: apartment houses demolished, trolleys overturned, and countless fires burning out of control. Hundreds of people were buried beneath the rubble. Cries for help seemed to come from everywhere. Sol could not have imagined the extent of the damage.

It was then the Rosenbergs realized how fortunate they were not to be left homeless. Miraculously, their apartment building had emerged unscathed. Froim and Chaya hurried their family off the street and up to sanctuary in their apartment where Froim locked the door and tried to think things out.

The day after their return, Sol heard a loud knock. Hesitantly, Froim opened the door; two of his brothers rushed in. Trembling, they told Froim and Chaya they had decided to flee to the east;

they wanted to seek security behind the Russian lines before the Germans advanced into Warsaw. They urged Froim to join them before it was too late: "If not for yourself, then for the children's sake," they argued. "Warsaw will not be safe for the Jews once the Germans arrive. We must act now."

Froim looked at Chaya, who sat in stunned silence. The intensity of their plea bewildered Froim. Everything was happening too fast for him to deal with. "I need time to think. To leave everything I have, everything with which I am familiar and comfortable for an unknown fate is unthinkable."

His brothers begged him to make a decision immediately. "We are leaving in the morning," they said. They wrote down a time and meeting place. "Be there and we shall all go together. If you aren't there we will leave without you. Time is not your ally. You must decide now." They kissed and embraced the children who had sat quietly during the conversation, hugged Chaya and Froim, and rushed from the apartment.

Froim was torn by conflict. He could not avoid a decision, but perhaps, by going along with German decrees, the family could maintain a semblance of normalcy. Shaken and depressed, Froim decided to discuss the issue with his twin sister, Bella.

Bella was roughly six feet tall, and stout, but attractive in her own way. She and her husband Leon were childless, so they treated Froim's children as their own. They lavished time and presents on them and the two families were very close. Bella and Leon owned the Zalcman Bakery, located in an upper middle-class area of the city. Of all the family, Bella and Leon had achieved the greatest economic success, in part due to Bella's shrewdness and common sense. Also, through fortunate timing they had secured contracts to provide fresh bread to a nearby military base. Their profits were invested in property and they had accumulated substantial assets.

Froim had the greatest respect for Bella and Leon and usually agreed with their advice. Moreover, Leon had become very friendly with many Polish officers on the base, both person-ally and professionally. After he closed the bakery, he would spend many hours socializing with them in card games or having a beer. Froim hoped these contacts would give Leon added insight into German intentions.

Froim walked nervously to their apartment. Bella was alone. Leon, she said, had mysteriously disappeared during the invasion and she did not know what had become of him. She indi-cated she believed he was safe and had been given refuge by his friends in the military. While concerned, Bella did not appear overly worried. Whatever she thought she kept to herself. Welcoming Froim into the apartment, she and Froim sat down and discussed the possibility of fleeing to the east. Without hesi-tation, Bella advised against it. "Why," she asked, "would you want to live in Communist Russia? It is a dictatorship and Stalin is as evil as Hitler. Life is hard. Times are bad there. There are no jobs and the future looks bleak. Besides, we can't expect to give up everything when the worst thing to happen to us here will be forced labor for the Germans."

Froim listened intently. Relieved, he had heard what he wanted to hear. He did not want to give up his home and the busi-ness he had worked so hard to create in order to take his family to an uncertain future with little hope of work and even less chance of locating a roof to put over their heads. Furthermore, he did not want to leave his mother who was too old to travel. The decision was made. They would not join his brothers. They would stay in Warsaw and weather the storm.

Froim could not foresee the calamity that awaited him and his family. He steadfastly believed that confinement to a ghetto would be the worst fate that could befall the Jewish community of Warsaw. "To resist," he later told the family, "is futile, and flight is too risky a venture. We must pray that the Germans moderate their anti-Semitic attitudes here in Poland. And if they don't, France and Britain will liberate us from German domination soon." He could not envision the horror the Germans intended for him, his family, and his people. He could not have imagined that his entire community was marked for extinction by Germany, long revered for its culture and sophistication by other Western Europeans.

Warsaw surrendered on September 28, 1939. The entire population of the city was gripped by panic and fear of what was to come. It was not long before their worst fears were realized. On September 30, the German army entered Warsaw unopposed. Sol wanted to watch the German entry into Warsaw, but his parents forbade it. Instead, like most of the citizenry, the Rosenbergs remained huddled in their apartment with the curtains drawn and door locked.

In the coming days as German troops and half-tracks moved into the Jewish Quarter, Sol caught his first glimpse of German power; he was stunned by it. He had never seen so many well-armed and formidable looking soldiers. From the outset of the Occupation, their attitude of arrogance and brutality was evident. Daily he saw scenes that made his blood run cold. Jews, in particular, were targeted for persecution, with religious Jews singled out for special victimization and humiliation. Their beards were yanked, and many were beaten. Then they were ordered to shave off their beards and cut their side locks. The Germans demanded that they give up whatever possessions they had such as watches or jewelry. To ensure that they had recovered everything of value, the soldiers conducted body searches of the frightened victims; while keeping his distance, Sol could hear the boisterous laughter of the soldiers halfway down the block.

In October 1939, most of Western Poland was incorporated into Germany, while a sizable chunk of Eastern Poland was annexed by the Soviet Union. Then, a number of directives against the Jews in the newly truncated Polish state were put into effect. All Jewish-owned businesses were ordered to mark their establishments with the Star of David symbol. Moreover, liquid

assets had to be transferred to a central bank and cash with-
drawals were limited. This was followed by further decrees
imposing heavy taxes. The ostensible purpose of the taxes was to
defray the costs of German occupation and to compensate the
Germans for losses sustained in the war. But the end result was to
further impoverish the Jews.

In addition, the Germans distributed work cards or
Ausweiss. Those who did not have these sought-after permits
could be arrested and sent to resettlement camps. Moreover, all
Jews were forced to sew on their coat sleeves yellow patches with
the Star of David emblem on which was written "Jude." The
purpose of the arm bands was to identify and to isolate the Jews
from the general population. Resentful and bitter, Sol ignored the
decree and regularly removed the stigmatizing insignia.

Over the next few months the character of Sol's neighborhood underwent drastic changes. The Rosenbergs watched with
incomprehension as their district was flooded with people expelled
from Western Poland. Almost 150,000 Jews were squeezed into
their small district, causing conditions to deteriorate to a crisis
stage as overcrowding passed the point of saturation. German
directives announced that this was the initial step in the process of
creating government-sponsored ghettos, a concept that Froim, an
avid reader of history, noted had not existed since the Middle Ages.

Sol listened in shock as the frightened newcomers
discussed their ordeal. Apparently confiscations and killings had
become commonplace. All had been stripped of their homes and
been forced to abandon their possessions. They were funneled
into the old Quarter where they tried to set up housekeeping in
abandoned basements, on rooftops, on the sidewalks, or along the
alleys of the Quarter. Lack of housing for the newcomers meant
that tens of thousands became street dwellers with no money and
few belongings other than the clothes on their backs.

By spring 1940, city services that had previously been
haphazard had become nonexistent. Many shops were shuttered

and curtains were drawn in the apartments. Electricity became sporadic and water service was irregular. In front of the few stores still open stood long lines of tired women, many of them gripping little children by the hand or carrying crying babies. Hunger stalked the Ghetto from the outset as food supplies dwindled due to German curtailment of shipments. Daily, children, lost and crying, wandered aimlessly through the streets looking for their families. Cries of anguish were overheard day and night as the uprooting continued. Even the most basic elements of safety and hygiene soon vanished. Trash began to pile up on every block. Scattered human excrement was visible in the alleys and on street corners where the homeless huddled.

News of the sudden and unexpected fall of France in May 1940, seemed to destroy all of Froim's hopes. The scope and magnitude of Germany's victory meant a long war and harsh occupation. Froim, well versed in history, took the long view. "This will pass," he said in low measured tones. "Jews endured tyrannical regimes throughout history and survived." In the meantime they could only hope that Nazi brutality would ease. Perhaps once German rule was established, life would return to normal or at least the Germans might grant them some sort of existence. "There is no recourse except to suffer in silence. The Germans have defeated us and are the victors. It is futile to resist. As the new Government, they can do whatever they want. We have lost control of our destiny and must accept the verdict of history. Still, we must persevere. We must not lose faith. We will overcome our trials as we have in the past."

Froim's words did not satisfy Sol, but he was mature enough to realize his father was paralyzed by pessimism and defeatism. Sol would have preferred that his father get angry and express his hatred for the Nazis. Instead Froim counseled patience, a wait and see attitude. He downplayed the seriousness of the situation while hoping everything would turn out for the best. Sol simply could not accept this. But, while he could not agree with his father's point of view, outwardly he remained quiet and loyal. Sol was anxious to ask questions, but thought better of it because he knew it would only upset Froim and hurt his sisters. So he listened quietly even though it was difficult. He never challenged or provoked his father by word or deed. He would not openly reproach him. Sol knew his father had enough to contend with without having his son contradict him. However, Sol had no doubt that his father was gripped by self-deception. Sol wanted to defy the occupiers and defend his family, but he was at a loss as to how to do this.

Then in mid-October 1940, establishment of the Ghetto became an official policy. All Jews living in Warsaw were ordered into the restricted zone. Confinement was enforced by harsh decrees, and Jews were forbidden to leave. The twenty-two entrances to the Ghetto were sealed. Life grew increasingly difficult for Warsaw's Jewry as new legal restrictions limiting freedoms were imposed daily: Jews were forbidden to change their place of residence, they were forced to register all property and possessions, and barred from restaurants, taverns, and public parks. Before the residents had time to adapt to the first set of humiliating decrees, new ordinances were announced that were even more tyrannical and threatening. Jews were stripped of citizenship rights, schools and synagogues were closed, and practice of the Jewish religion was outlawed. Furthermore, a stringent curfew was imposed and German checkpoints and barricades were set up at key intersections.

As the Jewish community reeled from the restrictions, the Germans increased the oppression by undermining the Jewish economic foundation. Jews were fired from their jobs, their pension and retirement funds were seized, as well as their personal and professional assets, and savings and checking accounts in banks were forfeited to the Nazis. This left most Jews without a livelihood and without any reserves to draw upon to support themselves and their families.

Such was the nightmarish world with which Sol and his family had to contend. Confinement to the Ghetto did not bring security from attack. Jews were beaten for forgetting to remove their hats in the presence of a passing German. The slightest pretext could trigger a German outburst, and the threat of danger also came from Poles. Sol had heard that Poles were granted immunity from any attacks on Jews or Jewish-owned property. This rumor seemed to be confirmed by the countless acts of violence he witnessed: senseless beatings, shootings, the looting and firebombing of Jewish synagogues, businesses, and apartments, as well as other individual atrocities. Under the watchful eye of the Wehrmacht, hundreds of Polish hooligans were dispatched almost daily in German-inspired pogroms. These thugs ran rampant through the streets, looting, vandalizing, beating, raping and sometimes murdering the inhabitants.

Daily, trucks with loudspeakers drove slowly through the Ghetto announcing new German edicts. Special "flying squads" of SS troops followed closely, arbitrarily arresting suspected leaders of the community. The prisoners were then force marched down the streets in full public view to Pawiak prison, where the Ghetto inhabitants disappeared, never to be seen nor heard from again. The destructive forays by Poles and Germans led to further intimidation and hopelessness among the inhabitants. Sol watched the suffering and was tormented by it. He had been proud and defiant before the war. Now he was shaken, uncertain, and overwhelmed by dread. He spent the nights in his apartment asking his parents,"Why?" and "What will happen to us?" His parents had no easy answers. They carried their burden in silence and tried to downplay the dangers so as not to alarm the children.

The winter of 1940-41 under the occupation was an especially cruel one in the Ghetto. The distress of the residents was made worse by extreme cold, deep snow, and scarcity of fuel for heating. Electrical blackouts were common and power was virtually nonexistent after nightfall. Sewage and water pipes burst due to the cold. Since toilets no longer functioned, human waste was dumped with the garbage into the streets. Eventually, the filthy and unsanitary conditions resulted in a typhoid epidemic.

As Sol walked the streets, he was sickened by the grim reality of everyday life in the Ghetto. People weakened by starvation and illness sat alone on the sidewalks waiting to die of hypothermia, their bodies swollen from malnutrition. Even children as young as three or four, too weak to cry, sat begging with outstretched hands for scraps of food. Soon the streets were littered with corpses, which froze quickly and were covered by snow after just a few hours. The corpses were then covered by newspapers until they could be removed. The following morning, men whose faces were covered by handkerchiefs arrived by wagon; they picked up the dead bodies and dumped them in mass graves outside the Ghetto walls adjacent to the Jewish cemetery. Sol, aware of the futility of their situation, prayed for the safety of his own family.

As sanitary conditions deteriorated, basic hygiene became impossible. With no water for drinking, cooking, bathing, or lavatory facilities, the Rosenbergs became dependent on Sol to scavenge for water. Baths and laundry became dispensable luxuries. The family was forced to use the foul-smelling public lavatories even though these too were out of order and filled to overflowing.

Most of the time, the Rosenbergs, like the others who were lucky enough to still have shelter, huddled in their cold dark apartment. There they bundled up in layers of clothing and blankets for warmth. Gradually, numbed by the deteriorating conditions which were worsened by uncertainty, they sank into a state of exhaustion.

Not a single day went by without the murder of at least some Jews. Sol's family was not left untouched by the killing. One day, German troops appeared on Powonski Street at the small apartment where Sol's seventy-six-year-old grandmother lived alone. They rushed up the steps and beat on the door. Hannah, afraid of the intruders, hesitantly answered the knock.

The soldiers burst in demanding to know where her son-in-law Leon was; since Leon had vanished, Hannah replied honestly that she did not know. She was struck by an officer and killed instantly. After searching the apartment, the soldiers left. It wasn't until several hours later that frightened neighbors looked in on Hannah only to discover her body. They quickly notified the Rosenbergs, who rushed over to find Hannah dead.

After hurriedly making arrangements and contacting relatives, the Rosenbergs walked sadly back to their apartment, where they gathered around the kitchen table. They talked of Hannah's life and what a good mother she had been to her ten children. While Sol did not participate in the discussions, he sat quietly and recalled her frequent visits to the apartment. He remembered her as frail and stooped, but kind and generous. Indeed, every time Grandma Hannah appeared she always had a small gift for each of the children. Her loss and the nature of her death stunned Sol. He couldn't make any sense of it.

Froim took the loss of his mother hard, shaking as he spoke of her. Sol felt especially vulnerable as he saw his father grieve. He had thought his father would be more angry about his mother's murder, but reacting calmly was part of his father's nature. If he did feel any anger, he never let it show.

The next morning, the day dawned dreary and overcast; the funeral was somber and stark in its simplicity. Hannah's body lay in a plain wooden coffin at the funeral parlor. The Rosenbergs sat through the brief service numb from the pain. Following the memorials delivered by friends and family, Froim and Chaya haltingly rose from their seats to receive those in attendance. The muted condolences and ashen faces of the mourners left a lasting impression on Sol. He was close to most of those filing out of the funeral parlor: uncles, aunts, cousins, and family friends. He did not know then that he was seeing many of them for the last time. For the Rosenbergs, the reality of the threat of German occupation had set in.

Although the Rosenbergs were not observant Jews, they still spent the next week at home sitting *shiva*, the ritual for bereavement, in Hannah's memory. They ate the sparse meals brought by family and friends. Froim did not shave during the week and the bakery remained closed. Visitors came and went constantly. At the end of the week, formal mourning came to a close. The family tried to return to a semblance of normal routine, but Sol could see that Froim was having a difficult time handling his grief. With a member of the immediate family struck down, the Rosenbergs could no longer distance themselves from what was happening all around them. Normal family life had become impossible; the happier more carefree days of pre-war Poland were only a distant memory.

For Frania and Tobcia, the changes in their circumstances brought about changes in their personalities. The giggles and playfulness of typical children living a normal childhood vanished. Now that the children were barred from attending school, their parents kept them busy with assigned chores. The girls refused to be parted. At night, they were afraid to go to sleep; they lay awake sobbing inconsolably. The slightest sound unnerved them. Even normal bickering, the kind all siblings engage in, ceased. They were afraid to leave the apartment for any reason and were suspicious of all strangers. They would sit silently on the sofa, hardly moving, staring vacantly straight ahead for hours on end. When they did speak, their voices had an air of hysteria.

Their appearance also mirrored these changes. Their hair hung in limp disarray and their eyes were puffy and swollen. Both Frania and Tobcia seemed listless and strained. It hurt Sol to see his sisters so distraught. He often put his arm around their shoulders to try to comfort them, but there was little he could do.

Every night, the family talked about their fears and anxieties, real as well as imagined. They were all growing more and more worried about their future. There were many arguments and endless discussions. However, they did not reach any decisions because there did not appear to be any options. Froim and Chaya were anxious about their children's safety and well-being, as well as their future livelihood under the occupiers. Sadly, the parents watched helplessly as a gradual role reversal took place. The family had become more and more dependent on Sol to forage for food and other basic necessities of life. They were overwhelmed by conflicting emotions: they feared for Sol's life every time he went into the streets, yet they realized they needed him for their very survival. They had been reduced to impoverishment and had depleted their savings on the high-priced yet meager food allotments permitted in the Ghetto. Now with scarcely any money and experiencing persistent hunger, the family was faced with a critical situation. Indeed, Chaya told Sol, circumstances could not be worse. Without Sol's help, they would face imminent starvation. They constantly warned Sol of possible danger. "Salik," Chaya would say, "you must be cautious. Don't get involved in any trouble. Stay away from the Germans. Be careful where you go and what you do. We love you too much to see anything happen to you."

In the meantime, Froim and Chaya considered it their duty to persevere and make whatever concessions were necessary to the new order. "What other choice do we have?" Froim asked repeatedly to no one in particular.

At the same time, Sol's parents did not seem bitter. More and more they talked about earlier and happier times. When they did talk about the uncertainties of the present, they tried to maintain their composure.

Chaya seemed to dominate family discussions. She had always been the person around whom the family was centered. Certainly, Froim's role was important, but he had been busy earning a living. Now the children listened to Chaya. She revealed her selflessness and kindness: she did not speak of vengeance, rather she forgave with humility.

Chaya had always had unbounded energy and she continued to display it in spite of worsening conditions. She continued to prepare meals, perform household chores, and protect and guide her children. She even devoted two hours a day to structured classes for the children so that their schooling would not be neglected.

She bore the misfortune with a strength of character that made Sol proud. However, the intense stress was beginning to tell. Her flashing smile was gone, her eyes were glazed, and her expression reflected her anxiety. She seemed visibly subdued, quieter, and her face wore a veil of wary sadness. The financial burdens, physical discomfort, and daily uncertainty tested her to the utmost. But in spite of the difficulties, she remained strong-willed and perpetually upbeat, ignoring her own needs to concentrate on the family. She did her best to maintain a normal family life, boost morale, and channel conversations to more pleasant subjects. Her way of dealing with the pain was to stay busy and pretend nothing was wrong. Sol had always admired his mother. But now his love for her increased immeasurably.

Circumstances forced Sol to grow up very quickly. He realized his day-to-day existence had changed forever. Survival depended on ingenuity. As flour rations for his father's bakery were reduced, Froim and Chaya relied on Sol to replenish their meager supplies. At night Chaya would carefully count out the money on the kitchen table that Sol was to use to buy flour on the black market. Sol would then leave the apartment carrying empty sacks on his back and go to prearranged meeting places in the Quarter to carry out the unsanctioned deals. After the Germans shut down the Rosenberg Bakery, Sol helped his father build a small oven in their apartment. He was amazed that his father could construct a workable oven and do all the wiring in the confined space of the kitchen. The family continued to turn out loaves of bread both to sell and to eat at home. When their neighbors and relatives no longer had money to pay for the bread,

Froim continued to share what little he had baked. When friends and family members had exhausted their resources, they resorted to bartering and neighborly swaps. Thus, a gradual and ever expanding voluntary support network of mutual-assistance developed. Although their income had virtually disappeared, the family was still able to eat and maintain a minimal existence in the early days of the occupation.

Life in Warsaw's streets became more dangerous by the day. Threatened both by the German Army as well as by Polish thugs, people ventured out only for the most basic of necessities. One afternoon, Sol was in a jewelry store owned by the father of a close friend. Two young Poles entered and demanded two clocks. The owner said they could not take the clocks, but he would be happy to sell them to them. The boys then became more menacing, snarling ominous threats. Sol, who had been standing nearby with his friend, intervened and told them to leave. The taller and more belligerent of the two turned and mocked him. "What are you going to do, Jew boy?"

Sol had no intention of backing down. Seeing that they were unarmed, Sol approached them, holding his right hand in his pant's pocket. Pretending he had a gun, Sol threatened them: " I will cut you to pieces. Moreover I have friends outside. Either pay or get out," he warned the would-be thieves. Instantly the arrogant look on the faces of the Polish boys vanished. They looked at each other and then fled the store. The bluff had worked. For one of the few times during the occupation, Sol felt a sense of satisfaction.

A few days later, the family was sitting around the kitchen table discussing the rumors and incidents they had heard about that day. Froim and Chaya then turned to Sol; reluctantly, they told him that they had decided that it was no longer safe for him to remain in the apartment. Security forces had been in neighboring buildings checking documentation, including work permits, and those without the proper forms had been shipped off to resettlement camps. Due to his age and lack of skills Sol had not been issued an *Ausweiss*, or work permit, which would have allowed him to work in the Ghetto. It was, therefore, simply too dangerous to remain at home. Sol could see from the look on the faces of his parents how difficult this decision had been for them. Chaya's eyes filled with tears as she got up from her chair to hug him and tell him how much they loved him. Sol was taken aback. Confused, he didn't want to leave his parents and had become very protective of his sisters. To go would be to abandon them, to desert them in time of need.

"When will I see you?" Sol asked.

Chaya hesitated. "You can return anytime you wish. We will be all right and you will be safer, Salik."

Sol was filled with conflicting emotions, but at the same time he knew they were right. He had no choice.

"When should I leave?" he asked.

"Tomorrow," Chaya responded. "We have talked to Aunt Bella and she will always have a place for you, day or night, whenever you appear. In fact, she expects you and looks forward to your being there to keep her company now that Uncle Leon has disappeared."

And so, the next night, Sol began his life on the run. Sometimes he stayed with Aunt Bella. Other nights, he stayed with the families of friends. From time to time, he was able to remain with his own family. He did what he had to do to survive, even though he felt unsettled and frightened. He tried to see his family daily, eagerly looking forward to these visits, however brief. But his time with his family could not overcome the overwhelming feeling of loneliness. Each day Ukrainian, Latvian, and Lithuanian guards arrested thousands of Jews who did not have the proper papers, confirming the wisdom of his parents' decision. The guards did not hesitate to shoot or beat their prisoners. As Sol watched the roundups, he was shocked and bewildered by the savagery. He could not believe what he was seeing, nor could he understand the reason for what was happening. The looting, bullying, and unpredictable nature of the sweeps and arrests threw him off balance. What he did know was that he could not allow himself to be caught; he had to remain on the move.

Sometimes there was no escape from the daily brutality. One night in early 1941, when Sol happened to be at home, there was a loud noise from downstairs. Sol and his family listened as Ukrainian guards in the apartment below yelled and cursed. Fearing that this was another search for undocumented workers and that Sol would be taken away, they locked the door to their apartment. They sat frozen, as the sounds of doors slamming, objects crashing, and loud footsteps came ever closer. Soon the guards were pounding loudly on their door, demanding to enter. While Chaya anxiously gathered the children around her, Froim walked fearfully to the door to unlock it. The guards rushed in, almost knocking Froim to the floor. They glanced around, glaring at the Rosenbergs. Then, as the family watched in stunned silence, the guards raced through the small apartment, grabbing anything they thought might be of value. They tore paintings off the walls, took three sculptured crystal horses that had been a gift from Froim's father, seized Chaya's fur coat, and ripped the chandelier from the kitchen ceiling. Within minutes they were gone, off to ransack another apartment. The entire incident lasted less than thirty minutes, but the family was devastated by it. The girls sobbed and Sol could see from the look on the faces of his parents how totally helpless they felt. The material loss of precious family heirlooms was bad enough; worse yet, they realized to what extent they were at the mercy of totally unpredictable forces. The danger was clear: they had lost any sense of security they once had had. Froim's previous hopes that life could not get worse were dashed. However, there was no choice but to try to survive one day at a time.

During the brutal winter of 1940-1941, the *Judenrat* or Jewish Council, which had ostensible civil authority in the

Ghetto, issued Sol a temporary work permit. He was ordered to shovel snow at the Okiecie Airport outside Warsaw. Sol was glad to have short-term work outside the Ghetto because it would mean extra money and hopefully added food rations to help his family. Moreover, it wouldn't be the backbreaking labor most of the work gangs were forced to endure outside the Ghetto. It also would give him a break from the continued tension in the Ghetto.

Each day he was picked up with about forty other workers at an assembly point and taken by truck to the airport, where they put in long hours. But one day the workers were told they would be moved into Polish military barracks and confined there until further notice. No one was allowed to leave the base, so there was no way for Sol to notify his parents. Sol knew they would be worried about him, but there was nothing he could do. Indeed, it was some time before he would see them again. He could only hope their concern for his safety would not overwhelm them.

The barracks lacked space and were spartan and confining. But they were relatively clean, the beds had blankets, and there were latrines and showers. Moreover, the workers were given adequate meals three times a day, usually the same food the German airmen received. However, they were required to eat either before or after the Germans went to the dining hall. In the evenings after work, the laborers were free to socialize on the base. One evening, Sol noticed an attractive young girl with shoulder-length blond hair outside the Officers' Club. After they made eye contact, she smiled and came over to Sol. She asked him his name and where he was from. Sol introduced himself and learned that her name was Amy. She was slightly older than Sol, about fifteen, and most surprising, she was the daughter of a German officer stationed at the base. She flirted with Sol and he in turn was attracted to her. Over the next two days, they saw each other during Sol's work breaks and had hurried but pleasant conversations. Sol looked forward to their brief meetings, as it was an escape from the drudgery of the menial jobs he had to do.

Almost every night, there were parties for the German airmen at the base. Somehow Amy was able to arrange for Sol's assignment to the Officers' Club as a waiter, although he never knew how she managed this. Since Sol was fluent in German, his grandfather's native tongue, and most of the other waiters were Poles who knew no German, Sol was in great demand. There he got to see Amy nightly, and after he finished serving and clearing the tables, he was even able to dance with her. Sol, who loved to dance, enjoyed himself immensely. One evening, even Amy's mother asked him to dance. The Polish waiters could not believe their eyes. They were jealous of Sol's acceptance by this high-ranking officer's family. They suspected Sol was a Jew and could not understand how he had gained so much favor with the Germans.

In time, Sol managed to get a different daytime assignment as well. He was assigned to clean and paint the homes on base, including the one in which Amy and her parents lived. One afternoon, while Sol was polishing the furniture, he and Amy began talking. Their conversation soon became physical. They were lying on the bed, fully-clothed, kissing, when, unexpectedly, Amy's mother came into the room. Though surprised, she did not forbid them from seeing each other again. And, while she didn't ask Sol directly, she told Sol she guessed he was Jewish but she liked him and would never betray him. She urged restraint and caution on both their parts. Later Amy told Sol that her parents weren't close, and he did not have to worry that her mother would ever tell her father what she had seen.

At first, Sol did not think about the consequences of this involvement. He was too caught up in his attraction to Amy and by the thrill of having an affair with the daughter of a German officer. Nor did Amy appear worried, even when Sol confirmed that he was a Jew who refused to wear the Star of David. In fact, she began to make plans for their future, including marriage and children. She wanted him to run away with her to her grandfather's farm in Germany. For Amy, Sol was the first boy she had ever loved. She would tell him, "My heart belongs to you, Solly, and your heart belongs to me."

Sol's fellow workers, however, warned him of the danger of getting involved with a German girl, especially the daughter of a German officer. He began to think seriously about what the Germans would do to him if they found out about this relationship. Common sense finally prevailed. He decided that he had no choice but to leave. One morning he asked one of the truck drivers bringing schnapps to the Officers' Club for a ride back to Warsaw. The driver dropped him off in the city and Sol made his way back to the Ghetto. He never said goodbye or left a note to Amy explaining his sudden departure. It took a long time for Sol to get over this, his first love; but he knew that, under the circumstances, their relationship was impossible. Amy had not understood what the Germans were doing to the Jews. She was either unwilling or unable to accept the truth.

Back in the Ghetto, Sol's brief break from reality was over. Sol's parents were very relieved to see him, but like other Ghetto inhabitants, they felt demoralized. Hope was disappearing, as the congestion, filth, disease, and death toll mounted, made worse by the cold. Through it all, Sol tried to help his family survive. In the following months, he managed to get temporary work permits for a variety of short-term unskilled jobs. These jobs lasted from three days to a few months. Sol worked in warehouses, shops, a brewery, and even as a rickshaw driver. The work, for the most part, was menial, backbreaking, and low-paying, but what little he earned was used to buy food for his family.

One job, which he held for three days, was at a brewery in Praga, a Warsaw suburb on the eastern bank of the Vistula River. Each morning a truck came to pick him up together with several other boys, and drive them across the river. There he spent his workday loading barrels of beer from the conveyor belts onto trucks, which carried the brew to German Officers' Clubs and military bases in the Warsaw region. On his third day at work, he and three other boys were hoisting a barrel aboard a truck when it fell to the pavement, splintering into many pieces. The German officer supervising the work team was so infuriated he ordered the boys to lick up the spilled beer from the pavement. The frightened boys dropped to their knees and did as they were commanded. Afterwards they were fired and told not to return. For Sol, the entire experience was degrading. It deepened his hatred of the German sense of superiority and his dread of German power.

Several days after Sol returned, Froim and Chaya calmly told Sol how worried they were about the family's survival. Chaya said they had sold her jewelry, but that they had not received enough money to purchase what they needed on the black market. Moreover, Sol's part-time jobs, while helpful, still didn't provide enough to meet the family's minimal needs. Their food supplies were virtually depleted; indeed, even by rationing the limited supplies they had, there was barely enough food to last several days. Basic necessities such as eggs, meat, fruits, vegetables, and milk had been completely prohibited by German decree. The meager allotment of less than two hundred calories a day per person could not sustain them. There just was not sufficient food allowed into the Ghetto. Sol knew the neighborhoods and had friends from school on the other side. In desperation his parents asked him if he would accept the risk of becoming a smuggler. Although this would involve a great deal of danger, they could think of no other alternative. Sol could see that his parents were very upset. He could only imagine the long discussions that had led to this difficult request. He knew his parents were more concerned for his safety than their own and that they would not ask him to do this if there were any other option. He answered without hesitation that he would do what they asked. Sol saw the relief on his parents' faces. He knew his immediate response had eased their despair.

That night as he lay in bed, Sol wondered how he would manage and whom he could contact on the other side. " First," he thought, " I must cross the wall and begin to scout safe crossing points. Then I can establish my contacts. I will begin tomorrow night," he decided, confident that he would succeed.

However, there were a number of barriers that stood in Sol's way. Not the least of these obstacles was the standing order that all Jews found outside the Ghetto were to be executed. Soon after the Ghetto was created in October 1940, work had begun to encircle the ghetto by nine-foot walls topped with barbed wire. Less than a year later, on October 15, 1941, Hans Frank, the head of the General Government, issued a decree that any Jew found outside the Ghetto without permission was to be sent to a special court and sentenced to death. Moreover, anyone aiding a Jew was to receive the same punishment. However, due to limited police manpower, it proved very difficult to effectively enforce this decree. Therefore, on December 16, 1941, new orders were issued which did away with the previous judicial pronounce-ments. The new decrees directed police to shoot on sight any Jews found outside the Ghetto.

In spite of the increased danger, Sol always seemed to find a way to leave the Ghetto on his own terms. Over time, he perfected his routine; he learned the safest crossing points and discovered hiding places in abandoned basements or apartments. He established a supply network with Poles willing to do business with him in defiance of German edicts forbidding trade with Jews. Trusting no one, he worked alone, even though he came to know many other boys his own age who in order to survive were engaged in the same type of clandestine activity. Every move had to be calculated, every sound was a threat, every person was a potential enemy, each moment of the crossing was taut with tension. Sol had to be constantly vigilant and exercise extreme caution. The difference between life and death could depend on the smallest of incidents.

Sol always tried to prepare in advance for the crossing. In order to blend in with the Polish population on the other side, he paid special attention to his appearance. He wore clean, pressed clothes which he kept at Aunt Bella's. Oftentimes, after obtaining food on the Aryan side, he would give it to one of several women in the Ghetto who, in exchange, would wash and iron his clothes. He was also aware of his grooming; his hair was combed back and his hands and face were always clean so he didn't look as if he came from the Ghetto. He wore special Bata running shoes which his parents had bought him shortly before the German invasion. They were black and laced up above the ankles. These shoes gave Sol the speed he needed to help him avoid capture.

Sol and the rest of his family were usually up before dawn. Nervously he paced the kitchen floor, frequently peering out the curtains at the dark and deserted street below. His parents and sisters sat quietly. Before leaving, he hugged them as if for the last time. They were all aware of the danger and cautioned Sol never to take unnecessary risks.

Sol moved quickly through the empty streets to the wall on the Ghetto side, alert to any unusual sights or sounds. He knew that guards were stationed at intervals along the wall, but in time he identified those areas that were lightly guarded. Approaching one of several dead-end alleys, he would scale the wall or use the extensive maze of underground tunnels or clandestine passageways between buildings, sometimes even the sewers that had been built for drainage, steam or electrical wiring. His movements were rapid and resolute. There was no room for error. Each time he left the Ghetto, Sol knew he was taking a grave risk. Indeed, he could hear the sound of random gunfire almost nightly and assumed other smugglers had been captured or shot. But Sol was not deterred; he realized his family's survival depended on him.

Once on the Aryan side, he walked at a normal pace, trying to lose himself in crowds and hide his nervousness. He tried to avoid German soldiers and to remain anonymous. He was always on the lookout for provisions for his family or friends. Since repressive laws forbade Jews from purchasing eggs, meat, milk, or bread, these were priority items for Sol. For his family and friends, Sol's success meant the difference between hunger and minimal sustenance. But Sol was not always successful. Sometimes, he could not even get staples such as bread or potatoes at any price. Then Sol would be forced to return to his apartment and pack the few remaining family heirlooms into a knapsack which he carried on his back. He would then try yet again to exchange his precious possessions for something to eat.

One day, once over the wall, he discovered a long line of people waiting patiently to buy a few scraps of meat. Joining the line, he saw a classmate he remembered from school. As his friend approached him, Sol became alarmed. They began to talk. "You are not supposed to be here," warned the boy.

Sol asked him to speak quietly. "I know," responded Sol, "but please don't inform on me. I am just trying to buy some food for my family. Then I will leave. Pretend you don't know me. Forget my name." His friend nodded his understanding silently and left. After Sol had bought the meat, he recrossed the wall, returning to the Ghetto. Timing, good fortune, and a knowledge of out-of-the way crossing points had once again enabled him to survive another day.

Much of Sol's time was spent helping other residents of the Ghetto who were desperate for food. He gathered money and valuables from friends and family, carefully noting what was given to him and by whom. Then he would make a second list, a "wish" list of things each family needed. He told the desperate residents when he was planning to cross the wall and what they could expect to receive in exchange for their goods or money. He also had to make time-consuming arrangements on the Polish side with his contacts there and establish prearranged meeting sites and times.

Sol became very adept at smuggling for the Ghetto. His Polish contacts brought him butter and grease in large tin cans. Occasionally they would also include sacks of food. Often Sol had to make several trips to the wall, lugging his heavy contraband, while trying to appear as inconspicuous as possible. Once at the wall, he tried to find a secure location where he could hide the cache before returning for more. When all of his goods were safely in position, he placed wooden crates against the wall to boost himself to the top. Then, with difficulty, he hoisted the contraband over the wall and into the Ghetto. Finally, Sol delivered his goods to his delighted "customers," who sometimes waited up for him most of the night. The entire process usually required half a dozen trips back and forth across the wall. Most nights Sol did not return until dawn to whichever safe house he happened to have selected.

Many times, in spite of his best efforts, the results were disappointing. Often, the Poles Sol dealt with cheated him, taking his money and giving him only part of what he had paid for. In many cases, it was not money the Poles wanted so much as jewelry and furs; they demanded exorbitant amounts of goods in exchange for food. Not only did the Poles frequently shortchange Sol, but they often failed to show up at a meeting place at the appointed time. This forced Sol to take many unnecessary risks. As the number of futile trips across the wall increased, Sol became more and more bitter. The Poles, if not implicitly supporting the Germans, seemed to be indifferent to the plight of the Jews. At worst, they collaborated with the occupiers. Sol found it increasingly difficult to distinguish between the Nazis and his fellow Poles. At home at night, Froim and Chaya tried to ease Sol's growing resentment. They told him that there were good Poles as well as collaborators, that non-Jewish Poles could be shot for aiding Jews in any manner, and that to provide food and shelter to a Jew was a capital offense. Reminding him that his only contact was with those Poles who were out to make a profit from the misery of others, they urged him not to judge all Poles by those with whom he dealt.

Sometimes, if Sol could not buy or trade for food, he would steal it. Like so many others, Sol was forced to turn to petty crime just to satisfy his family's most basic needs. In fact, over time, Sol became so successful, that his friends began to call him the "Warsaw ganiff (thief)."

Whenever possible, Sol slipped out of his safe house late at night and, staying in the shadows, moved quietly through the deserted streets, on the lookout for any opportunities. One night he walked to the rear of the Bata Shoe Store. The crooked alley was deserted. When he reached the building, he found the rear door to the store bolted shut. However, with the aid of a metal rod, he was able to pry the steel latch loose from the bolts. He entered, found the storage area, and hastily selected ten pairs of running shoes. Sol packed them in his knapsack and was gone in less than fifteen minutes. He kept several pairs of shoes in his apartment; the others were given away to his friends.

Another time, he broke the lock to the side door of a pickle factory. There he stole a five-gallon container of pickles. The pickles were also given away to friends. Yet another time he broke into the Walther C. Tobbens Clothing Complex, where he stole several spools of thread and articles of clothing. It took him a number of trips and most of the night to carry the goods back to his parents' apartment. Later that week, he loaded the stolen items in a backpack, making several trips across the wall to sell or trade the goods to eager Poles in exchange for sugar and bread for his family.

However, eventually lack of sleep and the stress of these efforts caught up with Sol. Late in February 1942, Sol had been out all day in the bitter cold without proper clothing or nourishment. When he returned to his apartment his concerned parents were waiting for him. With just one look, they realized that Sol was seriously ill. Fearing typhoid, they immediately summoned a doctor. The diagnosis was pneumonia. The doctor used leeches to draw blood and told the Rosenbergs to move Sol to the basement of the apartment building where a small amount of coal remained to heat the furnace and provide some degree of warmth. By now all the apartments in the building were cold, dark, and drafty and the doctor was convinced Sol might not survive under these conditions. Sol's fever raged for several days. During that time he was completely delirious. Finally, due to Sol's youth and physical condition, the fever broke. One of Sol's parents or sisters was always with him; they took turns keeping him company so that he was never alone. After a week of recuperation, Sol started to regain his strength and before long, he was back on the streets.

On July 22, 1942, the Nazis began the forcible removal of Jews from the Warsaw Ghetto to the Treblinka death camp. Notices were posted throughout the Ghetto proclaiming the deportation to resettlement camps in the East; there, supposedly, work and improved living conditions would await them. All residents were expected to comply except for those who were exempted because their occupations were deemed essential to the German war effort. Sol read the notices and was frightened for himself and his family, none of whom possessed the work permits or employment necessary to avoid deportation. Sol ran to the apartment to tell his family of the German decree. When they heard the news, their disappointment and anxiety were evident. All hope seemed to vanish.

Since Sol was constantly on the move and met many different people, he had easy access to the many rumors, both disturbing and hopeful, that swept the Ghetto daily. Given the harshness of living conditions, the residents were desperate enough to grasp at any promising news. Although Sol was still not sure what was happening, he felt pessimistic. He reasoned that no one had ever heard from those Jews who had already been deported from Warsaw. Nor did anyone know the ultimate destination of the trains.

Deportations began immediately. Supervised by a small army of collaborators, including Ukrainians, Latvians, Estonians, Polish "Blue" police, as well as Jewish Ghetto Police, hundreds of Jews were marched daily to the *Umschlagplatz*. This was the central gathering place for deporting Jews to Treblinka, which was located less than sixty miles to the northeast, or to Auschwitz, one hundred sixty miles to the southwest. The loading yard was located at the northernmost point of the Ghetto, next to the rail yards. There, the Jews were stuffed onto trains for departure.

The pace of deportations was relentless. By August 2, the twelfth day into deportations, more than 76,000 Jews had already been sent to their deaths. For seven weeks, the forcible expulsions continued. The scope of these roundups spread terror throughout the Ghetto; the terrified residents no longer had any hope.

At first, Sol managed to avoid capture. During the summer of 1942, he was able to get temporary work permits that allowed him to leave the Ghetto for brief periods. His first job was to transport leather to a shoe factory. Later he worked in Praga, helping load and truck in bales of cloth for use in sewing German military uniforms.

However, Sol knew that he was still at risk. He especially feared the actions of Jewish collaborators, particularly those known as the "Thirteen." The "Thirteen," named after the address of their headquarters at 13 Leszno Street, really numbered about 500. They worked in factories helping German security identify those who did not have valid work permits. One could always identify these informers by their green hats, in contrast to the blue hats worn by the Ghetto police. Sol always tried to maintain a healthy distance from the "Thirteen," several of whom he had known previously. He realized that if the Germans had not chosen these particular collaborators, they would have found others willing to do their dirty work out of fear or self-preservation. Although the "Thirteen" were armed only with whistles and rubber clubs, the Ghetto residents distrusted and feared them. Sol mocked them from a safe distance, derisively referring to them as the "whistle schmucks." To him they were all traitors.

Sol had several confrontations with the "Thirteen." Crossing the wall early one morning, he was surprised by a policeman in the normally quiet alley. Although he knew the area well, Sol became nervous, as he was carrying fifteen pounds of Polish sausage; he ran into a dead end, with the policeman in close pursuit. He hoped to squeeze through a narrow passageway by turning slightly sideways, but his burden prevented him from doing so. He could have escaped by leaving the sausages, but he refused to do this. The food was too valuable to the Ghetto inhabitants. By this time, the policeman, breathing heavily, had caught up with Sol; trying to catch his breath, he haltingly demanded that Sol give up the sausages and accompany him to headquarters. Anticipating compliance, the policeman was not prepared for Sol's response. Sol jumped up, kicked the policeman hard in the stomach and threw him backward to the pavement. Sol fled, carrying his sausages with him. He peered over his shoulder as he ran. His last view was of the policeman, caught off balance, writhing on the ground in pain, his arms and legs flailing. Sol had managed to complete one more mission, but the danger was deepening.

One afternoon several members of the Thirteen recognized Sol carrying a sack of smuggled goods over his shoulder. They immediately gave chase. Whistles blew and Sol fled. In spite of the heavy load, Sol, who was younger, stronger, faster, and more familiar with the neighborhood than the collaborators, again managed to escape. His older pursuers chased him for a short distance and then gave up. They were no match for him.

Another day, several members of the Thirteen approached him. Sol recognized a lawyer, a teacher, a painter, and a shoemaker from pre-war times. They asked Sol to stand still momentarily and hear them out. Sol, who was nevertheless suspicious, kept his distance and prepared to run. They said they had a proposition for him. They offered him money to buy them cigarettes and food when he went over the wall again; in return, they promised to turn a blind eye on his activities. Sol agreed and for several weeks both sides mutually fulfilled their end of the bargain.

Less than two months into the deportations, Sol was finally captured by another unit of the "Thirteen." Unfortunately,

Sol did not recognize any of its members. Quickly and without warning, the police, aided by Ukrainian security personnel, formed a human barrier around a block. This time there was no escape. One of the policemen grabbed Sol by the shoulder. Frightened, Sol broke the grip and fled. Several security men immediately gave chase. But this time Sol's luck had finally run out. He was run down and captured. The guards beat him and dragged him to the second floor of the deportation center on Stawki Street. There he was thrown into a "Special Room for Tough Guys." Once the Czyste Hospital, the drab four-story building had been converted by the SS into a selection and embarkation center for deportation from the Ghetto. The commander of the Ghetto, SS Brigadier General Jurgen Stroop, maintained his office and supervised the deportations from a nondescript building across the street. Next to the former hospital there was an enormous cobblestone courtyard surrounded by a high wall. The top of the wall was embedded with pieces of broken glass and barbed wire to prevent escape. After the prisoners arrived at the center, the guards separated them into different groups. Although Sol did not know it at the time, one group was slated for labor gangs in the Ghetto, while the other group was to be sent to the death camps. Those chosen for extermination were jammed into the courtyard where they waited to be loaded on trains. Sol wanted a chance to get his thoughts together. Two other boys in the room had asked to go to the bathroom down the hall and had been escorted out. Sol also asked permission to go to the bathroom, and the sole Ukrainian guard on duty granted his request. From the narrow window in the bathroom, Sol could see the crowded courtyard below. In the *Umschlagplatz*, SS Guards holding the leashes of vicious looking Alsatian attack dogs patrolled the yard and maintained order. A platform extended to the far end of the yard and a long train of empty cattle and freight cars waited nearby. A rectangular shed ran alongside the platform where the selectees were herded. Sol could see the guards ripping possessions away from the prisoners before they were forced on to the trains. Jewelry, money, and any other valuables were seized. All bulky possessions were carried to a large oven alongside the shed where they were burned to make room for more people on the cars.

Sol had seen enough; he knew he had to escape. He and the two other boys who had gone to the bathroom quickly decided on a plan. They agreed they had to act immediately before the guard outside in the hall became suspicious. Since the guard was armed and they didn't think they could overpower him, the window was their only chance. Sol eased the window open as quietly as possible. One by one, they jumped into the yard, scaled the brick wall in spite of the embedded glass and sharp wire, and fled through a narrow alley. To Sol's surprise, the glass and tangled wires caused only superficial cuts. But he hardly had time to think about it. Sol ran as he had never run before. He felt as if his lungs would burst; his heart was pounding as he dashed through narrow alleyways. Sol heard shots, but he and his new found friends managed to evade the bullets. With a sense of relief, they separated and disappeared into the Ghetto.

Sol was too frightened to slow down. Fearing he might be pursued, he continued to run until he reached home. Breathless and trembling, he burst into his apartment. There Chaya calmed him down. When he could at last speak, Sol told her all that had happened. Gratefully, Chaya gave thanks that he had managed to escape and was back with them.

However, this was not the last time Sol narrowly escaped capture. Several months later, he was again caught in a surprise sweep. The street where he was walking was sealed off. Soldiers, divided into search teams of three to four members, moved quickly into different apartment blocks. "Juden! Raus!" (Jews! Outside!) the soldiers shouted angrily. The Jews, panic-stricken, were driven out into the streets. The sick and elderly, and all those who could not march fast enough to the assembly point, even infants and children, were hurried along. Some were even forced to their knees, and then gunned down. Family members screamed and pleaded with the soldiers to stop shooting. When the terrified Jews tried to comfort their loved ones, they were dragged away. Soon, the street was littered with dead and wounded.

Trapped and with nowhere to run, Sol was swept along with the others in the expanding dragnet. As he joined the lines of frightened residents, he forced himself not to panic; he knew he would have to react quickly if he were to find a way to escape. Warily he surveyed his surroundings. He knew the neighborhood well. He realized that if he left the line of deportees he might be shot, but he had to take that chance. As the column made its way to the plaza, Sol saw an unattended rickshaw near the entrance. He took a deep breath and, easing out of the line, grabbed the rickshaw; instantly, he transformed himself into a driver. He calmly began to pedal the rickshaw away from the guards and throng of people. Blending into the crowd on the congested street, he made good his escape. A few blocks later, he abandoned the empty rickshaw and fled, not slowing to a walk until he was several blocks away.

After this latest narrow escape, Sol stayed on the move, living precariously, never remaining in one place or at one job too long. He kept a wary eye on all strangers. From various hiding places, Sol watched the daily procession of refugees to the *Umschlagplatz*. More and more apartments were emptied, their occupants led away under guard. He saw the prisoners force marched, carrying their small bags containing their few belongings. At the *Umschlagplatz*, they clustered together in fear, waiting for hours for the next train. Sol wondered how some of the elderly men and women, many obviously bedridden and sick, were able to get to the *Umschlagplatz* fast enough to avoid being gunned down.

Many of those taken away were children younger than himself. But, at that point, in all his confusion and in the effort of just trying to stay alive, Sol did not even question why children would be sent to work factories. He could not imagine the reason for the deportations. All he knew for certain was that he did not want to be a part of this journey to the Unknown.

With deportations increasing daily, Chaya became even more protective of Sol. Contrary to her previous belief, she was now convinced of the dangers on the street, and imagined the worst possible outcome. Each time Sol returned to the safety of the apartment, Chaya begged him to stay. Sol would not disagree with his mother, but she could see his answer from the look on his face. She would always relent with the customary "Be careful, Salik." When it came time for him to leave, Chaya hugged him, and told Sol how much she loved him. It was never easy to say good-by to his family or to tell them how he felt, but Sol knew his survival and that of his family depended upon constant movement.

One beautiful clear morning in late August 1942, just before he left the apartment, Sol's mother turned to him and said, "Watch yourself! Don't get into trouble. Quit running. See if you can get a job in a factory. Always remember how much we love you, Salik." They kissed and embraced each other. Then Sol hugged his sisters to reassure them and told them to be strong. For a moment they all looked at each other in silence. Sol left, not realizing that he was seeing his mother and sisters for the last time. Chaya, as well as Frania and Tobcia were rounded up later that day and put on transports headed east to Treblinka.

When Sol returned to the apartment that evening, he found his father sitting at the kitchen table. After just a glance at his father, Sol knew instinctively that something was terribly wrong. Froim struggled to breathe as he sat hunched over the table, dazed and disoriented. He was pale; his eyes were glazed over, and he was shaking. In a halting voice, choked with grief, Froim was finally able to tell Sol what had happened. The Germans had come, he said, while he was out. The block had been cordoned off, and then all of the women and girls in every apartment in the block had been seized. Any Jews who resisted were shot, their corpses left in their apartments or the stairwells where they had fallen.

Sol was shocked and confused. What had happened to his mother and sisters, he wondered. Were they all right? Where would they be taken? Did they have time to pack some belongings—dresses, shoes, sweaters, anything? And did they have time to prepare food in case the Germans didn't feed them? So many questions swirled around in his mind, but he knew he couldn't ask his father. Somehow Sol had known this dreaded day would arrive. Everything he had witnessed in the streets indicated it.

Sobbing, Froim reproached himself over and over for his inability to save his wife and daughters. The sight of his father crying uncontrollably combined with the terrible news was too much for Sol to bear. Losing his composure, he too broke down and began to sob. Overwhelmed by grief, he let go of three years of stifled tears. Father and son hugged and tried to comfort one another. But for Sol, seeing how vulnerable his father was only increased his sorrow. Froim made no attempt to disguise his sense of helplessness and intense shame for failing to protect his family.

Sol could see that Froim had given up. In the following days, Froim became increasingly withdrawn. Indeed, his voice was barely audible and he could no longer make decisions, take the initiative, or carry on a thoughtful conversation. Even the most basic tasks were left undone.

A week later, Sol went to visit Dorka, a girlfriend in the Ghetto. When he left the apartment, his father was wearing one of Sol's thick sweaters hand-knitted by his mother. It was too big for Sol, but fit Froim perfectly. The shock and grief of his loss had caused Froim to become very emotional. "Salik," he said, "you are all I have left. Please be careful. Don't do anything rash. I can't afford to lose you too." Uncharacteristically, he reached for Sol and held him, finally letting go so Sol could leave. That was the last time that Sol was ever to see his father. When he returned home from Dorka's apartment, Sol learned that the police had come and taken Froim away.

Sol burst into tears, but this time there was no one to console him, no one to share his pain. In just seven days, the sixteen year old boy had lost his entire family. For months, he had tried to stay strong for his family; now there was no longer any reason for restraint. Sol stayed alone in the apartment, having lost all track of time. Finally, he composed himself and left.

From that time on, Sol was alone. He rarely spent two nights in the same place. Many evenings he stayed with Aunt Bella. To her, Sol was the son she had never had. She gave him her total support, counseled him, fed him, and tried to lift his spirits. More importantly, she warned Sol to stay "invisible" to elude the Germans.

When Sol wasn't with Bella, he sought out friends with whom he could stay. Sometimes he slept on the hard concrete of one of the many tunnels that formed a huge underground labyrinth beneath Warsaw. Yet, no matter where he was, Sol lay awake at night remembering his loved ones. It was always hardest at night when he was obsessed by memories. Some evenings he lay awake for hours thinking about his family; this only made him miss them all the more. At the same time, cut off from his past and facing an uncertain future, he was forced to deal with the present danger.

One afternoon, when Sol returned to the family apartment, he was shocked to find it in total disarray. The complex had been entered and looted. As he walked through the rooms, he saw smashed dishes and glassware, the contents of cupboards, shelves, and drawers flung all over the floor, furniture overturned and broken, and those clothes that had not been stolen tossed about and trampled. Even personal mementos had disappeared.

The sight of all this destruction and the fact that the home where he had once been so happy had been looted left him even more bitter and angry. He remembered the pride his mother had taken in keeping the apartment neat with everything in its place. Now he barely recognized it. Even more painful, his family, everyone he had loved so dearly, was gone, and now he had nothing left to remind him of them. Not a single photograph remained. Frania, not yet eighteen, Tobcia, only thirteen, and his parents, both thirty-six, had vanished as if they had never lived.

Sol had to deal with the disappearance of his family and the death of his childhood simultaneously. The world Sol had known was gone forever; he was overwhelmed by a sense of deep despair and helplessness over events beyond his control. He looked around one more time. In spite of all the destruction, the apartment still linked him to his family. He could feel their presence, hear their words, and recall their touch. The memories were just too painful. Overcome by emotion, he threw himself on the couch and pounded the pillows; he cried out in the empty apartment, cursing the Germans. Then he buried his face in a quilt and cried until the quilt was soaked with tears. After what seemed to be an infinite period of time, he got up, brushed away the tears, and washed his face. Confused and sick at heart, he turned to leave, never to return.

Frightened and alone, Sol was nevertheless determined to evade the ever-widening roundup. However, this became increasingly difficult. His Aunt Bella's apartment on Nalewki Street was next to Mila Street, close to the "cauldron" or "sluice" set up by the Germans as a selection site. Without warning, the street would be sealed off and entire apartment buildings and blocks would be emptied of their residents. The Ukrainian guards shouted and pounded on the doors, methodically searching the buildings from cellar to attic. They forced their way into the apartments to search, rape, and rob, stealing the valuables, the privacy, and the dignity of the residents. All Jews were ordered downstairs and into the street at gunpoint. Children were beaten in front of their parents to force them to reveal secret hiding places. Those who hid were located and shot. Women, the elderly, and the sick all were kicked and senselessly brutalized. Once, German soldiers entered an apartment on nearby Mila Street, shooting or beating to death all nineteen people jammed into the tiny complex. This calculated and cold-blooded massacre shocked the inhabitants.

Late one afternoon, as Sol was walking through the Ghetto, another selection process was underway. Terrorized Jews, with all avenues of escape cut off, were being herded to the train station. Sol hid in the entrance of an apartment complex and watched with mounting anger. He saw a soldier push an attractive young girl out of the crowd into an abandoned burned-out building. Sol guessed she was about thirteen. After the prisoners had passed, Sol ran across the street and peered in the window of the deserted building. He saw the soldier pulling the girl's clothes off and heard her muffled screams.

Sol was overcome by rage. Without thinking, he rushed inside and, before the surprised German could react, he grabbed his uniform, violently shoved him against the wall and punched him in the face. He then pulled the dazed and bewildered soldier toward him, and slammed his head into the German's face. Thrown off balance, the soldier fell to his knees as his legs buckled. Holding his hand in his pocket as if he had a gun, Sol ordered the German to leave the girl alone.

"You no good barbarian. Who do you think you are? Don't ever touch this girl again. You don't have any right to do this." The soldier pleaded with Sol not to kill him, moaning as blood flowed from his nose. Sol tore the rifle from the German's shoulder and threw it to a far corner of the room. Controlling his anger, Sol told the trembling girl to leave. As she fled silently, she nodded her gratitude. Turning to the soldier, Sol warned, "Don't ever do this again. Don't worry. I am not a barbarian like you. I will not kill you."

Sol then shoved the frightened soldier to the floor and escaped to Nowolipki Street. There he cut through a deserted factory and took a back alley to Smocza Street. No one followed.

For the first time in many months, Sol felt good about himself. He didn't know if his act of defiance would ensure the girl's survival, but at least he had fought back.

For a time, Sol worked legitimately as a rickshaw driver. One day, he was hired by two German soldiers. After one got off at Stawksi Street, they entered a deserted narrow alley. The other soldier began to harass Sol. Since it was common for the Germans in the Ghetto to bait the Jews, Sol usually ignored their insults. However, this time, exhausted by the long hours of pedaling, Sol could no longer restrain himself. Oblivious to the consequences, he took a safety pin from his shirt and stuck it in the tire. He then told the German the tire was "kaput" and he could not repair it. The German became angry and startled Sol by slapping him. Sol stood up to the German.

"You slap me one more time and I'll beat the shit out of you. I'm a boxer and with my bare hands I can kill you. Who do you think you are, you Germans? You think you control the world? Someday you will not!" Sol retorted. The German was also young—about nineteen—but he was thin, lacking Sol's solid build. He was taken by surprise and began to back away. Sol started to beat him; the German cried out, pleading for his life. Fortunately for him, Sol decided he would not sink to the level of the Germans and would let him live. Sol knocked the soldier unconscious and left with the rickshaw. But, first, he took the German's gun. He later hid it in a pot in the cellar of one of the many bombed-out buildings.

Afterwards Sol told his friends about the gun. One of them, who was with the underground, asked to buy the weapon. Sol had reservations. "Why," he asked, "since the Germans will retaliate and kill Jews if this gun is used to shoot a German?"

The friend said it was difficult to get weapons since the arms trade with the Poles on the other side of the Ghetto walls had been drying up and every weapon was desperately needed. He persuaded Sol to give the gun to the resistance.

Shortly thereafter, Sol was standing by his rickshaw at the entrance to the *Umschlagplatz*. He was on the side of the street as it narrowed into the courtyard. A black Mercedes drove up and tried to ease by him. It screeched to a halt unexpectedly, and a well-groomed, but visibly agitated SS officer, accompanied by two soldiers, got out. The angry-looking officer strode up to Sol, struck him across the face with his glove, and impatiently ordered him to move the rickshaw to make room for the car: "Obersturmbannfuhrer (Lieutenant Colonel) Adolf Eichmann cannot be kept waiting!" he shrieked.

Chapter III

Treblinka

The day after Christmas, 1942, Sol was again captured and sent to the *Umschlagplatz*. The day had dawned bright but bitterly cold. While Sol was walking down Nalewki Street, a unit of the Jewish Ghetto Police poured out of a courtyard on one of their periodic sweeps. The entire street was cordoned off. Police were advancing from all directions. Sol fled, confidant he could outrun the police, but with all exits blocked, he was trapped. Frantic, he looked for someone he knew in the police unit, but this time recognized no one. Along with many others, Sol was marched to the *Umschlagplatz* which was already crowded with prisoners. They were ordered to sit in the square so that the guards could better observe them. Anyone who stood or attracted the attention of the guards was beaten or shot. When the freight cars were ready, the police immediately ordered the prisoners into the waiting rail cars. Those who did not move fast enough were pushed and beaten by the Ukrainian guards. As Sol observed the guards forcing the prisoners on board, he couldn't help but think how much the guards seemed to enjoy their work.

Sol estimated each car was meant to hold no more than sixty to seventy people. Yet, at least twice that number were packed in so tightly that there was only room for them to stand; the doors could barely close. To Sol's horror, several people were shot to create more room. When the train was loaded to capacity, the doors were locked.

In early evening, the train set off for the short trip to Treblinka. Due to frequent stops at sidings to take on the water needed to power the train, the trip lasted all night. The over-crowded car was dark; a narrow opening along the long walls just below the roof of the railcar allowed in the only light from the moon. The air was suffocating; people were gasping, sobbing, and struggling desperately for breath. All during the long night, Sol could hear the screams of babies, as well as moans, and pitiful cries. While some people seemed resigned to their fate, others were hysterical. Some people fainted; others in a panic tried to climb on top of one another; still others banged on the walls. Sol was overcome by loneliness, fatigue, and helplessness.

Sol saw several frail or elderly prisoners quietly slump unconscious to the floor. Within hours the railcar was filled with the stench of the dead. There was no food or water; nor were there toilet facilities. The odor of urine and excrement added to the suffocating smell. Cold air rushed in through the wooden slats of the car, but Sol couldn't feel it. He was crushed against the wall of the boxcar and desperate for fresh cold air. Taking his knife from his pocket, he used it to cut openings in the wooden slats; he then put his mouth against the small holes to suck in fresh air. When he tried to enlarge the holes, his knife blade broke. His mother had warned him several times about carrying the knife, but now that it was gone, Sol felt that he had lost his only security.

Peering through the holes, Sol could now see the Polish peasants at various stops. In spite of the cold outside, the oppres-sive heat inside the car caused terrible thirst. Several prisoners became delirious and cried out for water. The peasants were willing to give it to them, but only in exchange for gold or other valuables. "You may as well give up your valuables. You are going to die anyway," one old man yelled. These words erased any doubt Sol had about their fate.

The Ukrainian guards drank heavily; but from their vantage point on the caboose they were still sober enough to watch for any escape attempts. Several prisoners in Sol's car did indeed try to escape by squeezing through the narrow air openings beneath the roof; however, all such attempts were cut short by rifle fire. Sol was now more alarmed than ever.

The trip through the dense Polish forests brought them to a place which appeared to be another country station, Treblinka. Only a few months before, it had been a penal camp near a gravel quarry. Sol felt the transport jerk to a halt. Then he heard sporadic rifle fire from the Ukrainian guards stationed on the steps at either end of the boxcar. He didn't have much time to think before a section of about twenty cars was coupled to another locomotive and pulled into the camp. As he felt the train move slowly forward, Sol didn't know what to expect: on one hand he was glad the nightmarish journey was over, but at the same time he feared what lay ahead.

As the door of the train slid open, the prisoners were greeted by stern-faced guards, bristling with hostility. After the guards unlocked the cars, they began to pull people out. Sol, though groggy from the heat and cramped conditions in the boxcar, could not help but notice a peculiar odor. He did not know at the time that it was the thick smoke containing smoldering human remains. He choked from the stench, finding it difficult to breathe.

The railcar was about three feet above ground level. Many of the prisoners, infants and elderly alike, injured themselves as they jumped or were pulled to the ground. But they were given no time to compose themselves. The guards used brute force, striking the prisoners, including women and children, with whips and rifle butts to hurry them along. This was the German way, to disorient and confuse. SS guards holding whips yelled, "Schnell! Schnell!" (Hurry! Hurry!) to keep the prisoners moving and to enforce order. Sol, along with the others, jumped to the ground. He observed the people around him, some injured, all exhausted. He saw that some of the prisoners were covered with excrement from the long trip. Facing the frightened prisoners was a line of SS guards with menacing-looking German shepherd dogs; their function, it seemed, was to viciously attack those who dared falter or step out of line. The constant barking unnerved Sol even more. The SS watched the prisoners' every move with icy stares. As he was carried along in the midst of the crowd, Sol noticed that they were being funneled toward a wide gate in the fence near the rail spur. At first glance, the fence looked like it surrounded a forest, but as he drew closer Sol noticed barbed wire protruding through the branches of the trees. It was then Sol's worst fears were confirmed; he realized he was entering a concentration camp, not a relocation center.

Looking anxiously about, Sol thought he noticed a familiar face among the prisoners. After a closer look, Sol recognized Moniek, a friend who had lived on his street in the Ghetto. Moniek, who was about Sol's age, tall and slim, with dark hair, approached Sol carefully. Although all slave laborers were prohibited under penalty of death from the slightest contact with new arrivals, nevertheless, Moniek dared to try to help Sol. More frightened than ever, Sol froze and listened closely. Grimly, Moniek told Sol to immediately throw away the warm cap covering his ears so that he wouldn't appear to be a recent arrival. "No uniforms are required for the inmates here," he said. "Just follow me and do everything that I do so that you can blend in with the workers and not be noticed by the guards. Don't ask any questions. I'll explain everything to you later." There was no time to think, no further chance to talk. Instantly Sol made the decision to trust Moniek. Sol realized instinctively that this might be the only chance to save himself. He followed Moniek through the milling crowd to an area near the camp entrance where a group of workers was standing off to the side.

These prisoners were called platform workers or *Bahnhof Kommandos*; their job was to clean out the rail cars and remove the clothing and any other objects of value belonging to the victims. Sol followed Moniek's lead, as they joined others already busy cleaning out the rail cars. Moniek told Sol what to do to remove all traces of the passengers who had been on the train with Sol before it returned to Warsaw for its next load of human cargo. But Moniek had not prepared Sol for what he would see in the boxcars. Upon entering his first car, Sol was shocked by the sight of half a dozen corpses scattered amidst the baggage. Several were tiny infants; they appeared to have suffocated to death, their mouths wide open as if gulping for their final breath. The car reeked of a terrible stench. The personal belongings and bodies lay in puddles of excrement and vomit.

As Sol stared in disbelief, Moniek rushed over to him, warning him to get to work before the guards outside the railcar fired at them. Sol recovered, returning to his ghastly task. He and Moniek and other members of the work party unloaded the baggage left by the deportees, piling their meager belongings onto a two-wheeled wagon; they then pulled the wagon inside the wooden front gate to a large warehouse near the SS barracks. As they went to the "sorting area," they passed long ditches. There Sol saw the bodies of those who had died on the transports and then were dumped in the ditches for later burning. Within hours after each convoy arrived, all that remained of the hundreds of deportees was a huge mound of dirty clothes, luggage, and other personal effects which grew higher and higher as the day wore on.

While Sol watched the pile of personal possessions grow, he wondered what had happened to those who hadn't died on the train, where they were being sent and how they would ever recover their belongings. However, he did not have time to ponder these questions for very long, as the guard kept screaming "run, run." Sol learned quickly that life in the camps would be lived on the run.

As Sol went back and forth between the platform and the sorting area, another long line of boxcars appeared. He heard the blare of the loudspeakers in the station announcing to the new arrivals in several languages, "Leave your belongings where they are. Good care will be taken of them. You will now proceed to the showers for disinfection,"

Sol was overwhelmed by the inescapable stench, the strident sound of the loud speakers, and the horrible sight of so many dead bodies in the overflowing ditches. In order to retain his sanity, Sol realized he had to deny the reality of what he was experiencing. He tried to erect an emotional shield to protect himself.

Late in the afternoon, a black Mercedes with snow chains veered noisily by Sol's wagon and came to an abrupt stop by the platform. Several well-groomed SS officers wearing well-pressed uniforms got out and walked directly to a warehouse. In a hushed tone, Moniek told Sol that they came regularly to load cartons of gold, watches, rings, and other valuables into the trunk of the car. Sol was furious. "We ought to kill them all," he said. "They are turning us into slaves and stealing our possessions."

Moniek quieted him. "If you want to survive, say nothing, do nothing. Just hide your thoughts and feelings. Be as inconspicuous as possible and do as I do." Furious, Sol nevertheless went back to work.

As darkness fell, still shaken by the events of the day, Sol accompanied Moniek to his barrack, Camp Number one. There Sol discovered that the living conditions were just as primitive and forbidding as he had feared, judging from the rest of the camp. Sol found an empty bunk with a smelly straw mattress covered by a single threadbare blanket. Located between the building where the prisoners had gone to "shower" and the platform where the trains arrived, the wooden building was drafty, unheated, and foul. Behind the barrack was a small latrine fenced in with barbed wire. It consisted of a deep ditch with rough boards arranged in a ladder-like pattern laid over a hole filled to overflowing with waste. The stench was overpowering and nauseating. In addition, several filthy excrement and urination bowls were placed in the barrack. These were to be emptied in the outside latrine in the morning. For running water, there was an exposed pipe located outside in the rear of the barrack. These were the only sanitation facilities. There was no soap or cleanser of any kind.

While Sol was still inspecting his surroundings, Moniek warned him of the upcoming evening roll call. Fortunately, said Moniek, the count was conducted by their Ukrainian guards who were indifferent, and not nearly as meticulous as the Germans. The chief guard, a stocky and crude man named Boris, kept no names or numbers of the constantly changing prison population. So in that sense Sol was safe. However, the headcount could be an extremely dangerous time. The prisoners, said Moniek, could be arbitrarily whipped for any "crime," real or imagined. Moniek warned Sol to follow his example and not to give the guards any excuse to beat him.

Shortly before the roll call began, the inmates rushed out of the barrack and lined up in several parallel rows, one behind the other. Frightened, Sol stood erect in a back row next to Moniek. His heart was pounding for fear that he would be discovered, but as Moniek had indicated, Boris took only a perfunctory headcount. Sol's relief, however, was short-lived; following the count the prisoners were forced to continue standing at attention for over an hour in the bitter cold while the guards argued over how many of those who had died or been killed in labor details that day should be included in the final tally to be turned over to the Germans.

After this lengthy wait, the prisoners lined up for dinner. They were served a thin slice of coarse black bread and a meager allotment of meatless, watery soup in which floated a few scraps of unpeeled potato. While unsatisfactory, the hot liquid warmed Sol and temporarily revived him. After a few minutes the prisoners were sent back to their bunks. Although Sol was physically and emotionally drained, his mind was racing. He had so many unanswered questions. Also, he could not bear the intense cold in the unheated barrack. Although exhausted, he could not sleep.

The next morning, the prisoners were roused from their bunks early. They were forced to stand outside for a hurried roll call and given a watery cup of coffee. Then they were ordered to report to their work stations, as several transports were expected that day. As Sol stood near the platform waiting for the train, he heard rifle fire even before the train came into view. Sol feared that the guards were shooting prisoners before the train could reach the camp. A short time later, the first of several transports arrived. Sol stood to the side, waiting for the trains to empty. He watched helplessly, as the exhausted, bewildered, and terrified prisoners unloaded from the train were brutally beaten in a replay of the events of the preceding day.

Moniek took this opportunity to walk over to Sol. Somberly, telling him that it was better for him to know the whole truth, he began to tell Sol about the gas chambers. Moniek pointed to the upper camp where the murders took place. The gas chambers were located there, he said, in an area blocked from view by a barbed wire fence interspersed with branches and foliage. "I heard from another prisoner that they were installed last summer, shortly before I arrived here. Since then the mass killings have gone on every day the transports have come. The Germans will kill all these people before the day is over." Sol turned to Moniek and stared in disbelief. "Don't be so surprised, Salik. Everyone here knows what is going on. They are killing us by the thousands each and every day." Stunned and unable to utter a single word, Sol could not believe what he was hearing. He could scarcely comprehend the enormity of the catastrophe. The thought was just too horrible.

When the platform and train were cleared of the new arrivals, Moniek motioned to Sol to follow him. Still dazed, Sol mechanically followed Moniek to one of the loading platforms. There they loaded luggage and other personal effects aboard a wagon.

However, numerous cans of food discarded by the detainees proved too much to resist. In the privacy of the boxcar, Sol and Moniek gulped down enough fruits and cakes to satisfy their hunger. Then they pulled the wagon to the warehouse and unloaded it.

After they finished, Moniek pushed the wagon to the side of the building and told Sol to follow him. "There is something you must see, Salik." They walked through a gate to a large open area which was fenced in. This was known to the prisoners as "Transport Square," *Transportplatz*, or the "Undressing Square." They pretended to be collecting discarded garments, but at the same time were able to observe everything. Sol watched as the workers meticulously examined the victims' clothing, squeezing them to make sure valuables were not sewn inside. Then they removed names or any other indications of ownership or religion, separating the items by specific categories, and tying them into neat bundles.

While feigning work, Sol watched as the exhausted arrivals were hurried into the square. Upon entering the "reception" area, the men were sent to one side, and the women and children were sent to the other. Then they were divided into two groups: those selected to live, the young and able-bodied, were sent to the barracks; the second group was directed to two long huts located on either side of the square. Dazed women and children were rushed into the building on the left; there they were ordered to undress, leaving their clothing before going to the "showers" for delousing. After the shower, the guards told them they would be permitted to retrieve their clothes. Similarly, the men were sent to the hut on the right. Those who did not undress fast enough were lashed with whips by the guards.

Once undressed, the women and children, clutching each other, sobbing, hugging, kissing, and saying their last goodbyes, were forced to run up the narrow fenced path, about ten to fifteen feet wide, through a gauntlet to the "showers", in reality the gas chambers. The men followed soon afterwards. The Germans called this path *Himmelfarbstrasse*, the "Street to Heaven." The prisoners called it "Death Avenue." The guards, stationed in rows on either side, resorted to knifing, shooting, and smashing their rifle butts against the skulls of those who could not keep up. Those who fell unconscious were shot. The rest of the prisoners were driven to the chambers, running as fast as they could to avoid the blows, naked in the bitter cold, stripped of all dignity. Sol could not see the path from his vantage point in the corner of the yard, but he could hear the screams and cries of the victims as well as the curses of the guards.

The whole process of disrobing and being driven to the gas chambers lasted eight to ten minutes for the men and about fifteen for the women. The women were forced to have their heads shaved before being sent to their deaths, thus accounting for the extra time. It was only years later Sol learned that the women's hair was used as filler for mattresses in Germany.

The gas chambers, located in a massive brick structure, were a short walk from where Sol worked. They were operating at full capacity at the time of Sol's arrival. Afterwards the bodies were burned in enormous ovens. The identity of the prisoners as human beings was completely erased. Later the ashes were collected by slave laborers and spread as fertilizer in nearby fields.

To Sol, everything seemed to happen so fast and so routinely that he could not fathom the enormity of what he was witnessing. His hands began to tremble and he felt sick in the pit of his stomach. He could not erase the terrible sights, sounds and odors from his mind. Moreover, he realized how hopeless his situation was: an orphaned slave laborer who would likely die with the rest of his people. Angrily he turned to Moniek and sobbed. "I can't believe what is going on. I am so mad. I want to grab a machine gun and kill all the Ukrainians and Germans. I would rather die here doing something and taking some of them with me than do nothing. I hurt so badly."

It was not until this moment that Sol finally realized the full extent of the horrible truth. It suddenly dawned on him what his parents and Frania and Tobcia must have experienced just a few months before. As he watched the agony of the new arrivals, he could visualize what must have happened to his own loved ones. The magnitude of his terrible loss was more than he could bear. There had always been a part of him that refused to believe his family was gone forever. He had prayed he would see them again. Clinging to this belief had helped him cope during the harrowing days he was living through. Now random thoughts flashed through his mind. Did his parents and sisters know of the fate that awaited them as they were forced to undress? Were his sisters and mother together? Were they beaten and clubbed as they were forced to run the gauntlet to the gas chamber? What were their last thoughts as they were driven into the gas chamber? How deep was their anguish and despair? Why did the Germans hate them so? He had no answers. He broke down and sobbed bitterly.

Moniek tried to console Sol, but there was little he could say. "I know how you feel, Salik. Don't you think I am angry too? But, if we are to survive you must keep your rage under control. We need time to think of a way out and we can't do it if our heads aren't clear. I, too, carry a lot of pain inside of me. You are not alone, Salik. I share your anger and grief," he said sympathetically.

They left the undressing square and returned to the wagon. Sol didn't have the slightest idea of how much time had passed, but it couldn't have been long. The rest of the day was a blur, pulling the wagon back and forth from the train platform to the storehouse, loading and unloading. So this is what resettlement was, Sol thought. How could they have trusted the Germans? How could they not have known? Why hadn't they been warned? The transports rolled in that day, five in all, carrying several thousand people. None of the new arrivals seemed to have the slightest idea of the horror that awaited them.

"Who could know?" thought Sol. "Who could ever anticipate such brutality?" Sol was so overwhelmed by the enormity of what was happening, he couldn't even speak. Words simply refused to come. The pain was too deep. For the first time, he felt like giving up.

That night, after another sparse meal and lengthy roll call, Sol lay on his mattress. As tired as he was, he still could not sleep. He thought about his family, now lost to him forever. All doubts as to their whereabouts had disappeared. Any hopes he had left for their survival were gone. He thought about his parents and sisters and realized how much he loved and missed each of them. He thought, too, about the warmth and security of his family life. The Germans had taken all this from him and reduced him to a subhuman slave laborer.

The more he thought, the more he was consumed by utter rage. He was convinced that to avoid the same fate as his family, he had to find a way to escape—sooner rather than later. He was overcome by a sense of urgency: he must think of a plan. There had to be a way out, he thought; he had to find it before time ran out. For if he did not act quickly, he knew he too was doomed.

The next morning Sol and the other prisoners were awakened by the Ukrainian guards while it was still pitch dark. Sol had slept in his clothes for warmth and because Moniek had told him there would be no time to dress in the morning. The prisoners were first allowed to go to the latrine. Then the guards repeated the same lengthy roll call exercise as the night before. For Sol and the others, the effort of standing stiffly at attention in the darkness for over an hour was excruciating. They had to endure a numbing wind, sub-zero temperatures, and hunger. Sol had chosen to stand in the last row to better shield himself from the cold and the attention of the guards. At long last roll call came to an end. Coffee and a slice of stale bread were distributed. Then the prisoners were shuffled under guard to their stations to begin a twelve hour workday lasting from 6:00 A.M. to 6:00 P.M.

While working at the railway station the previous day, Sol had noticed that rather than guard the individual railway cars, the Ukrainian guards usually went into the caboose to escape the penetrating cold. He also observed that the guards did not shut the doors of the empty railway cars until their last walk through shortly before the trains left for Warsaw to pick up the next victims. All at once Sol realized he had a way to escape, although he knew that if he made any mistakes at all, he would be on the next march to the gas chamber. However, he realized that to remain at Treblinka was in itself a death sentence.

As they cleared and cleaned the railcars, Sol talked with Moniek and another young man, Fawv, who was in his twenties. A salesman before the war, Fawv knew the area well from his travels in the region. Fawv told them he too had been thinking about the same thing. "Our only means of escape," Fawv said, "is to use the transports. I will go whether you come with me or not. Do you want to join me?"

Moniek and Sol agreed enthusiastically. Sol told the others of the unlocked train doors; this sealed the agreement. Later that afternoon, while working in the rail yard, the three prisoners hoisted themselves undetected into one of the cars. They closed the doors on one side. Then, standing erect and motionless, arms pressed over their heads against the side of the car for what seemed an eternity, they tried to blend in with the deepening shadows. After some time, they overheard low voices speaking Ukrainian. Rigid with fear, their hearts pounding, they remained stationary. As they shuffled by, the guards pushed the doors shut; fortunately they did not look inside. It was dusk and vision was limited.

Soon, Sol and his friends felt the train begin to jerk to a start. They were overcome by a sense of relief. Lowering their hands from the wall, they sat on the floor to plan their next move. However, some time passed before they could bring themselves to talk. Moniek, shaking and frightened, defecated in his pants. Fawv and Sol also were terrified. The train slowly wound its way through the forest, making several stops. When it halted, the guards got out of the caboose to smoke and talk. Sitting motionless, Sol could hear their chatter through the narrow slits in the walls.

After the train resumed its journey, following the third stop, Fawv finally broke the silence. They must leave the train before it reached Warsaw and the heavily-policed *Umschlagplatz*, he said. They all agreed, but worried about where to leave the train. Fawv suggested they jump about ten to fifteen kilometers outside of Warsaw. The area, he said, should have few German troops, and yet be near enough so they could reach the city on foot. He told them that he knew how to jump safely, and would teach them what to do. He opened the door about halfway; they could see light snow falling and were hit by a frigid blast of cold air. Fawv repeated his instructions: "You cannot jump when the car is going straight. You jump and you get killed. You'll break your leg. You have to watch and see when the train is approaching a little hill. After we begin our descent, we jump. Don't jump with your feet. You must hold your hands over your head, crouch, like this, bend your head down, and somersault down the hill." He paused: "I will tell you when to jump." He then peered out into the night, watching for inclines. After a period of quiet, he finally shouted, "It's time! Let's jump!"

Moniek pushed the door wide open. Freezing air rushed in, first shocking, then invigorating the three. Fawv jumped first, followed by Sol and then Moniek. Sol landed with a crunch, rolled down the hill and rose quickly without a scratch. Fawv hurt his hip in the fall, but he assured them he was able to reach Warsaw. Although they were relieved to be free, they all knew they were still far from safe. At Fawv's suggestion, they decided to separate. At least one of them had to get to Warsaw to inform the Ghetto leadership of what was happening at Treblinka. They agreed: this was the most important part of their mission. To remain together would make it that much more likely they would be recaptured. They said their good-bys. Sol never saw them again; nor was he ever able to learn of their fate.

Through brutal weather conditions, Sol began the lonely trek back to Warsaw. A thick mantle of snow covered the ground and a silence enveloped the forest. He tried to think of a plan of action as he walked. He realized that since he did not know the countryside and could not trust its inhabitants, any of whom might be collaborators, he would have to depend on his instincts to survive. Afraid to stay on the highway since it was used by military vehicles, he took a parallel course through the wooded areas and fields, trying to remain as inconspicuous as possible.

Finally, Sol could go no further. He was overcome by the bitter cold, gnawing hunger pangs, and exhaustion. He wished he still had his knit cap for warmth. Shivering from the cold, he stopped often to massage his feet and rub his hands to avoid frost-bite. But as soon as he had finished, he could feel the cold return. The thick layer of snow and ice which covered the ground made footing treacherous and each step difficult. He had tried to avoid seeking help, but he was so weak that he had to take the risk. He knew he needed to find shelter to escape the cold. Stopping at a store, Sol went in to ask for assistance. The Polish shopkeepers, frightened by Sol's unkempt appearance, told him to leave. Then, about one hundred yards away, Sol saw a group of farmers. Approaching them, he told them he was a Pole who had been bombed out. He said he was hungry, and that the car he had been waiting for had been confiscated by the Germans. He asked if he could stay with them until he could get a ride to Warsaw.

One farmer nodded, but there was a condition. In exchange for assistance, Sol would have to help with the work. Sol agreed, but was not pleased to discover that the farmer's business was hauling human waste to be used for fertilizer. For two days Sol shoveled waste. He rode in the wagon, which was filled with excrement, until the stench became too much for him. At the end of the second day of hard labor, the farmer dropped Sol off at his house while he went into the nearby town for supplies. Sol took off his filthy clothes and threw them into the stove. For the first time in weeks, he took a long, leisurely bath, and then helped himself to some of the farmer's clothes. He kept only his shoes, which he cleaned thoroughly.

After leaving the old farmer's house, Sol marched another day before finally reaching Warsaw. As he walked, he tried to reflect on all that had happened and sort out his feelings. He was torn between despair and anger. Sol was sure of only one thing: he knew he had to alert those in the Ghetto to the atrocities he had witnessed at Treblinka.

Chapter IV

The Ghetto Uprising

Sol moved quickly through the city, then jumped over the wall into the Ghetto. Once inside, he knew that he had to make contact with the secret organization known by its acronym, "ZOB." With the first mass "resettlement" in the summer of 1942, a small group of Zionist youths had founded a Jewish resistance organization called *Zydowska Organizacja Bojowa*, or Zionist Fighting Organization. Its purpose was to resist the Nazis in any way possible and with any weapons available. "Better to Die with Honor" was its motto. Sol was determined to link up with ZOB in order to avenge the horrible deaths the Germans had inflicted upon his family and people.

After making inquiries, Sol succeeded in finding ZOB member Jacob Jacobovich, a soccer hero before the war from Sol's neighborhood. Sol told him of the mass killings he had witnessed at Treblinka. Jacobovich asked Sol to come with him. Walking from Nalewki to Mila Street, they crossed through underground tunnels and deserted alleys. At last they arrived in a small dimly lit room where several men were seated around a large table. Most were smoking and a stale gray haze filled the air, making it difficult to breathe. Standing silently against the wall were two armed men. Scattered around the room were empty milk cans. As Sol's eyes became accustomed to the semi-darkness, he looked closely at the men and recognized some of them as members of the Jewish Ghetto Police units. Jacobovich approached a good-looking young man with a sturdy frame who was taller than the rest. He then introduced Sol to Mordechai Anielewicz, the ZOB commander.

Anielewicz asked Sol to tell him everything. Sol slowly and carefully recounted everything he had seen and heard during his two days at Treblinka. He paused frequently to try to remember every detail. Each time he looked around the table he saw the others staring at him intensely. "Treblinka means death! All the people that have been taken there have been killed, and so will we," he concluded. There was silence in the room when Sol finished.

Anielewicz nodded and replied, "We are already doing something about that. We are the Jewish Underground. Whatever you see here, don't mention to anyone. Don't tell anyone what is going on." Anielewicz then quizzed Sol on some specifics, wanting to know about the number of kapos at Treblinka, the name of the commanding officer, the Ukrainian guards, how many he had seen, and how they carried out the slaughter of so many. Since he had not been there very long, Sol did not know all the answers. However, Sol suspected from Anielewicz's questions that the underground already had information about Treblinka and the killings there. He guessed they were using his information to verify earlier reports. When the questioning ended, Sol asked hopefully whether anyone had heard from Moniek or Fawv; no one in the room had any news of either of them. Perhaps, Anielewicz suggested, they had reached a farm where they were being hidden.

Sol then told Anielewicz that he was a member of the Betar youth movement and was anxious to become involved in the underground. Anielewicz said that Sol would be welcome as an individual, but that disagreements about the organizational structure of the resistance movement made it impossible for the ZOB to accept Betar into the organization. Sol readily agreed to the condition of joining ZOB as an individual.

There was one more matter that Sol was anxious to discuss with Anielewicz: he wanted to be trained as a fighter. Anielewicz assured him that his time would come, but in the meantime, he had to remain silent about where he had been and what he had seen. He asked Sol to start collecting milk cans, soda water bottles, and any other containers he could find; he told him to search at night, as the Germans ruled the streets during the day. He also warned Sol to be careful, because if he were caught, he would be hauled back to the *Umschlagplatz*. Jacobovich said that the organization would be in touch with him; Sol was then taken back to Nalewki Street by a different route.

Sol walked slowly through the Ghetto, thinking over his meeting with the underground. He had come to see things in a different light. He, like so many others, could scarcely have suspected the horrible truth. He had come to realize that silence created doubt; it was this uncertainty that kept the residents from giving up. For if they knew the truth, they would no longer have any reason to hope. Sol now realized he must speak of Treblinka to no one except the members of the underground. To do otherwise would create panic and despair.

Sol walked to the only sanctuary he could think of—Aunt Bella's apartment. He approached anxiously, not knowing what to expect. Much to his surprise and delight, Bella was still there. She looked older, more tired, and strained. But Bella hid her feelings well, and did not talk of herself. As she showed him in, she put her arms around him and hugged him. She was thrilled to see him. She offered him what little food she had and comforted him. Bella had always been a source of strength to the family. Now that the rest of his family was gone, Bella was like a second mother to Sol, representing the only family he had left.

Bella told Sol she had missed seeing him the last several days. She asked where he had been and where he had slept. At first Sol hesitated, but with Bella's encouragement, he quickly forgot the promise he had made to himself and told her the whole story of his two days in Treblinka. Bella did not reveal any shock, although she tensed as Sol's words spilled out. When he was done, she praised him for his courage. While her voice remained calm, it betrayed deep concern. Apparently, thought Sol, she had already guessed the worst.

After they finished talking, Bella told Sol she had a secret to share with him. She walked him through the apartment to a stairwell that led to an underground cellar. She explained that that was where she lived with several other women whose husbands also had vanished. It was, said Bella, a secret hiding place, and all the women were involved in the resistance. She never revealed their exact role in the underground nor did she ever say any more about her husband, Leon. This surprised Sol, but he was determined not to bring up the subject unless she initiated it.

After they returned to the living room, Sol decided it was time to leave. "I must let my friends know I am all right. Don't worry about me, I can take care of myself."

Again, Bella hugged Sol. "Don't be cocky. Don't take any chances, whatever you do. Better to be safe than sorry," she cautioned. "I love you too much to see anything happen to you. Someday this will end. In the meantime, please take care of yourself, Salik. You must survive this. You cannot let them win." Sol pulled away. Bella's eyes were tearing; she was losing her composure and Sol wanted to leave before she began to cry. For the next few hours he walked aimlessly around the neighborhood. Many of the tenement buildings had already been emptied of their occupants, the silence giving an eerie sensation. Sol was at a total loss; he didn't know which way to turn. Eventually he made his way to a friend's apartment where he was welcomed and given a couch to sleep on for the night.

Several days after his return to the Ghetto, the ZOB approached Sol and put him in touch with other members of the resistance with whom he would be working; they asked him to be part of a smuggling operation within the Ghetto, rather than joining

resistance forces developing outside the walls. Several boys who
had left the Ghetto to join the partisans in the forests outside
Warsaw had been killed by the Poles and stripped of their possessions. This news further confirmed Sol's distrust of the Poles.

Much to Sol's surprise, he discovered he already knew
many of the ZOB members from his prewar school days. Most
were in their late teens. Some, several years older, roughly twenty
to twenty five years of age, were familiar, as they were from his
old neighborhood or were fellow athletes from the Maccabee
Club. In the coming weeks, a strong bond developed among all
the boys. Sol grew to like them immensely and trust them uncon-
ditionally. All had experienced similar traumas, most having also
lost their families; yet, rather than complaining, they were all
determined to exact revenge from the Germans for their suffering,
no matter how unequal the odds. When Sol was discouraged,
their high morale helped to boost his spirits. In time, although
they could not replace Sol's family, they did help to fill an
emotional void in his life.

Among Sol's friends in the newly organized smuggling
band was Felek. Like the others, he was a native of Warsaw.
Other members of the group included Julek, Lolek, and Schlomo.
Julek was quiet and unassuming, with a boyish face, but efficient
and dedicated; Lolek was just the opposite. Broad-shouldered and
hardened by life in the streets, he was a born hustler, cocky and
arrogant. He took chances and almost seemed to enjoy the danger,
even appearing at times to be indifferent to life. However, he
could be counted on to gather vital intelligence on the German
patrols on the other side of the wall; he also helped with the
movement of smuggled food and supplies into the Ghetto.
Schlomo was a tall, emaciated looking ex-student. Blond and
with a fair complexion, he could blend in easily with the Polish
population. His knowledge of the neighborhoods outside the
Ghetto walls allowed him to act as a guide when the smugglers
crossed to the other side.

Other members of the group included Meyer Berkowitz, one of Sol's fellow soccer players in after school pick-up games. Meyer was a cautious but skilled member of the smuggling team. Moishe Teitlebaum, like Sol, had been a rickshaw driver during the early months of the German occupation. He and Sol had become friends at the time, as they shared their problems while waiting for passengers at the rickshaw stops. Moishe was an extrovert with a ready smile and a penchant for gallows humor, always trying to make light of the dark days they were enduring. He was only a few years older than Sol, but the stress of the times had aged him considerably. His eyes seemed permanently ringed with circles and he bore a tragic look. Always calm and composed, Moishe became Sol's mentor and instructed Sol in "street smarts." Leon Lefkowitz and Bolek Speigleman were both tall, powerfully-built former boxers from the Maccabee Club. The hardships they had endured had transformed them into born leaders, tough and determined young men who went to great lengths to carry out their missions for the underground.

Sol's activities in the resistance also brought him into contact with his own extended family. On his father's side, Abraham and Schlomo Rosenberg, both first cousins, were active in the underground. More surprising to Sol was the presence of Mania Rosenberg, an attractive twenty-year old with a smooth complexion and long black hair. Her education, like that of the others, had been cut short by the war. She had joined the struggle early on and carried out the same assignments as the boys. Sol also met a cousin on his mother's side, the fiery red-haired Daniel Deurschmann. Of average height and slender build, Daniel had a ready smile, but a tough, no-nonsense approach to his missions. He refused to admit defeat and would do whatever was asked of him.

In the weeks that followed, Sol faithfully carried out his orders from Anielewicz. He waited until workers at the Schultz Bottling Plant on the Aryan side were leaving. This was a good time; the streets were crowded and Sol could lose himself in the congestion. He took as many empty milk bottles and petrol cans as he could find and carry. He even stole directly from the Germans; when no one was watching, he took full petrol cans that were tied to the sides of their trucks and hid them in an abandoned storefront near the wall. At night he climbed back over the wall to retrieve them. Very carefully, so as not to spill a precious drop of fuel, he carried the cans back to the wall one at a time and hoisted them over to the other side.

He also went to bakeries that remained open in Warsaw and placed orders for hard bread. This bread was later put into bags and hidden in the cellars of the Ghetto. In addition, he helped to fill and store bottles of water at numerous locations scattered throughout the Ghetto for future use.

Having obeyed his orders to this point, Sol wanted to obtain a pistol and learn how to use it. Unfortunately, though, there were more resistance fighters who wanted weapons than there were guns available. Instead, Sol was told that when the time for action finally arrived, he was to run to dead or wounded Germans and strip them of their weapons, ammunition, and helmets; he was then to scurry back into hiding.

At night, in violation of the strict curfew imposed by the Germans, he was sent out on clandestine raids. Together with several other members of his band, he was ordered to steal German military uniforms from a warehouse on Dzielna Street. The break-in was to take place under cover of darkness, after all the security personnel had left. The uniforms were to be carried to a nondescript building across the street from a prison where Jews were being held. The plan was carried out without a hitch. At the time, Sol was not given any reason for the theft. Only later did he learn that the underground was planning a raid on the prison in an attempt to release the prisoners.

Following the success of the raid on the warehouse, Sol was given a much more dangerous assignment. He and four others were ordered to again cross the wall, where they were to meet a Polish couple at a prearranged site on Okopowa Street. The couple had a truck, supposedly carrying potatoes, that would be parked on the street. Sol was told that hidden under the potatoes would be sacks of much-needed bullets; they were to smuggle the bullets back to the resistance. Scaling the wall, they moved quickly through the shadows until they saw the truck. As they approached it, the man and woman standing near the rear of the truck began to push the potatoes aside, revealing bundles hidden underneath. With few words, they helped Sol and the other four boys place the heavy packages into knapsacks on each of their backs.

The knapsacks were filled quickly, but each one weighed well over one hundred pounds. The trip back was excruciatingly slow and physically agonizing. They had to halt often to rest, even though to stop was to risk detection. Exhausted, they decided to reconsider where they would recross into the Ghetto. Slowly, breathing heavily, they made their way to the Muranowski Street crossing. There they stacked wooden boxes one on top of the other to make scaling the wall less difficult. After what seemed like countless hours, they finally arrived at the resistance headquarters. There they unloaded their ammunition, much to the delight of Jacobovich, who was patiently awaiting their return. The bullets were then placed in a two-wheeled wooden wagon and pulled to secret arms caches in the maze of tunnels beneath the Ghetto.

Since the demand for munitions was so great, the ZOB thought up a number of ingenious methods to secure weapons for the Ghetto. Sol was assigned to one such operation. The Germans permitted the dead to be placed in makeshift caskets which were then carted off in wagons to the Jewish cemetery located outside the Ghetto walls for burial. The ZOB took this opportunity to smuggle live people hidden in the caskets out of the Ghetto. Whenever possible, ammunition or supplies were clandestinely brought back through German lines in the "empty" wagons. Sol made several such trips, and although the risk of getting caught was always present, the Germans never searched their wagon. For Sol, each trip was an achievement because he was assisting others to escape and at the same time bringing in much needed supplies. It gave him a sense of fulfillment that he had perhaps helped to save someone's life and at the same time it reduced his sense of powerlessness.

On another occasion, while Sol was trading for food with Poles outside the ghetto wall, something quite unexpected happened. A slow rain had turned into a hard-driving storm. Sol decided to try to find shelter on the Aryan side.

Sol was familiar with German decrees imposed on this side of the wall as well. Although the ordinances were not as onerous as those in the Ghetto, the Poles were also suffering under the occupation. One such ordinance was a 9:00 P.M. curfew which was strictly enforced. Sol knew that this hour was fast approaching and anyone on the streets after this time could be shot on sight. Kazia, a classmate from school whom he had visited several times, lived nearby. He ran through the downpour to her apartment, knocking loudly on the door. The entire family was at home. Kazia was surprised and pleased to see Sol; she greeted him with a big smile and welcomed him inside. When Sol asked if he could spend the night, Kazia told him to wait in the hall while she asked her father for permission. A few minutes later Sol heard Kazia's father.

"Let the Zydek (Jew) stay overnight since it is storming outside. Also, tell him I have grease and sugar to trade for money."

Although Sol was angry at Kazia's father, who knew Sol's name, but had derisively referred to him as "the Jew," he gave no outward sign and accepted their hospitality. Indeed, he was grateful for the shelter because he knew Kazia's family was risking German retribution. After drying off, Sol visited with Kazia's parents. He also purchased several items not available in the Ghetto from Kazia's father; he bought several pounds of sugar and a few cans of grease with money from the ZOB. As the storm outside worsened, the family decided to retire early. Sol was shown to an empty bedroom next to the room belonging to Kazia's brother.

Later that night, long after her family had gone to sleep, Kazia slipped into Sol's room, quietly closing the door behind her. She woke Sol as she slipped into bed with him. They spoke for a short time and then made love. Although Sol was attracted to her he did not feel any deep emotional attachment. Following this brief sexual encounter, Kazia blushed and expressed concern that she might have to go to confession; she was afraid that Jesus would discover her sin and consider her a bad person. "How is he going to find out?" Sol asked. "You don't have to tell him. I promise you I won't," Sol whispered.

She shrugged and told Sol there was something else. She was worried about what people would think if they learned she was having sex with a Jew. "Salik, I never made love with a Jew before," she cried. Sol sensed he was not her first lover. He believed that she was more frightened of what would happen to her if German authorities or her parents ever learned of her relationship with Sol. He tried to reassure her that no one would ever find out about their encounter, so nothing would ever happen. After several moments of silence she seemed to relax.

"You had best leave now," he whispered, "so that your parents do not discover you here. Our secret will be safe with me." Kazia left Sol's room quickly. The next morning, Sol rose early and left the apartment before the family awoke.

On January 18, 1943, the inevitable finally occurred. German troops entered the Ghetto intending to destroy it and make it *Judenfrei*, or free of Jews. The day dawned bitterly cold. In a surprise move, German tanks, half-tracks, and jeeps moved slowly through the main streets of the Ghetto followed by columns of troops. The dilapidated buildings crumbled as the soldiers fired indiscriminately; the residents were gunned down as they fled their demolished apartments. By this time, most of the Jews had already been removed from the Ghetto, but over loudspeakers the Germans warned those who were still hidden away in the attics and basements of their tenements to surrender or be killed. With surrender came the promise of food and work in the factories of labor camps. For some, the offer appeared too good to refuse. Many of the exhausted and starving inhabitants, clinging to the illusory hope of a better life in the resettlement camps, hesitantly emerged from hiding, allowing themselves to be taken away.

However, things did not quite go according to German plans. As a group of deportees was being herded to the *Umschlagplatz*, a dozen armed men who had intermingled with the prisoners suddenly opened fire on the guards. Anielewicz and the small group under his command had had little opportunity to plan or coordinate their attack. Nevertheless, they still managed to surprise the Germans, who did not anticipate any opposition. At a given signal each resistance fighter opened fire on the guards. Several Germans fell, the rest retreated, and the surprised detainees fled. After the initial shock, the Germans regrouped and attacked again. This time their overwhelming firepower quickly killed or dispersed the attackers.

In spite of their losses, news of their stand caused a wave of euphoria in the Ghetto. German casualties, heretofore unthinkable, stunned the Nazis and forced them to rethink their tactics. During the next three days their incursions into the Ghetto were tentative and marked by a concentration of force in a small area. The raids did nab several thousand prisoners, mostly elderly or infirm, who were quickly dispatched to the death camps. Those capable of eluding the dragnet, now imbued with a sense of hope and pride, fled. On the fourth and final day, the Germans took out their frustrations. All restraint disappeared. Rather than arresting Jews, they were determined to kill as many as they could find. Over a thousand Jews were brutally slaughtered, most of them women and children.

By now the Ghetto had become an empty shell. In block after block burned out and abandoned buildings stood silent. In fact the Ghetto reminded Sol of a deserted cemetery. Pedestrian traffic on the street was virtually nonexistent. Those few who did venture out did so under cover of darkness. The remaining inhabitants lived in basements, bunkers, or the apartments of those previously deported. Most of them were ravaged by malnutrition or typhus. Everyone knew that the end was near; there was no doubt that the Germans planned to liquidate the Ghetto. However, knowing the intentions of the Germans, the survivors were more determined than ever to resist to the end. So while there was a temporary respite from German attack, the survivors spent the next few months in frenzied preparations for what they knew would be the final assault. ZOB Commander Anielewicz seemed to be everywhere at once, encouraging his forces to prepare for the imminent attack. To Sol, he was the type of dynamic leader who inspired men to do the impossible.

Sol and a number of other young orphans were placed under the supervision of Marek Edelman, a member of the central command, who also oversaw several additional squads. Edelman gave the impression of being older than he was. His look was intense and there was a certain hardness, which commanded respect, in his voice. Edelman told the boys to continue their activities. In addition to monitoring Sol and the other boys, he informed them about the overall situation in the Ghetto. Furthermore, he introduced a semblance of military discipline and during slack periods, led the boys in discussions on a variety of topics.

Sol stayed busy; he was constantly on the move, in search of more cans for the petrol bombs that were being readied, or stocking bread and water in key locations in the cellars, or running messages. When the group was not busy smuggling, Edelman took Sol's band to an abandoned burned out building on Nalewki Street. There he showed them how to prepare a hiding place or bunker in order to defend themselves during the German attack. They were told to do the excavation work at night, when German patrols normally avoided the Ghetto.

The boys divided into two work shifts, digging on alternate nights. Gradually, over four weeks, the shelter took shape. The interior was bare. No sleeping or sanitary facilities were constructed and no electrical connections were installed. However, vents through the roof and narrow slits in the walls facing the street allowed in fresh air. The entrance and exit were camouflaged with debris so that they were invisible from the street, and the walls and roof of the basement were built up with sand to help withstand direct German artillery or tank assaults. A maze of underground tunnels connected the bunker to other bunkers and to nearby basements. Water and small amounts of food were stockpiled for a long siege.

The squad ate all meals together. Breakfast consisted of loaves of bread with ample amounts of jam. Boiled potatoes and tasty vegetable or lentil soup were prepared for dinner in the kitchen of a nearby abandoned apartment.

On the evening of April 18, 1943, the resistance learned that plans for the final destruction of the Ghetto were to be implemented early the next morning on Passover, one of the holiest days of the Jewish calendar. The German attack force consisted of over three thousand soldiers and SS troops. Their orders were to liquidate the remaining Jews in the Ghetto, now reduced to approximately fifty thousand.

Lying in wait were the members of ZOB. The approximately twelve hundred fighters were armed with an assortment of cast-off and stolen weapons, many of which were defective or of little use in street fighting. Months of pleas to the Polish underground, the AK, had gone unheeded; the Poles were either unwilling or unable to meet the demand for weapons for the Ghetto. Still, the enterprising fighters had managed to acquire, in addition to their various weapons, thousands of rounds of ammunition, water pipe grenades, and Molotov cocktails, as well as food, and medical supplies. These were scattered and hidden in bunkers throughout the Ghetto. In addition, the fighters had learned rudimentary street-fighting tactics, had planned evasive maneuvers, and had organized themselves into battle groups with chains of command. Given the circumstances, they had done all they could do to prepare for the unequal struggle.

Sol felt very much at ease with the men and boys in the bunker. Over three months' time, a strong sense of solidarity had developed. The composition of the small groups in the bunker changed constantly as the fighters were shifted about. But on that Passover morning, Sol's good friends Smulek and Lolek were with him, as were several other close acquaintances from his old neighborhood. In addition, a man named Teitlebaum, who was not related to Sol's friend Moishe, had moved into the bunker a couple of weeks before the German attack. He was older and married, and served as a father figure to the boys. In the days that followed, he comforted them, advised them, and tried to reassure them. He grew close to all of them, constantly checking on their morale and providing words of encouragement. His presence served as a stabilizing influence and calmed their jittery nerves. When he wasn't in the bunker, Teitlebaum baked bread for the underground. Also, shortly before the attack, Sol's second cousin on his mother's side, a dentist who had fled Germany in 1939, joined them in the bunker. Sol had heard Chaya speak of him, but had never met him until circumstances brought them together. Strong-willed and outspoken like the other Deurchmanns, he kept the boys focused, and tried to ease the tensions.

When the fateful morning of April 19 arrived, all those in Sol's bunker were quiet, although Sol sensed an undercurrent of restlessness. No words were spoken, no one moved; their thoughts were focused on what the day would bring. Sol was overcome by mixed emotions: on one hand he was nervous and afraid of what was to come; on the other, he was relieved that the

time to fight back had finally arrived. Sol was confident his group
would give a good accounting of themselves. If there was fear, no
one showed it. What was visible was a grim determination to try
to gain some measure of satisfaction. Sol knew they would not
give in without a struggle, even though they had very little with
which to resist the Germans. No one had any military training.
Only the two older men in the bunker were armed with small
caliber pistols. The others had no weapons except about one
hundred gasoline-filled bottles, which they planned to hurl at the
enemy. In addition, Teitlebaum had a two-way radio that allowed
him to speak to fighters in the other bunkers. Through his
earplugs he could hear the other transmitters; he then relayed the
news or orders to the rest of the group.

Mordechai Anielewicz ordered those with weapons not to
shoot until they were told: "I'll give the order when to shoot," he
said emphatically. The Germans were first to be allowed to enter the
Ghetto. Until then there was to be silence. "Remember," he said,
"you are fighting for our lives and dignity and honor. If you run out
of ammunition, use your fists. Use your teeth. Bite off their noses!"

Sol waited anxiously. He didn't consciously think about
losing his life. He was pumped with adrenaline and was eager to
fight. But nerves were getting the better of him. His hands were
sweaty and his heart was racing. From a small opening he
watched the column of armored half-tracks, jeeps, large trucks,
light cannons, and soldiers crawl slowly up the street. The resistance fighters in their hiding places remained silent, waiting for
Anielewicz's order.

Finally, at about 6:00 A.M., when the order came to fire at
will, Sol felt his entire body stiffen. It was not long before the
Germans' sense of invulnerability was dashed. Petrol bombs and
Molotov cocktails that Sol had worked so hard to prepare rained
down upon the invaders; grenades exploded everywhere. Several
German soldiers fell to the pavement, while the rest fled for
cover, stunned by the defiance.

It was all over in less than twenty minutes. There seemed to be little serious damage. The German withdrawal resulted in a wave of exultation in the bunker. Teitlebaum glanced around the room, "Is everyone all right?" he asked. Everyone nodded. No one was injured and all appeared relieved to have overcome their fears and to have survived their first battle. Teitlebaum praised their spirit and told them how proud he was of their courage. "Get some rest," he said. "They will be back." A strange silence fell over the bunker the rest of the day.

During the next week, German columns advanced into the now devastated Ghetto each morning at approximately the same time. The result was always the same: the defenders hurled grenades from their bunker hideouts. The incendiary bottles spread panic and death among the Nazi forces. Sharpshooters picked off German stragglers. Bullets seemed to ricochet everywhere. The fierce resistance succeeded in turning back the German attack. But the following day the Germans returned to renew their assault.

For seven days the resistance steadfastly withstood the German attacks. The initial German reversals had an extraordinary impact on the resistance and especially on young Sol. During lulls in the fighting, he rushed into the street to pick up whatever the Germans had dropped during their retreat. He pulled the helmets off dead Germans and retrieved ammunition and weapons. Sol felt so elated when he found his first helmet that he scratched a Star of David on the back of it. Crying tears of joy, he was finally able to gain some measure of revenge for the deaths of his loved ones. Sol regained his confidence; he naively believed they were near victory. The "invincible" Army of the Third Reich seemed to be crumbling before the might of the ZOB. Sol was proud of himself and the other fighters and felt a sense of fierce exultation that they were at last fighting back. During the first few days of the battle, he rejoiced when he saw the German columns withdrawing and the dead Germans lying in the streets. His fears diminished and he was eager for retribution.

In the evenings, after the Germans had withdrawn, Sol and the other members of his squad left the bunker and took to the streets. There they breathed fresh air and talked enthusiastically with other members of the resistance. It was an exhilarating time. Despite his weariness, Sol felt rejuvenated. However, his perspective was limited. He did not realize that the Ghetto fighters' stocks of ammunition were dangerously low, food and water supplies were very close to depletion, and the dead and wounded fighters could not be replaced. Indeed, by the seventh day the boys in Sol's bunker were limited to one glass of water and several slices of moldy bread a day.

Shortly before dawn on the eighth day, the Germans changed their tactics. They now began to liquidate the Ghetto block by block. First, they unleashed a concentrated artillery bombardment. A storm of flames and destruction swept through the Ghetto. The earth shook and buildings blew apart. This was followed by low-level pinpoint bombing runs by the Luftwaffe on the orders of SS Brigadier General Jurgen Stroop. Incendiary bombs readily ignited the nineteenth century wooden buildings. Windows exploded, raining shattered glass on the streets below. Roofs collapsed, as tongues of flames soared skyward. The defenders were overcome by intense heat and suffocating smoke. Ashes from the burning buildings seemed to be everywhere. For the next two weeks, with the exception of Easter Sunday, the Ghetto was raked by a combination of withering bombing runs and murderous artillery fire. And, while Sol's bunker withstood the murderous assaults due to the layers of fill and debris which protected it, the results were nevertheless devastating. The Ghetto became a raging inferno of gutted buildings and rubble.

To Sol, the whole world seemed to be aflame. Everything was so hot it was impossible to even touch the bricks. Temperatures in Sol's bunker became unbearable. It was difficult to speak and almost impossible to breathe. Most of the boys took off their shirts, but relief was negligible. Sol saw people jumping from burning buildings to their deaths. Many choked to death in clouds of smoke. Others were crushed when their hiding places collapsed. Still others turned their weapons on themselves rather than face deportation or execution. Those who fled the oppressive heat in the bunkers for the open streets were killed instantly by withering German fire. Sol was haunted by images of death in the man-made firestorm. Charred bodies and severed limbs were visible everywhere. He could not believe the horror all around him. Even on the one day, Easter Sunday, when all attacks ceased, flames continued to devour the ramshackle buildings in block after block. But for the first time in days there was no sound of exploding artillery shells. In its place, Sol could hear the church bells from cathedrals across Warsaw. He could visualize the crowds kneeling in prayer on this Holy Day. "How could they be so pious?" thought Sol, when thousands were dying just a few minutes away. Could his fellow Poles be that indifferent to their plight? "They must smell the burning and see the smoke and fires. Why won't they come to our aid before it is too late? The Ghetto is dying. Why won't they help us battle the Nazis?" he wondered. But Sol knew these hopes were futile; he had long since lost confidence in his fellow Poles.

Later that night, under cover of darkness, Sol and other members of his squad ventured outside to escape the broiling temperatures in the bunker. Accompanied by Lolek and Schlomo, Sol headed down Nalewki Street for several blocks. There, at the site of two bunkers which the Germans had been unable to penetrate earlier in the week, the boys finally came to realize just how illusory the belief was that they could stand up to German force. Following their first failed attempts, the Germans had poured large concentrations of automatic weapons fire into the area and then launched a large-scale troop attack. It was at that time Teitlebaum had lost all contact with the two bunkers.

Now, as the boys surveyed the area, it looked like a wasteland of scorched earth. Isolated fires were still burning out of control. The Germans had made no attempt to put out the fires and the heavy smoke caused the boys to choke and their eyes to burn. As Sol looked around, he could no longer recognize the streets or neighborhood. All landmarks had been obliterated, replaced by block after block of rubble. When they reached the site of the bunkers, they found the narrow opening partially blocked by fallen bricks. After clearing the debris away, they proceeded down the narrow stairwell to the cellars. The buildings had burned down to their very foundation, the smoldering embers creating intense heat. As they descended into the tunnel to the connecting bunkers, they could hardly breathe. The air had literally been sucked out of the cellars.

After the boys reached the basement level, their eyes adjusted to the darkness; they were stunned by what they saw. In the two bunkers, at least one hundred people, including many women and children, lay dead in twisted heaps. There were no signs of bullet holes. It looked as if all had been asphyxiated; there was no indication of life. Sol tried not to imagine how terribly they had died and the agony they must have endured. This seemed to confirm the rumors Sol had heard that the Germans were pouring poisonous gas into the bunkers. The bunkers had become silent tombs. The three boys stared in disbelief, first at the corpses and then at each other. The carnage was appalling. Sol had seen enough. He turned to leave, followed by the others. They groped and stumbled their way back through the passageway and up to the street as fast as they could; then they returned silently to their own shelter, each deeply immersed in his own thoughts. Sol was now prepared for the worst. His earlier euphoria had turned to deep despair. Shock and fear began to set in.

With most of the Ghetto leveled, in order to flush out any remaining Jews like Sol still hidden deep in the underground bunkers, German engineers began to systematically dynamite the remaining buildings. This was followed by a methodical sweeping of the ruins by German soldiers using flamethrowers.

The fires doomed anyone who had managed thus far to survive. The final one hundred and twenty fighters of the ZOB leadership committed suicide rather than surrender after gas bombs were lobbed into their bunker under Mila 18. Anielewicz, whom Sol had looked upon as a role model, was among those killed. Later the Nazis blew up the bunker.

The dense smoke and suffocating heat enveloping the Ghetto caused the few survivors to panic. By design, the ZOB had issued no escape plans. There was to be no retreat and no surrender since there was nowhere to go and they could expect no mercy from the Germans. All fighters were expected to fight and die at their posts. However, the hopelessness of the situation caused the survivors to abandon their bunkers and flee to the sewers, cellars, and maze of tunnels beneath the streets. Stroop blared messages on loudspeakers into the sewers ordering the diehards to surrender; the demands were ignored. Now the confused and shell-shocked fighters could think only of trying to remain alive. All hope had vanished. Like the others, Sol felt a desperate need to survive.

Following the other boys, Sol hurried through the narrow alleyways. They descended through an open manhole and lowered themselves into the darkness of the foul sewers. As he began to slosh his way forward through the sickening brown sludge, Sol was immediately overcome by the nauseating odor. The narrow pipes were wide enough for only one person to move forward at a time, and due to the low overhang, it was impossible to stand upright. Sol's feet kept sliding in the muck and his hands slipped on the green slime of the brick walls; but he pushed forward as fast as his exhausted body would carry him. Some of the others were swept away by the rushing sewage. Sol tried to plunge in to save one boy, but it was hopeless. Sol did not know where they were heading. He wanted to stop and rest, but the walls were too slippery to grasp, so he continued struggling along in the wake of the others.

Finally, Sol realized the Germans had indeed poured poison gas into the sewers. One of the ZOB members told Sol to urinate on his hands and then put his hands to his nose to help him breathe. Sol tried this, but he continued to gag. At last, Sol managed to follow a group of boys up a ladder through an open manhole out to the street. The burst of sunlight temporarily blinded him, and he felt disoriented.

Recovering, Sol recognized where he was and ran frantically. However, the street seemed to be swarming with German soldiers. Sol was trapped on Nalewki Street by SS troops and their German shepherd attack dogs. Raising his hands in surrender, he was escorted into a courtyard. There he was ordered to sit with a number of other prisoners.

As he looked around, he noticed a girl, perhaps nineteen or twenty years old, and a tall, good-looking boy in his early twenties wearing a leather jacket. One of the Nazi guards turned to the boy and said, "You must be the leader." Before he could reply, the guard shot him, killing him instantly. Then the guard pointed his gun at the girl and said, "You must be the leader," and shot her in the face. He then sprayed the ground of the courtyard with machine gun fire.

Shocked by these murders, Sol quietly began to dig a hole in the ground behind his back. He knew he had to bury his gold chain and pocket watch. The watch held special meaning for Sol: Aunt Bella had given him the watch, which had belonged to her husband Leon, soon after Leon had disappeared. It was his only connection to the past. But to keep the watch might give the impression that he was also a leader; Sol knew he could not afford to take this risk.

As Sol sat burying his watch, the guards continued to interrogate the fifteen or twenty people remaining in the court-yard. Sol feared these were his last minutes left on earth. One guard walked straight over to Sol, who by now was trembling. Ominously he asked Sol how many Germans he had shot; Sol took a deep breath and answered in good German that he had only been looking for food, for bread. "I don't know how to use a gun. I have never shot Germans. I am just a young boy," Sol blurted out. The soldier was startled by Sol's fluent German and asked him who he was. Sol answered that his people had come from Germany. The German lashed out that Sol was not a German, but a "Jude."

"Jawohl, jawohl." Yes indeed, answered Sol. The bewildered and frustrated German began to spray his machine gun wildly to vent his anger. Sol was afraid everyone would be killed.

Sol managed to bury his watch just in time; shortly afterwards he and the others in the courtyard were marched to the *Umschlagplatz*. There they were forced to sit or squat on the ground without moving. A deep silence fell over the square. As the hours passed, some prisoners collapsed. Others were beaten for no apparent reason.

Sol tried to pass the time by wiping the foul-smelling sludge from the sewers off his clothes. He had tried not to drink the sewage, but he had accidentally swallowed some of it and had been unable to avoid breathing the poisonous gas. Now he was sick to his stomach and felt like vomiting.

The quiet was interrupted by the sound of a distant whistle from a locomotive. As the train neared the station, he could hear the loud rumble of its wheels on the tracks. It was shortly after midday when the train pulled in to the platform. The guards reacted quickly, ordering the prisoners to walk to the open boxcars. There they were jammed aboard. Those who did not move fast enough were cursed at and struck with rifle butts. Finally, when the cars were full, the doors were sealed and the train set off on its journey. This time the train carrying Sol was bound for Majdanek.

Chapter V

Majdanek

When the last resistance crumbled in the Warsaw Ghetto in early May 1943, Brigadier General Stroop ordered the largest and most beautiful synagogue in the city dynamited. This act, more than any other, symbolized the destruction of Warsaw's one thousand year old Jewish community. Then, street by street and building by building, Stroop had the Ghetto systematically demolished, to erase every last vestige of its Jewish past. According to General Stroop's report to his superior, seven thousand Jews were killed in the fighting and thirty-five thousand were captured and shipped to Treblinka, Majdanek, or to other labor camps in the Lublin region. For his victory, Stroop was later awarded the Iron Cross First Class, Germany's highest award.

Sol was among the last resistance fighters to surrender. He and the few remaining survivors of the uprising, exhausted, and frightened, were crowded aboard boxcars. Unsure of their destination, Sol thought he would probably be sent back to Treblinka or perhaps Auschwitz. But others said they were heading for Lublin, in eastern Poland. When Sol asked what was in Lublin, he was told that Camp Majdanek was just east of the city. It was said to be a punishment camp where prisoners were worked to death at hard labor. Sol had not heard of it, but he was still relieved he was not returning to Treblinka.

None of the prisoners aboard the train from Warsaw, including Sol, knew what to expect in Majdanek, but he could not believe the camp could be worse than what he had experienced at Treblinka. Sol was hungry, tired, thirsty and still dazed from the defeat in the Ghetto, but he had been through this before. He resolved, however, to keep his thoughts to himself. There was no need to alarm any of the others in the railcar. He could only pray he could survive this time too.

Sol knew he had to remain still to conserve his energy. Very little ventilation came through the cracks in the walls and floor of the boxcar. Breathing was difficult in the suffocating heat, made worse by the packed bodies which were continually jarred by the movement of the train. Sol also knew there would be no water to drink. Nor was there any place to relieve himself. A bucket had been thrown into the railcar, but due to the crowded conditions it had never reached Sol. The hours passed slowly. Since he was wedged in the middle of the car surrounded by other prisoners, he could not peer outside to see which stations they passed through. This would have made the time go by more quickly, he thought, and given him an idea of their final destination. He was too uncomfortable to doze. With nothing else to do, he tried to think to block out his fear and uncertainty. He made up his mind to observe everything and to try to plan an escape as soon as he possibly could. There had to be a way.

Early the following morning, the transports pulled onto a railroad siding outside of Lublin. The doors were shoved violently open and the exhausted and filthy prisoners were forced out of the dark railcars into bright sunlight. Temporarily disoriented as he emerged, Sol tried to adjust and restore feeling to his body. After jumping off, Sol stretched his muscles from the cramped conditions in the railcar. Forcing himself to be mentally alert, he quickly scanned the faces of the other prisoners. He was relieved to see Bolik, Hanek, Lolek, Schlomo and other veterans of the Ghetto uprising. The sight of his friends was reassuring. They, too, had survived. At least now he knew he was not alone.

It was a short walk from the train to the gate, only a few hundred yards away. The main road to Lublin ran alongside the camp where a German military convoy was now passing. On the other side of the road, carefree Polish children were playing a pickup game of soccer while their mothers busied themselves planting in their gardens. It all seemed so surreal; they appeared totally oblivious to what was happening so close by. Sol turned his attention to the camp as he approached the gate. He glanced down momentarily and was stunned to see Hebrew inscriptions on the path. Looking more closely, he realized broken pieces of tombstones from a Jewish cemetery had been used as paving stones for the path. Sol felt even more apprehensive and tried to prepare himself for the worst.

As Sol approached the camp gate, he noticed several fields on the far side of the barracks, one of which seemed to be worked only by women. Even the guards appeared to be women. This seemed strange, but he had no time to think about it.

The armed SS guards supervising the prisoners hurried him toward some makeshift tables in front of what appeared to be the camp's headquarters. There he waited in line with the other prisoners while inmates serving as clerks filled out detailed questionnaires on each of the newly-arrived detainees. The line moved slowly, but the wait gave Sol a chance to look around. Hopefully this place wouldn't be another Treblinka, he thought. Everything appeared orderly and less menacing. There was no sign of the violence which had greeted him at Treblinka. The grounds were neat and clean and the guards, quite businesslike, didn't exhibit the same cruelty as at the previous camp.

When Sol arrived at the front of the line, he was asked to give his name, date of birth, place of birth and residence, vocation, and date of arrest. Sol answered the questions, stating that he was a baker, his father's occupation. But he was disconcerted by the suggestion that he had been arrested. "I wasn't arrested," he said. "I was captured following the uprising and sent here."

"I don't care how you were taken," replied the clerk, "just give me the date." Sol had lost track of the days, and when he couldn't answer, the clerk jotted down a random date, matter of factly asking him whom to notify in the event of his death. Again, Sol was taken aback; he could not think of one living family member except Aunt Bella. However, he didn't want to give her name for fear it would place her in danger. The clerk waited a moment while Sol tried to collect his thoughts and then drew a line through the space on the form. He then handed the form back to Sol and told him to give it to the clerk at the next table. As Sol glanced at the paper, any complacency he might have had quickly disappeared. He was struck by the words "sentenced to life imprisonment." In shock, he passed the paper to the next clerk who in turn handed him a piece of canvas with a number on it. From that moment on, Sol realized he had ceased to exist as a person.

Sol was then ordered to go to a nondescript one-story wooden building a few yards away. There he was told to disrobe and surrender all his belongings. Just as they did at Treblinka, the guards shouted, "Hurry! Undress completely!" Sol had nothing, but others were forced to turn over any money or other valuables they had hidden. Deprived of everything which reminded them of their life outside the camp, the prisoners were hurried through a dark, narrow hall to a large solid grey concrete room for delousing. A tremor of fear ran down Sol's spine. Naked and panic-stricken, he tried unsuccessfully to break ranks and retreat to the back of the room, but there was no place to run, nowhere to hide in the mass of humanity. Then he heard shrieks and hysterical screams. He looked up and saw several naked and shaved prisoners holding bundles of clothes running from the side door of the "showers." It was not until then that he realized he wouldn't be gassed. Relieved, he allowed himself to be carried forward in the line; however, his relief did not last long.

At the entrance to the "showers," Sol was ordered to stand naked with his legs wide apart, his arms outstretched, and his mouth open. A guard inspected him thoroughly, even examining his rectum to look for valuables. Attendants roughly hacked off his hair and shaved his entire body. Sol grimaced as the indifferent and careless workers slashed his armpits and genital areas, causing deep gashes.

Bleeding from numerous cuts, Sol was then ordered into one of two vats to "delouse." The vats contained brownish-colored foul-smelling water with a heavy concentration of disinfectant. When Sol hesitated, a forceful blow on his back pushed him forward into the liquid. All the open sores and cuts on his body were exposed to the chemical disinfectant, causing excruciating pain. He cried out in agony, but this only seemed to amuse the guard, who forcibly pushed his head under the cold water. Sol didn't know how much longer he could endure the pain or hold his breath. Finally, after what seemed an eternity, he was ordered to get out, and directed to a nearby table.

While waiting in line at the table, Sol wondered what good the disinfectant was supposed to do; he estimated that at least two hundred men had bathed before him in the same water. It was unlikely, thought Sol, that the Germans had bothered changing the water. These thoughts were interrupted by a clerk who shoved toward him a worn blue and white striped long-sleeved shirt and a pair of pants several sizes too large for him. Sol learned later that these clothes had come from murdered Russian war prisoners. Both shirt and pants were of such poor quality they were almost threadbare, providing little protection from the rain or cold. He was also given a small round blue and white striped cap, but there was not even a rag with which to clean off the disinfectant or dry himself.

On the back of the shirt were the letters "KL" for *Konzentrationslager,* or concentration camp. A yellow triangle with the word "Jude" in the middle was sewn on the upper right front. A guard motioned to Sol to give his shirt and trousers to a tailor sitting at the table. On the left breast of his shirt, the tailor quickly and efficiently sewed the patch with the number which Sol had been given earlier. The number was also sewn on the trousers. Sol saw that some of the other prisoners had a colored triangle with a letter inside it stitched below the number. He later learned that these letters designated nationality: "P" for Poles, "C" for Czechoslovakians, "H" for Hungarians, "B" for Belgians, etc.; but Jews were not given any letters for nationality. Moreover, the color of the triangle on which the letter was stitched indicated the prisoner's "crime." For example, homosexuals were given pink triangles; political prisoners, red triangles; common criminals, green, etc. Sol's triangle was yellow, referring to the "crime" of being Jewish. Like the other survivors of the Warsaw uprising, Sol was singled out for special attention. In addition to the yellow triangle pointing upward, he had a red triangle pointing downward. When sewn together, they formed a six-pointed Star of David. This insignia designated its bearer as a "Jewish Bandit of Warsaw," a contemptuous term the Germans used to refer to members of the resistance.

Sol was also handed wooden shoes but no socks. The clogs, at least one size too small, were extremely painful as they rubbed against his feet. Sol located a string he could tie around his waist to hold up his pants. In addition, he was issued a rusty bowl and spoon. He found a second string to wrap the spoon and bowl tightly around his waist so that he would not lose his utensils.

After dressing, Sol hurried awkwardly from the building. He noticed that all the other prisoners looked exactly the same: shaved heads, ill-fitting clothes, tight fitting clogs with no socks. No one knew what would happen next, but Sol sensed they all felt the same dread and uncertainty. Although Sol did not realize it at the time, by depriving the prisoners of everything which reminded them of life outside the camp and reducing them to nothing more than a number, the Germans had forcibly dehumanized the captives. But Sol did understand one essential element of survival: in anonymity, he could become invisible; he would try to maintain a low profile and disappear in the mass of humanity.

As he shuffled back from the delousing area, he saw women walking back to the camp from the fields where he had seen them working earlier. It was then Sol had another surprise: he saw his Aunt Bella. Her appearance startled him. Her head was shaved and her once stout frame was much thinner than he remembered. Although she resembled the others, something was amiss. After a closer look, Sol noticed that in defiance of German regulations, Bella was wearing the everyday walking shoes he had last seen her in in Warsaw, and not the standard issue clogs. "How did she manage that?" he wondered. He started waving to attract her attention and she nodded back at him. As she approached, she said in a strong voice words he would never forget: "Salik, behave yourself. Keep your mouth shut. And your eyes. Don't see things that you are not supposed to see. And don't be a Samson. This is a different place. You are not in Warsaw. To survive in this concentration camp you have got to keep your mouth shut and do what they tell you to do. You hear me, Salik?"

Then Bella was hurried away by the guards. Sol wanted to follow and talk to her, but he knew this was impossible. He did, however, think about what she had said. Her words had a chilling effect on him. At the same time, he wasn't sure exactly what she meant, but he knew he was in a situation that would test his will to survive.

Sol was also reminded of an incident from the early days of the occupation. Aunt Bella had asked him to accompany her to a shoe-maker; there she had the heels of her shoes removed and hollowed out. She then placed twenty gold pieces and a diamond wrapped in paper into the empty heels. The shoemaker then resealed the heels and Aunt Bella put the shoes back on. Seeing the puzzled look on Sol's face, Bella smiled and said: "Salik, we are in for difficult times. Money can buy favors or silence. I believe I can do business with the Germans. This will be my insurance in case it is ever necessary."

Sol was marched to Field IV, Barrack Number 21. This was a dark building, crowded with triple bunks crudely made of wood. Sol immediately chose an upper bunk; he preferred to be on top, rather than have people climb over him. Elsewhere in the barrack, inmates were quarreling over the bunks in several languages. In the middle of the noise and commotion, Sol looked around. Much to his surprise, the barrack appeared to be relatively neat and clean. The floors were swept. Although there were no pillows, all bunks were made up with a thin, dirty blanket covering a soiled mattress stuffed with straw. However, upon closer inspection, Sol noticed the blanket and mattress were infested with lice. The bunks were lined up perpendicular to the longer walls with an extremely narrow aisle between the walls and the bunks and a slightly wider space between the two rows of bunks facing each other. No showers or toilets were visible. However, Sol was told that latrines were located outside the barrack in a separate building. A long, narrow opening just under the roof allowed light in on two sides of the building. Two doorways at either end of the barrack were the only means of entry. The bunks of the block kapos, or barrack wardens, were located near the front entrance.

Sol looked around at the other prisoners. He could tell from their letters that they were of mixed nationalities. Poles, Czechs, Belgians, Hungarians, and Yugoslavs seemed in the majority, but there were many Jews as well. Many looked younger than Sol, and he assumed that most, like himself, were orphans. As Sol learned later, they represented different religions, various shades of the political spectrum, different educational levels, professions, and social positions. But one common denominator was that very few appeared to be able-bodied. Most of the inmates looked emaciated. Some had bruises from terrible beatings. Many were scratching themselves from the lice and others appeared to be sick with typhus. All looked depressed and exhausted, and all appeared very frightened. Sol wondered how long they had been there and what kind of terror they had been subjected to. It was a sobering sight.

Sol's thoughts were abruptly interrupted when two block kapos, both Jewish, entered the building. They called for silence and introduced themselves as Mosche Tofee and Naftula Gazle; Sol was surprised by this name, as Gazle meant "murderer" in Polish. Both men had a Kapo arm band, wore shiny boots, and carried whips. To Sol, they looked well-fed, formidable, and physically intimidating. Sol was prepared for the worst. He had heard about the kapos, many of whom were Jewish, and how they wielded the power of life and death over the prisoners. He had been told all were social misfits who had been selected because of their antisocial tendencies. They were indifferent to suffering, overbearing in manner, and in order to safeguard their own position, completely dedicated to the Nazis. Their task was to maintain harsh discipline over their barrack. In return, they were given a number of perks in the form of food and clothing.

The kapos' words and deeds soon confirmed what Sol had heard. He learned from the other prisoners that both kapos had been part of the prewar Warsaw underworld. They were both said to be collaborators with no decent qualities. They were also bisexual and pedophiles. They would select women from the camp to rape, but they also forced young boys to come to their bunks. Of the two, Gazle was the more vocal and seemed to be the dominant one. Sol later guessed that this was because he was more fluent in German and could talk with the SS guards. Both men reeked of alcohol and seemed to be under its influence; they had reddish complexions and their eyes appeared glazed. During the coming months Sol was to witness firsthand their frequent and unpredictable explosive outbursts of temper, especially when the two kapos appeared to have had too much to drink.

Gazle spoke first. In a blustering voice, he addressed the newcomers: "You are scum and don't you ever forget that. The letters on your back, K.L., mean you are in a death camp. You are imprisoned for life. There is no escape. No one will ever leave here alive. If you obey me completely you may survive—if the whippings, hunger, work, illness, or lice don't kill you. All of you are nothing except numbers. Forget your past life. It is over. It is behind you. From now on you are mine. Don't even think about escape because it is impossible. You have no hope, no salvation." He glared at them and then continued, "I am the king and you will do as I say and be happy doing it. Since you have all been brought here from Warsaw, I know you have hidden diamonds and gold in your possession. Several of you may have secreted jewels in condoms and swallowed them, hiding them in your intestines. If so, and you want to survive, then hand over your possessions to me. If you give them to me, you will make me happy and I will assign you jobs in the camp that will allow you to survive. If I am satisfied, you in turn will be pleased. Otherwise you will endure a hell you cannot even begin to imagine. Remember, I decide whether you live or die. I dish out your food rations and assign you to your jobs. Your life is in my hands. Don't cross me and don't do anything to anger me."

When Gazle finished, a silence fell over the barrack. It wasn't only what Gazle had said, but the way he had said it. Sol had no illusions. After Aunt Bella's warning, his worst fears were confirmed. To survive in this hell would take every ounce of his courage. While he was still pondering Gazle's words, Tofee stepped forward to address the inmates.

Cruder and less articulate than Gazle, Tofee reiterated Gazle's ominous warning. He threatened the prisoners from the outset, demanding anything of value they might have smuggled into the camp. "Keep me happy so you won't be punished. You are all Warsaw thieves. I know you have gold and diamonds. Give them to me for your own safety. If you don't, we will find them. If we find the jewelry, you will suffer as you never have before."

When Tofee was through with his threats, he addressed everyday routine. The prisoners, he said, were expected to keep the barrack clean, make their bunks neatly each day, and sweep the floors; Tofee would conduct daily inspections of the premises to make certain all was in order. He would be with the prisoners at all times. No one, for whatever reason, could remain in the barrack during the day; all would go to their work assignments. He indicated that he personally would inspect the barrack to make certain no one was hiding. The latrines and washrooms were in a nearby building; no one was to use them without prior permission. Nor would anyone be permitted to relieve himself anywhere except in the latrine unless approval was granted. As Sol later discovered, due to the lengthy lines at the latrine, it was impossible for many to get there in time. Therefore, many unfortunates were shot as they waited and their bodies were left lying in their own waste.

Shortly after the kapos departed, Sol and the other new detainees were ordered out into the square for yet another address, this time by the SS. The Germans warned the men that they were now housed in a concentration camp and they were to follow orders, carry out their assignments, and do what they were told; otherwise few would survive. Infractions would not be permitted. They were there to be trained to march and work.

Majdanek had been open less than two years. Unlike other extermination camps, it had originally been conceived as a giant forced labor camp for P.O.W.'s who were to produce war materials for the army on the eastern front. By the time Sol arrived, the original plans had been scrapped due to wartime shortages of construction materials. Indeed, only about twenty percent of the industrial complex envisioned in the earlier plan had been completed. Nevertheless, Majdanek's inmate population had mushroomed until it was second in size only to Auschwitz in the German penal system. In addition to interning mainly Jews and to a lesser extent Poles, the camp housed inmates of over fifty different nationalities, including thousands of Soviet P.O.W.'s. Majdanek was staffed by 1200 SS guards and several hundred kapos who enforced obedience through intimidation and terror.

Although the power of the kapos was absolute, the SS never let the kapos forget that they too were prisoners. They could be sent to the gas chambers as readily as any other inmates. Thus, their status was always precarious. This insecurity was reflected in the brutal treatment of the prisoners, partly to impress the SS. The result was a climate of constant fear and oppression among the prisoners, most of whom tried to disguise their hatred of the kapos beneath hypocritical obedience often unsuccessfully.

In the fall of 1942, the camp underwent a change in mission. The first two of an eventual seven gas chambers were installed and the mass killings began. When Sol and the other survivors of the Warsaw Ghetto uprising arrived in the camp during the summer of 1943, the death rate by gassing was at its peak. Transports from every part of Nazi occupied Europe arrived daily. Majdanek had become a vast killing machine. Death for the detainees came from every atrocity imaginable. Most were gassed, but there were also mass shootings, hangings, and beatings; death from starvation, disease, immersion in excrement, and the abysmal and unsanitary living conditions claimed thousands more. The constant brutality gave Majdanek the highest mortality rate of all the German death camps. Most prisoners lived less than ninety days before death overtook them. Only a small number of detainees survived the horrific conditions. By war's end, the death toll would number over 360,000.

The camp, built in the shape of a huge rectangle, was constructed in stages, first by Soviet prisoners of war and later by Jewish and Polish slave laborers. It was divided into six fields, although only five of the six fields were in use at the time of Sol's imprisonment. Each of the five fields contained what was virtually a separate camp. The fields mirrored each other in many respects. Initially, twelve identical long wooden barracks were situated on either side of each field. All five fields contained workshops, kitchens, latrines, and offices. Between the two rows of barracks in an extended open area known as the square, roll calls, hangings, and public beatings were carried out. Crudely constructed gallows occupied a central location on the square of each field. All were similarly built, consisting of a wooden stake approximately ten feet high with a metal hook jutting out from it. Between Fields I and II, nine gallows were in place for collective hangings, which were held with increasing frequency. The gas chambers were next to Field I, and the crematorium was adjacent to Field V.

All the Fields were enclosed by twelve foot high double rows of barbed wire, with the inner row electrically-charged. Elevated watchtowers manned by armed guards stood at each corner of the field and were situated along the camp's fence line roughly every hundred yards. After dark, searchlights in the towers scoured the camp's perimeter, augmented by lamps on the posts of the security fences. The net result was to give the guards clear visibility day and night, making escape virtually impossible. The camp eventually grew to contain one hundred forty-four barracks, each housing two to three hundred inmates, sometimes more.

Prisoners in the camp were separated by sex and status as combatants or civilians. The first, third, and fourth Fields housed male civilians, the second, Soviet prisoners of war and skilled prisoners employed in the camp workshops, and the fifth, women and children. It wasn't long before Sol discovered that the bulk of the prisoners in Fields Three, Four, and Five were earmarked for death in the gas chambers.

Following the stern lectures from the kapos and the SS, the new arrivals were given permission to go to the latrines. As Sol approached, he was sickened by the stench. The latrines consisted of a wooden box which had to accommodate over two hundred prisoners, the vast majority of whom were suffering from diarrhea. After waiting in line, Sol finally reached the overflowing box surrounded by puddles of urine and feces on the floor. To make matters worse, the wooden shoes worn by the prisoners tracked the feces back to the barracks.

That night, the newcomers were not given any food. Sol was overcome by hunger, which continued to stalk him the entire time he was in Majdanek. At 9:00 P.M., a loud gong sounded, marking the end of the day. The lights were turned off, except for a few bulbs which remained on all night. One of these small bulbs was almost directly above Sol; the light it cast caused him to toss and turn all night long. Furthermore, the kapos had warned the inmates that anyone who left the barrack after lights out would be shot. Some nights wooden buckets were flung into the barrack to allow the prisoners to relieve themselves. However, this was at random, so on most nights those inmates with weak bladders or with intestinal disorders had no choice but to soil their pants, adding to the stench and potential for disease.

Sol's fitful sleep did not last long. The first work parties left the barrack at 3:30 A.M., and less than two hours later, at 5:00 A.M., all other prisoners were roused from their sleep by angry shouts of "Raus" from the Kapos. Another workday had begun. Initially, Sol found the babble of several foreign tongues and the loud screeching of the kapos disconcerting. The kapos ran through the barrack, hitting the exhausted prisoners over the head to make them rise. But, as the days passed, Sol became accustomed to the routine and followed the lead of the veterans. They first had to carefully make up their bunks in strict military fashion so that there was not a crease showing on their threadbare blankets. Those prisoners who failed to satisfy the kapos were denied food and sometimes whipped; every single day the kapos always found some prisoners to punish for not making their beds properly.

After the bunks were inspected, the inmates were permitted to go to another wooden building where the washrooms were located. As with everything else at Majdanek, the kapos kept them moving along on the "run." This was not easy for the inmates in their ill-fitting wooden clogs. Then the long lines of the night before at the latrines were repeated. Sol heard yelling and cursing from inside and saw several inmates emerge covered in blood. He wondered what was happening. When he finally entered the washrooms, he first noticed there were no towels or soap. The inmate next to him began to take off his shirt to wash. The kapo standing behind him began to shout, hitting him over the head with a club: "Keep your shirt on, scum. Do you think this is a bath house?" When the others in the room saw this, they realized that all they could do was to scoop water up in their hands to wash their faces as quickly as they could.

Still, the kapos were not satisfied. "Who taught you how to wash?" the kapo yelled at another standing nearby. "You people can't do anything right." Then the kapo grabbed the man by the shoulder, spun him around violently, and punched him in the face. The groggy inmate stumbled out of the washroom bleeding profusely. Sol quickly finished slapping water on his face, gulped down a couple of mouthfuls of water, and fled the washhouse to avoid similar treatment. In spite of the early hour and the pitch black sky, he was now fully awake.

Sol ran in short, choppy steps back to the barrack. At 6:00 A.M., workers brought in a watery herb tea. Sol swallowed a couple of mouthfuls, but the taste was so disgusting he couldn't bring himself to drink anymore.

When a veteran of the camp, not much older than Sol, saw what he had done, he came up to Sol. He warned him that many prisoners in the camp had died due to sickness. Hygiene in the camp was almost nonexistent and contributed to the toll. Since there was a permanent shortage of water, the only solution was to use whatever liquid was available to try to stay clean. The tea, while it tasted awful, could be used for washing. "It isn't much, but it is better than nothing," he said. "Trying to stay clean is the first step if we are to survive." Sol knew he was right. He had always been aware of his personal hygiene, and to try to take care of himself, he thought, would be his first act of resistance. He would not allow himself to be reduced to the level of an animal. He told the other prisoner that he would take his advice and try to wash every day. As the months passed, Sol saw the wisdom in the counsel of his new friend. Those prisoners who succumbed to the filth and dirt seemed to lose the will to continue to fight. Sol maintained the ritual of washing with the hot water that he didn't use for drinking until the day he left the camp.

Their conversation was abruptly cut short by the kapos screaming "Achtung;" the inmates were ordered to line up in parallel rows of five for roll call. Sol quickly discovered this was little more than a selection procedure. The prisoners were required to stand at attention during a seemingly indeterminate number of counts. Even those who had died overnight were included. Their bodies were dragged out of the barrack and tossed on the ground next to the ranks of the living. In the meantime, the prisoners were forced to stand erect, motionless, and silent, regardless of the weather conditions or the state of their health. During the extended roll call, the kapos would walk briskly back and forth, often randomly clubbing prisoners without warning. Any infraction, real or contrived, could trigger savage reprisals. Even though they were dismayed by the screams of pain, Sol and the others who were fortunate enough to be spared couldn't flinch or even look to see what was happening; they were forced to stare straight ahead. Sometimes when the count did not equal the supposed number of prisoners, the kapos shrieked obscenities before beginning the count yet again. Often an inmate too weak or sick to drag himself from his bunk remained in the barrack. The kapos then pulled him outside and beat him, often until he was near death. If SS officers found the inmate first, they hanged him publicly for "trying to escape." Sol knew several of those killed in this fashion; he considered it almost a blessing for victims who were in so much pain. Some roll calls lasted for hours. During these periods, Sol tried to disassociate himself from reality and concentrate on his own thoughts. The ill-fitting shoes made it even more difficult to stand for such long periods, but he refused to give in.

On many mornings, after roll call and the barrack clean up were completed, the kapos would organize the inmates into paramilitary drill formations and force them to march, run on the double, and perform calisthenics, such as pushups and kneebends. Under a torrent of curses and clubbings, the prisoners were expected to perform without letup. Weather conditions were immaterial, never interfering with the kapos' whims. To Sol, the kapos seemed amused by the pathetic sight of the exhausted prisoners trying to run in their clogs. Every step Sol took caused pain to shoot through his toes and ankles, as his skin rubbed off and blistered. He just hoped he could tolerate the pain one more day.

At noon, the prisoners were given an hour for lunch. They were required to stand at attention in front of the barrack while the kitchen staff set up kettles of soup. The soup was made from vegetables, either potatoes or turnips, which were often rotten. The prisoners filed quietly by in line, holding out their bowls, while one of the kapos ladled in some of the liquid. Eventually, Sol learned, in spite of his hunger, to stand near the back of the line. Early on, he had noticed that the prisoners at the front of the line always had a very watery mix. The vegetables and richer part of the broth settled on the bottom of the kettle. So Sol waited patiently for his turn. If the soup was cabbage or nettles Sol altered his strategy, as the tastier part of this soup floated to the top. However, whatever soup he received was never enough, although the warm, but tasteless liquid and the hour's rest revived him; lunch was the only break of the entire day.

After lunch, work details were to leave for their assignments. But first, the kapos asked the new arrivals if any spoke German, for the Germans needed some prisoners who could speak German outside the camp. Sol felt that any excuse to get out of Majdanek was worth the risk. Without knowing where he would be going or what he would be doing, Sol volunteered. Any change, Sol reasoned, would be an improvement. Sol was informed that wounded troops were being brought in from the eastern front and were being placed in the second field. Inmates were needed to help bathe and care for them. The Germans admitted that these soldiers were all that remained of General Paulus' Army Corps, which had taken a beating at Stalingrad on the Russian front. For the next three weeks, Sol helped to tend to the needs of the German wounded. The work was not exhausting and the fresh air was invigorating.

Moreover, the Germans present in the second Field consisted mainly of nurses and physicians. The few guards left the prisoners to the supervision of the health care staff, who were too busy tending to the wounded to harass them. Thus, Sol had a temporary respite from the on-going reign of terror in the camp. He was even able to walk at a normal pace without having to look over his shoulder. As an added bonus, he was permitted to eat the same food as the wounded, thus finally satisfying his constant hunger.

Gradually, while working in Field II, Sol recovered his strength. However, he could never quite forget his precarious situation. On his daily journey from his barrack to Field II, Sol passed the gas chambers adjacent to Field I and the special facility with nine gallows located between the first and second Fields. On many days he would see prisoners' bodies dangling limply in the wind. The faces of many prisoners were so pulverized they were unrecognizable. On the return to his barrack, the long chimney of the crematorium on the far side of Field V was visible, belching forth its smoke and ashes daily. The odor of burning human flesh was unmistakable. Due to the daily ghastly reminders, Sol had few illusions, no expectations, and little hope. But he had to cling to something to survive; he willed himself to stay alive in order to defy his captors.

Unfortunately, this brief reprieve came to an end. After the German wounded were transferred to hospital facilities in Germany, Sol was told he was being reassigned to Field IV to perform heavy labor. Sol had been told that Field IV was reserved mainly for Jews. Of the five Labor fields, the prisoners considered this the most punishing. Sol had heard his bunkmates assigned to the rock crushing and road building teams talk about this work; moreover, he could see the toll the labor took on them. He prepared himself for the worst.

The following morning, after bunk inspection and "breakfast," Sol was plunged back into the reality of life in Majdanek. As the kapos shouted *Arbeitskommandos Formieren*, ("form up workers") the prisoners rushed from the barrack and lined up in parallel rows. So began another seemingly interminable roll call, as the kapos counted and recounted. Then, urged on by cursing kapos, the prisoners in Sol's work team, called "Kommandos" by the Germans, were forced to run to the gate. There they had to stop and stand at attention while the kapo reported the number of prisoners in the work detail to the SS officer. After that, one of the guards ordered the men to sing "Hatikvah," as they ran to the field. Sol reasoned that forcing the prisoners to sing must have given the guard some sort of perverse pleasure. Apparently, what the guard did not realize was that singing this song, which later became the Israeli national anthem, actually helped to revive the men's spirit.

For the next several weeks, Sol's days consisted of carrying heavy rocks to be used as fill on the roads. Sol could see no purpose to the work, other than to physically exhaust the prisoners. The ever-present guards forced the prisoners to run everywhere. "Laufen! Laufen!" (Run, Run) the guards bellowed, as the prisoners tried to keep pace with the commands. The guards seemed to be everywhere. There was never time to stop or even catch a breath. Sol had to pretend to be busy every minute and do so on the run. Not even one idle minute was permitted. Sol's feet, already swollen from the tightfitting shoes, were always in excruciating pain. Indeed, he could do little more than hobble. On mornings after all night rains, his clogs became stuck in the mud; each step took every ounce of his strength. On other days, when he could not move fast enough to satisfy the guards, he was ordered to remove his shoes and run barefoot over the sharp gravel. The rocks were heavy and their irregular shapes made them difficult to carry. His arms shook and his back strained as he lugged the rocks, gasping from the weight and the heat, rushing from one location to another. Sometimes a particularly sadistic guard would order Sol to pick up the heavy rock he had just put down and carry it back to where he had gotten it in the first place. Some days he was so tired he didn't think he could continue. But at times like this, he realized he had no choice. To falter or pause meant punishment.

At midday, the guards' whistles screeched and the exhausted prisoners sat down in groups. They were ordered not to move, as cauldrons of the watery brown soup were brought out onto the Field. Then the prisoners escorted by the kapos shuffled over to the soup kitchen. Although the smell was disgusting, the prisoners were starving. Those workers who had not done enough to please the guards were not given anything. After the fifteen minutes or so that they were allotted to eat, the prisoners were given permission from the guards to relieve themselves. They had to go into the Field to urinate or defecate in full view of all. Many prisoners, lacking the strength to even walk to the Field, relieved themselves in their clothing. Others, too weak to continue, died in their own excrement. To Sol this was just another means of humiliating and dehumanizing the prisoners. But once again there was no choice: to live he had to accept the system. In the afternoons, the stench from the excrement was overpowering; furthermore, as they resumed their senseless labor, the prisoners were forced to run barefoot through the waste.

After the short break, work began anew. Often the guards would interrupt the "work" with "games". They blew their whistles, ordered the prisoners to stop whatever they were doing, and line up at attention. Sometimes the guards would just smoke and joke among themselves, while the prisoners stood for what seemed an eternity in their long-sleeved shirts despite the heat of summer. Other times, the kapos would bark commands in quick succession: "Caps off! Caps on!" Those prisoners who became confused or failed to respond to the orders fast enough were hauled out of line and clubbed. In the meantime, the remaining prisoners were forced to continue to stand at attention and watch the beatings.

One day, an inmate near Sol too weak to continue, dropped a huge rock. Guards began to swear and beat him mercilessly. Instinctively, to protect himself, the prisoner raised his hands. The guard, shrieking that this was an additional offense, beat him even more savagely. It seemed to Sol as if the guards went out of their way to be cruel. They were more interested in degrading their helpless victims than in accomplishing any tasks. Sol made every effort to avoid those guards who seemed the most sadistic.

Sol estimated that on any given day there were several thousand slave laborers in Field IV. He was always on the lookout for those he knew. But because of the constant surveillance of the guards, it proved impossible to talk to any of his friends. He rarely looked up and learned to mask his expression. Some days, without warning, a shot would ring out from one of the watchtowers. The prisoners never knew if or when they might become a target. The uncertainty robbed many of the will to live. Sol could see the life slowly ebbing from many, but he no longer had the strength to offer them support. Finally, a little after 5:00 P.M., the guards called a halt to the day's work. The exhausted prisoners were lined up in formation and driven back to the barrack the same way they had come, with the aid of kicks, curses, and clubbings.

At the end of the work day, Sol was miserable. He could barely stand. He could never get enough water to drink; his mouth was dry and his lips were parched. He thought, if he could just get enough water, he could get through the ordeal. He willed himself to be patient until he could get to the washroom later that evening to drink water out of the rusty faucets. But for many workers the situation was far more desperate. There were always those who collapsed at the end of each day due to a combination of exhaustion, beatings, sickness and malnutrition. With the inadequate food and lack of sanitation, disease was commonplace. Diarrhea and dysentery ran rampant. For the starved and exhausted prisoners, these debilitating diseases usually proved fatal. Some prisoners were assisted back to the barrack by the more able-bodied among them. The remainder, those already dead or dying, were piled on top of carts or placed on stretchers and taken back to the camp; there, prisoners were ordered to push the lorries to the crematorium. Sol could never escape death. As he returned from the Field each evening he passed by the gallows. Much as he tried, he could not take his eyes off the bodies he saw hanging there. Sol wondered what small infractions had cost these prisoners their lives. Many were boys younger than he was. From their malnourished appearance, he guessed they had long since lost the will to live. At least the Germans could no longer make them suffer.

In the evenings, dinner, which was dished out in front of the barrack, consisted of a watery coffee, but with the taste of corn, and a small amount of bread or potatoes. It was never good, and never sufficient to satisfy him, but in spite of the taste, Sol gulped it all down.

Following supper, Sol and the other prisoners had their only reprieve of the day. They were allowed to visit other barracks in their Field. Sol always looked forward to this brief interlude, for he enjoyed the opportunity to talk to his friends. However, the prisoners were forbidden to set foot in an area five meters wide between the inner fence and the barracks. The prisoners called this the "Death Zone"; if they trespassed there they could be shot without warning. Hardly a night went by that Sol didn't hear rifle shots. By accident or design the killings continued even during "quiet hours."

In the evenings after they used the latrines and washroom, the prisoners were lined up for evening roll call. If the count didn't equal the kapos' numbers, this could take as long or longer than in the morning. Moreover, the men found it much more difficult to remain standing than in the morning due to their physical exhaustion. Normally Sol chose a place in the back to avoid any problems. The prisoners would stand closely together and try to use each other for support. When the roll call was over, the inmates were ordered back into the barrack. Lights out was thirty minutes later.

The nights were as hard as the days, but in a different way. The frantic pace of the day's activities allowed no time for the prisoners to think or truly assess how bleak their situation was. In the evenings, however, the reality and pain set in. Most nights Sol gently massaged his hands and feet which had been rubbed raw. Every nerve seemed to be exposed and was sensitive to the slightest touch. The throbbing pain was so intense that some nights he could not get any sleep. Moreover, when it rained particularly hard, water dripped into the barrack through holes in the roof. Sol, in his top bunk, was soaked; once more he went without sleep. The following morning at roll call, Sol shivered in the chilly air as he stood at attention. It was not long before he caught a cold which hung on for many weeks. He had a runny nose and a constant cough; yet as he looked around him, he realized he was one of the lucky ones: most of the other prisoners were far worse off than he.

While the Jews worked in the Field, the Polish prisoners and those inmates of other nationalities who could speak German were farmed out to work in Lublin's defense industries. The labor detachments left early in the morning for the aircraft plants, clothing works, munitions industries, or construction projects in Lublin. They seemed to fare much better than those who toiled in the fields, as they returned to the camp neither beaten nor exhausted; Sol tried desperately to get transferred to this work detail. He realized Gazle's power to issue work assignments could be the difference between life and death. Since almost half of the camp's inmate population was hired out to production plants in Lublin, Sol thought the odds were good that more workers were needed; hesitantly he approached Gazle several times, emphasizing his willingness to work and fluency in German, but to no avail. This was a desperate attempt by Sol, but he knew he had to take risks if he were to remain alive. The type of work he performed could determine whether he lived or died. If he didn't get a change of assignment, he knew he was doomed; it was only a matter of time. However, Gazle said he was needed where he was and there would be no reassignment. Sol was devastated by Gazle's refusal, but at least Gazle had not taken out his anger on Sol as he had on so many others.

Sol was aware that those prisoners not assigned to factories in Lublin were, after a few months, funneled to the gas chambers. The path along which these unfortunate victims were marched was not far from Field IV. On many days, as he struggled with his rocks, Sol looked up to see a pathetic file of prisoners, usually numbering from fifty to one hundred; they were clubbed mercilessly by the guards, as they headed to their deaths. They must know, thought Sol, that these are their last few minutes on earth. He wondered what they were thinking. Sometimes they passed so close to him that Sol could see the tears running down their cheeks. He over-heard several murmuring the "S'hma Yisrael. " He gazed in disbe-lief at their expressionless faces. What was happening was beyond his comprehension. "I won't let that happen to me," he said to himself. "I won't leave here through the chimney. They won't put me out of my misery that way." Yet, even on those days when Sol didn't see prisoners on their death march, he knew when victims were being gassed even though the Germans would turn on tractor engines to muffle the cries of the dying.

Due to its inadequate size and frequent mechanical breakdowns, the crematorium could not dispose of the large

number of dead. The SS, therefore, began to burn the bodies at
night in huge grates over deep pits. During Sol's time at
Majdanek, he would watch the flames light up the night sky,
turning it red. The thick, black smoke was suffocating; it
permeated the barracks, causing Sol and the other prisoners to
choke on the odor of burning flesh, bone, and hair. Sol would
lie awake at night thinking of what was happening just a few
hundred yards away. When he finally did fall asleep from sheer
physical exhaustion, his sleep was restless and fitful. Tension
and fear remained with Sol constantly, night and day.

One of the most sadistic kapos in Field IV was a tall, trim,
blue-eyed, light-haired, and muscular Czech known to the prisoners only as "Blondie." Sol guessed he was no more than in his
late twenties. He wore a green patch to distinguish himself from
the Jewish collaborators and was never seen without his whip.

Blondie, like many of the other kapos, was one of the many
Volksdeutschen, or honorary Germans from the Sudetenland, who
served as guards or kapos in the camps. All were collaborators from
occupied countries who slavishly supported the Nazi cause. Most
could speak little or no German, but all were loyal to the Germans
out of fear or ideology. Most were convicted criminals; many were
murderers. All were social misfits who came from the worst
elements of society. Nevertheless, all were considered superior to
the Jews. In order to curry favor with the Germans, they committed
acts of savagery equal to or greater than those of the SS. They
enforced iron discipline, inflicting unspeakably brutal corporal
punishment for even the slightest transgression. Whippings were
commonplace and savage. The kapo's whips, made from belts,
resulted in many deaths.

Sol had heard that Blondie, like many others, was a
convicted murderer; this did not seem surprising as he displayed no
compassion or regard for human life whatsoever. Whether his
cruelty and inhumanity were from true conviction or to gain
approval from his superiors, Sol could never be sure, but regard-

less, all the prisoners feared him. There was never a flicker of pity or compassion on his face. He exuded an undercurrent of contempt and hostility for the prisoners. He seemed to be obsessed with power, wanting to control every move the inmates might make. His eyes were clear and intense and even his laughter had a menacing quality to it. He would deliver his orders in a ranting, furious voice, which reflected his unstable nature. Many mornings Blondie would enter the barrack, single out a sleeping prisoner, walk directly to his bunk, and without any warning or provocation, beat him savagely. He continued until the victim quit jerking and lay still. Sol lay tense on his mattress as he listened to the pleas for mercy. When the beating was over, Blondie threw a blanket over the bruised lifeless body and stomped out. Shortly thereafter camp guards would supervise the removal of the corpse from the barracks.

Normally, when there were whippings, the inmates were required to stop whatever they were doing and watch. Sol was sickened by what he saw and tried to distance himself emotionally. To Sol's knowledge, superiors never questioned Blondie's actions nor the actions of any of the others.

In the evenings, the kapos called out the numbers of those who "talked back," did some kind of damage, or did not do precisely what they had been ordered to do. One night, Sol's number was called. Sol froze; he could not think of anything he had done wrong. He didn't know why he was being singled out. Frightened, and caught off guard, he didn't respond until the kapo had called his number a second time. This time, Sol replied reluctantly. "That's me," he murmured.

The kapo, hot-tempered and impatient, bellowed, "You will be whipped twice because you didn't answer right away." Two kapos grabbed Sol roughly in a viselike grip and dragged him out to the field. There he was ordered to remove his shirt. He was pushed face down onto a hard bench. The kapos stretched his arms, secured his wrists, and inserted a device over his neck to prevent any movement. Sol tried to brace himself for the all too

familiar ordeal, though he had previously experienced it only as
an observer. He heard the count "Eins, zwei, drei, vier . . ." as the
kapo flogged him unmercifully on his bare skin. The kapo
appeared to be in a frenzy. The pain was so excruciating, Sol
soiled his pants. He mouthed a silent prayer to blot out the agony.
Initially he tensed his body anticipating each lash, but after the
first blows he remembered little. He wanted to scream out but he
was determined to remain quiet, because he knew that those prisoners who resisted usually received even more lashes. He gritted
his teeth and tensed his muscles, but it was impossible to suffer
in silence. Each time he felt the pain, he heard himself grunting.
The blows caused deep gashes all along his backside, shredding
his pants, searing his legs, slicing his buttocks and back, and
falling with particular ferocity on his neck and head. After
twenty-five lashes, he lost count of the number. He was whipped
on both sides of his body until he passed out. When they had
finished, the kapos left. Sol's friends in the barrack carried him to
his bunk, gently laying him on his stomach.

All during the night Sol drifted in and out of consciousness. When he came to early the following morning, it was still
dark outside. He was in unbearable agony. His vision was blurred,
he could barely speak, and what little he did say was incoherent.
He could not stand on his own nor even move, except for involuntary twitches. His entire back was swollen and discolored. His
body was wet with sweat and drenched in blood; indeed, his thin
mattress was soaked through with blood. In defiance of German
orders, two of Sol's friends slipped out of the unlocked barrack to
collect dirty water in their cups from the washroom. They quietly
returned and gently dabbed at his wounds.

That night, as a result of infection, Sol came down with a
fever. His friends offered support and looked after him as best
they could, but he could see them shaking their heads, even as
they tried to console and reassure him. His strength ebbing away,
Sol sensed he was losing the battle. There was no hope of

receiving medical treatment because none existed for prisoners. Sol lost track of time. During his conscious periods, he tried to take stock of his situation. He knew he was badly hurt and in excruciating pain. He began to talk to himself and pray for the fortitude to overcome this ordeal. One friend, Moniek, who had been in the camp over a year and had lost his toes to frostbite, gave Sol a small amount of potatoes and a piece of hard stale bread he had hidden in his mattress. Sol, however, was too nauseous to eat. Sol's pants were so badly shredded they could no longer be worn; another friend, who worked in the kitchen in Field III, had stolen some pants; he gave Sol two pairs removed from recently murdered prisoners. However, his friends could not locate any clean underwear, so Sol was forced to stay in the same filthy underpants he had been wearing. Sol knew he had to live; he could not let himself die now after all he had endured. He must not let the Germans win. He would fight back. Calling on every ounce of strength he possessed, he willed himself to recover. He refused to give in to despair. Beyond his pain, the only emotion he had left was his hatred of the Germans. He was determined to use this to fight back. He would not let his tormentors win. "I will not die," he said over and over to himself.

Sol hoped and prayed. He had been stripped of his humanity. He had been robbed of his name, his family, his education, and his hope for the future. He owned nothing; he had nothing. Even the clothes on his body weren't his own. His only hope for survival was to draw on every bit of inner strength he possessed.

Sol had been in the camp long enough to know what it meant to remain in the barrack the next morning. Any prisoners unable to report for roll call and continue working were immediately sent to their deaths. Although every move caused searing pain, Sol willed himself to sit up on his bunk. With his friends' help he struggled to put on his pants and shirt while wincing in agony from even the slightest movement. His friends helped him

limp to the twice daily lineups. They stood close to him to prop
him up and keep him from collapsing during the extended roll
calls, which now seemed even more unbearable than ever.
Finally, they did their best to shield him from the notice of Nazi
guards in the Field. For several weeks he worked in agony in
almost a trance like state while his wounds healed slowly. At
every opportunity, his friends also tried to rebuild his will to live.
A close friend and fellow Pole, Sam Radoszewski, told him: "You
can do it. You must do it. You can't let them beat you. Just don't
be a hero. Do what you are supposed to do. Keep your mouth
shut. This hell is not Warsaw. There may never be an end to this,
but we must keep going in case there is."

Considering the lack of medication, rest, nutrition, or
hygiene, Sol's recovery was remarkable. The pain was slow to
leave him, but his wounds gradually healed. It was his spirit and
emotions that took much longer. However, this was not the last
time Sol was beaten. After regaining his strength, Sol returned to
the mindless routine of strenuous labor and sparse meals. One
evening, after a particularly tiring day, Sol was standing in line
for soup. He was especially hungry that day, so much so that even
the thin watery gruel looked good to him. He extended his bowl,
but Moshe Tofee poured only about half the usual amount. Sol
asked him to fill the bowl to the top as he normally did. Tofee
exploded with a torrent of abuse, snarling: "Who are you? You
think you are a big shot, don't you? Well, you're not. You are
scum." Without warning, he lifted the hot metal ladle from the
soup pot, and before Sol could react, he smashed the ladle several
times across Sol's head and shoulders. Momentarily dazed, Sol
flinched and dropped the bowl, splashing the precious liquid to
the ground. Tofee stood grinning, holding the ladle as if he were
preparing to strike again. Sol backed away. Now there would be
nothing for him to eat and he would have to return to the barrack
even hungrier than usual. He didn't know what was worse—the
beating or losing his meager ration of food.

However, in the weeks that followed, Tofee did give Sol the same meager amount of soup he ladeled out to the other prisoners. No further attempts were made to short-change Sol or single him out. Sol was never sure why Tofee backed off, but he was grateful that he did.

But this incident taught Sol another lesson about survival. In the future he would heed the advice of his friends to remain silent, no matter what abuse he had to accept. The beatings he had already endured made him realize how vulnerable he was: he could be singled out for punishment at any time. The Germans demanded total submission. He decided he would do whatever they wished, trying at the same time to stay invisible to those who could harm him. He would try to anticipate their actions, and thus stay one step ahead of them. Caution would dictate his every move in order to avoid punishment. However, inwardly he seethed with rage.

The sameness of his everyday routine caused Sol to lose all track of time. Days, weeks, and months no longer mattered. He knew that winter had turned into summer, and summer had in turn given way to the first cool winds of autumn. Beyond that, he was unaware of anything outside of his immediate circumstances. He did not even know who was winning the war. The routine of prolonged roll calls, meager food rations, and long brutal days in the fields followed by evening roll calls left him physically exhausted. Every muscle ached, every joint was tender.

Sol used Sunday, the one day prisoners were not required to work in the fields, to rest and restore his energy for the coming week. He tried to force himself to use the day wisely. However, on many Sundays, he was so sore he could barely move. As he knew that an unkempt appearance could mean a trip to the gas chamber, he tried to make his soiled clothes appear as presentable as possible. This was not easy to do, since after working all day he had to sleep in the same clothes at night. Indeed, although Sol had long-since become accustomed to the horrors of

Majdanek, he could never get used to the foul body odors and the
stench of the barrack. Therefore, each week he washed his
clothes in water from the outside washroom and then put them
back on wet. However, the combination of overcrowded
barracks and lack of basic sanitary facilities made it difficult to
maintain his personal dignity.

Sundays, though, were not always free of turmoil.
Sometimes the relative peace could turn into terror if or when
"Blondie" appeared. There was no pattern to his coming and going
and he was just as likely to appear on a Sunday as on any other
day. When he strutted into the barrack with an evil scowl on his
face, his presence brought a sudden silence. The prisoners waited
anxiously to see whom he would single out for abuse this time.

After selecting his victim at random, Blondie ordered all
the prisoners to leave the barrack. Trembling, the weary men
followed Blondie outside, as he laughed and cursed at them. After
a ferocious beating, the unfortunate victim lapsed into uncon-
sciousness. Finally, Blondie tired of his "game." Leaving the prisoners frightened and shocked, he disappeared as suddenly as he
had arrived. For Sol and the others, this psychic terror kept them
off balance. They never knew when it was coming, or who would
be the next target. No one ever felt secure. Unpredictability was
a constant of life in the camp.

The unsanitary conditions made lice and bedbug infesta-
tions another serious problem. During the day, Sol was so busy
working in the Field that he forgot about the lice. But at night, as
he lay in his bunk, he could feel the bugs biting him. He tried to
pick them off or slap them away, but it was a losing battle. He
could never rid himself of the lice which covered his entire body.
Indeed, his skin had turned a mixture of red and dark gray. The
discomfort was intense; he was always hurting, always itching.
Dark scab-like crusts formed on his skin from constant
scratching. But the more he scratched, the more he broke the
scabs causing the pus to run, and risking more serious infection.

Sometimes he felt as if his whole body was covered with scabs and boils. Even worse, lice, the carriers of typhus, had already led to the death of thousands.

While there was little Sol could do about his appearance, he could control his fate in another way. Unlike many other prisoners, he refused to eat from the garbage. He would lie awake at night scratching and itching and consumed by his preoccupation with satisfying his hunger, but he refused to resort to digging through the garbage; nor did he ever use anyone else's eating utensils. He knew that to do so would expose himself to bacteria causing dysentery and death. For even to look ill could mean a death sentence.

Majdanek had become a savage reality. Conditions were unimaginable. Human life no longer had any value, death was everywhere, the terror never diminished. Night and day, in the barracks and in the fields, Sol heard the anguished cries of the victims. It seemed as if suicide in the barracks by men slashing their wrists or hanging themselves was a daily occurrence. The weakest were taken out of the barrack and shot. Some simply disappeared. In Sol's barrack, two men were permanently assigned to gather up the dead every morning; after the dead were counted during roll call, their bodies were loaded on wagons like cordwood and taken to the crematorium for burning. Not even the most elemental respect was shown for the dead.

Although he was weak from physical exertion and lack of food, Sol was more fortunate than others; he had been hardened by his life on the run in the Ghetto. Moreover, he had an idea of what to expect from his two days in Treblinka. Those who had arrived from the more temperate southern European countries had little opportunity to adopt to the harshness of daily life in the camp. They died by the thousands. In fact, many deportees were selected for death immediately upon arrival. Those who appeared incapable of work, including children, the sick, and the elderly were sent directly to the gas chambers.

For Sol there was no choice except to pretend to be fit and continue to work. He tried desperately to maintain his strength and resolve. In spite of the constant persecution, he was determined to survive the Nazi savagery. He tried to block out the horrors he witnessed daily and just focus on getting through one day at a time. Camp life had a way of numbing normal human emotions. Prisoners focused on themselves alone. Norms of morality that applied in the outside world were no longer respected. The only way he could survive was to withdraw totally within himself, speaking rarely, trying to block all normal thoughts and feelings. He also refused to think about an earlier time; thoughts of his parents and sisters were just too painful, especially thoughts of how they had died. Indeed, everything about his prewar life was too hurtful to recall and only drained him of whatever energy he had left.

The only exception to his self-imposed isolation was a handful of friends whom Sol knew and trusted, people with whom he shared a common background from the prewar days in his neighborhood in Warsaw. These hardened survivors lived in his barrack, and together they formed a mutual support network. The continued surveillance, the constant turnover in the prisoner ranks due to the many deaths and executions, and the steady stream of replacements by new arrivals reduced close personal contact among the other prisoners. This network was Sol's only solace. Bound as they were by their current situation as well as their past, an intimacy developed among them. Sol felt a great camaraderie and a genuine sense of support. They had become his family and the only ones with whom he could communicate openly. Anyone he didn't know could be a collaborator. Thus, he shared his thoughts with only a few; with all others he remained on his guard.

One prisoner who lived in his barracks and worked in Field IV with him was Sam Radoszewski. Indeed, it was Sam who had helped Sol so much after his severe beating. Sam, eight years older than Sol, had on more than one occasion given him the inner strength and discipline necessary to survive the ordeal.

In addition to Sam, Sol found support among several other slave laborers who had also been partisan fighters in the Ghetto. Like Sol, they were determined to resist. Zdziesek also helped Sol survive the ferocious beatings, as did Moniek, who in prewar days had harbored a crush on Frania, Sol's older sister. Moniek slept directly beneath Sol on the triple pallet they shared. Bolek and Smulek, both from Warsaw, and several years older than Sol, were other camp veterans. They labored together in the rock fields with Sol during the day and shared their thoughts about the terrifying uncertainty that lay ahead during the night. For, in the evening, after the lights went out, the prisoners were able to reflect. They were usually too tired or weak to engage in much conversation beyond their preoccupation with food. But sometimes, unwinding from the turmoil of the day, Sol and his friends would discuss the good times they had experienced growing up or their future options in hushed tones so as not to be overheard by the kapos. Sol looked forward to these few moments each day, no matter how exhausted he was.

On one occasion, after a particularly hard day in the field, as they were sitting on their pallets, Smulek whispered dejectedly, "We are not going to make it. We are all going to die here. There is no escape. None of us will survive." After a moment, Bolek changed the subject and asked the group what they would wish for if they did survive the war. Smulek said he just wanted to live through the war and see Germany defeated. Bolek said he hoped to survive, eventually have a family, and move to South Africa, where he had relatives.

When Sol's turn came, he said he believed in miracles and that he wished for three things: he longed for a loaf of bread to satisfy his nagging hunger, he hoped someday to marry a beautiful blond, and after the war he wanted to move to the United States. America, Sol said, offered more promise than Europe. He could live in freedom and raise a family without fear of discrimination. Then Sol told his friends they must continue to believe, to have faith: "We must never surrender the will to live. In the end Germany will be defeated and we will overcome." Sol's remarks were greeted with skepticism. As they lay there sapped by hunger, forced labor, beatings, and untreated illnesses, the little group had no reason to believe their dreams would ever be realized.

Chapter VI

Skarzysko-Czestochowa

In the early fall of 1943, after Sol had spent about five months at Majdanek, his life took a turn in yet another direction. Three large Mercedes, each carrying several SS officers, arrived at the camp. Sol and the others were surprised by this unusual sight, and wondered what it meant. The guards immediately began screaming orders for all prisoners to stop what they were doing, strip naked, and assemble for inspection. "Schnell, Schnell," the guards yelled, as the inmates hurried over from every direction. The prisoners were then ordered to form a line and proceed in single file past one of the cars. There, an SS officer, an obese man in a rumpled uniform, sat in the driver's seat with the door open, joking with his colleagues.

Sol and hundreds of others dutifully lined up. Unlike many other inmates, Sol realized immediately how much was at stake. Alarmed and somewhat disoriented by the suddenness of it all, he moved slowly, retreating as far back in the line as possible in order to give himself time to figure out what was happening. As the procession moved forward, Sol saw that the officer was dividing the inmates into two groups by a simple flick of his wrist. When Sol arrived before the officer, he saw the SS man focus on his feet which were smeared with dried blood from the constant rubbing of the tight fitting Hollander shoes on his ankles.

The officer looked up and waved Sol to the left. Instinctively, Sol knew something was wrong. He sensed that he had been sent with the ill-fated group which could only mean the gas chamber. At once, Sol was overcome by flashbacks of Treblinka. He realized what he would have to do. He knew the selection process, which showed no mercy, was based on physical appearance. People were sent to the gas chambers just because they had swollen legs, scratches, or bruises on their bodies, or perhaps because they wore eyeglasses, or did not stand erect. Sol had been in the camps long enough to know that the Germans kept alive only those they thought strong enough to work. Furtively, he slipped away from the group of those who had been rejected, working his way to the back of the original line. Seeing no guards present, Sol blended into the milling crowd of prisoners. He then ran to the rear of a building where there was a water pipe. Using the dirty water, he carefully cleaned the blood off his feet and vigorously brushed the dirt and grime off his body. He even pinched his cheeks to give himself a healthier appearance. Then he returned to the front of the barrack, sneaking back into the inspection line. He arrived a second time in front of the SS officer, who did not recognize him. Sol flexed his muscles for the officer, saying in German, "I want to work for Deutschland. Germany needs strong arms to work in the factories."

This time the officer said, "Jawohl, jawohl," and ordered him to proceed to the line of those inmates who had been spared. These prisoners were told to dress immediately and board nearby railroad cars. Sol recognized his good fortune; once again he had cheated death. He felt as if a great weight had been lifted from him. Without any doubt, he knew that those in the first group would be sent to the gas chambers at Majdanek. Sol's instincts proved correct. Shortly thereafter, Nazi executions by gas and mass shootings intensified. On November 3, an all-day mass killing on Field V resulted in the deaths of over 18,000 Jewish prisoners. Their bodies were dumped in three huge newly excavated ditches near the crematorium.

Once the fear of death had eased, the concern for survival became paramount. The transports were packed tightly with no room for movement. Frequently, when the train stopped, Sol heard rifle fire followed by the thud of falling bodies. Pleas for water were ignored. Sol's mouth was dry, and he assumed the guards were shooting those who could no longer cope with the heat or thirst. Sol prayed for rain, hoping that a few drops would leak through the cracks in the wooden roof and provide some relief, but none came. Sol knew he had to deal with his discomfort in silence, but the days and nights in the suffocating car seemed to drag on endlessly. There was little he could do except to stand motionless. Sol wondered where they were headed. While relieved to have survived the horrors of Majdanek, he was apprehensive about what lay ahead; indeed, he seriously questioned how much more he could endure.

Every few miles the train stopped for prolonged periods, but the prisoners were not allowed out. Sol could hear the guards outside the sealed cars joking and asking for smokes, oblivious to the cries of anguish from the prisoners within. Once a day, the doors were opened and pails of water and stale, hard bread were distributed to the prisoners. The meager rations neither satisfied their hunger pangs nor quenched their thirst. With no place for the prisoners to relieve themselves, the railcars were soon permeated by a sickening stench. Many of the prisoners were overcome by the odor, collapsing in silence. Conditions continued to deteriorate, with more prisoners succumbing each day. Several days into the trip, so many prisoners had died that there was now space to move about, though Sol had to be careful to step over the corpses that littered the floor. However, at least he could breathe and didn't feel suffocated by the mass of humanity. After what appeared to Sol to be about a week, the train finally arrived at Skarzysko, one of the most notorious labor camps in German-occupied Poland. It was located in a heavily forested area with barracks and factories interspersed among the trees to provide cover from Soviet air attacks.

The barracks at Skarzysko were dark and filthy, the wooden floors covered with dirt and grime. There was no heat, even though winter was fast approaching. There were no sanitation or sewage facilities. Nor were there any windows. The ceiling had several holes, which leaked when it rained. Privacy in the overcrowded building was nonexistent. Health conditions were atrocious. To Sol, the surroundings were as grim as any he had previously endured.

Sol knew that given these circumstances, he would need help to survive the coming winter. On the railcar from Majdanek to Skarzysko, he had stood next to Julek, a young Polish physician from Warsaw. Although Julek was about fifteen years older than Sol, they found they had much in common and formed a strong bond. Julek was later assigned to the camp hospital which was for Germans only; from time to time Sol would sneak over to see Julek, requesting medicines to combat cold, nausea, and dysentery. In spite of the danger, Julek never failed to help Sol. Thanks to his assistance, Sol remained relatively healthy.

Even though he knew what to expect, it was still difficult for Sol to adjust to the situation at Skarzysko. Guards were ever present, constantly berating and beating the prisoners, forcing them to work to their last ounce of strength. The guards were commanded by a particularly brutal Gestapo officer, a member of the Death's Head Battalion, known to the inmates only as Hecht. An older officer, he spoke seldom, but there was an unmistakable menace in his attitude. When he did speak, his only utterances seemed to be the obscenities he hurled at the inmates. He could often be seen riding his motorcycle throughout the camp; on more than one occasion, he literally ran over exhausted prisoners who could not clear out of his way fast enough.

To Sol's surprise, the supervisors of the camp were a Jewish couple, a Mr. and Mrs. Markowitz. Both seemed to receive special treatment from the SS. Dressed in the latest fashions, they always appeared very elegant; Mr. Markowitz wore polished new boots which Sol admired. They had total authority over the disbursement of food, supervision of the kapo wardens, and the conduct of the labor program. They even made the life or death decisions concerning the disbursement of drugs and entrance to the camp infirmary. In fact, they appeared to have complete control over all aspects of camp life. They knew the names of many prisoners by sight in spite of the huge turnover of inmates. Even more startling to Sol was the fact that, despite their religion, their relationship with the Nazi guards seemed friendly. There was much gossip about the private lives of the couple. For instance, both were rumored to have involuntary lovers among the inmates, and Sol was cautioned by his friends to keep a safe distance from them. Sol believed there was substance to the gossip, but he kept his thoughts to himself.

Directly under their supervision was Neumann, a kapo who was in charge of Sol's work gang. Sol detested Neumann, a collaborator known for his explosive outbursts. A day didn't go by when Neumann did not intimidate or terrorize a prisoner for some trivial infraction. Sol witnessed his cruelty first-hand on more than one occasion. Each day he seemed to choose a different target. On his daily inspection of the barrack, Neumann would walk directly to a bunk, yank the prisoner off his mattress, and begin to beat him, screaming, "Let's go to work." The frightened prisoner staggered from the barrack in a state of shock.

Sol could never understand the pathological rage behind Neumann's uncontrolled fury. His authority was absolute and his victims were powerless to resist so he didn't have anything to prove to the prisoners. Sol had seen this type of behavior many times before in the other kapos. The Nazis seemed to follow a deliberate policy of selecting psychopaths. Sol was filled with a deep revulsion and hatred for both the individual and the system he represented. In fact, there were times when he could barely conceal his contempt for the man; Sol just hoped that some day he would have the opportunity to get even.

Sol was soon put to work sorting and storing the belongings of murdered Jews. He was to collect bundles of clothing, which were to be separated into piles of shirts, pants, socks, and underwear. He was then directed to examine the clothing and remove all personal items, identification marks, and valuables. After that, he was ordered to carry the clothes to specific locations in the shed. When Sol had deposited the items, a kapo would count them, as Sol had a daily quota to fill; then the clothing would be packed and classified for future shipment.

Sol considered this work an opportunity to maintain a semblance of cleanliness and to satisfy his ever-present hunger. Since there were no showers nor any facilities to wash his clothes, Sol changed wearing apparel as often as possible. However, he had learned through bitter experience to be cautious. He would wait for the guards to take breaks and then quickly substitute fresher clothes from newly arrived deportees for his own dirty, tattered ones. At the same time, he began snatching clothing in order to trade it to Polish workers for food to supplement his meager rations. Even though the Poles were strictly forbidden to talk to or cooperate with the Jews, there was a ready market for expensive items such as fine double-breasted suits, as otherwise the Polish workers could not have afforded them. Sol had become an expert thief in the Ghetto and this training served him well in the camp. Sometimes he would even sell or barter the clothing off his back for food, cigarettes, or bread.

Among the warehouse guards, most of whom were Ukrainian, were several orientals wearing German uniforms. Sol thought they were possibly Mongols who had been captured Soviet P.O.W.'s, now serving as auxiliaries to the German Army. Several of them approached Sol, trying to communicate with him in a combination of broken German and Russian. They ordered him to give them any watches he found. Warily, Sol responded: "I know where to find watches. Give me several days more and I will get them for you. It won't be easy, so please be patient."

Sol never gave the Mongols anything, but his vague promise seemed to satisfy them for the time being and permitted him greater freedom of movement. Less than a week later Sol was transferred to another work station and never saw them again.

Sol was only one of many engaged in theft from the warehouses. Despite the consequences—an immediate death sentence if caught—there was a flourishing black market among guards and prisoners alike. Everyone from the commandant on down was involved in the thievery and profited from it. Ukrainian guards would take furs for their wives and Germans would seize leather coats, boots, jackets, watches, rings, and other assorted valuables for their families. Many of those taken prisoner, thinking they were being sent to work camps, would unwittingly wear their finest clothing. After they were sent to the crematoriums, their glasses, wedding rings, watches, shoes, and clothing were taken to warehouses, such as those where Sol worked. Even teeth were salvaged from the dead and placed in huge copper pots in the warehouse. The personal effects of the murdered Jews were then cleaned and items that had not been stolen or seized were sent from the death camps to Germany for distribution among needy civilians.

Although Poland had officially been declared *Judenfrei* by the fall of 1943, thousands of Jews remained alive, doing the Germans' bidding in the labor camps under SS control. The need for this forced labor clashed with Nazi ideology, but economics took precedence over idealism. For the Germans, the entire operation was highly lucrative. They had turned the extermination of Jews into a vast plundering machine by which they enriched themselves. Inwardly, Sol seethed with frustration and rage, for he knew his work sorting the possessions of his own people was helping his enemies.

One day, Sol sold the clothes he was wearing to a Polish worker, replacing them with the only items he could find in his size: threadbare pants and a torn shirt. A German soldier pointed Sol out to Neumann who happened to be standing nearby: "This man needs clothes. He cannot run around naked."

Guessing what Sol had been up to, Neumann gave Sol a penetrating look. Neumann's eyes narrowed and his shoulders stiffened as he demanded to know what Sol had done with the clothes he had been wearing. Sol assumed an expression of feigned innocence, as Neumann looked back at him with sheer contempt. Frustrated, he signaled for Sol to accompany him from the warehouse to the crematorium. They came to a place with piles of dead bodies emitting an unbearable odor. "Take the clothing from them," Neumann ordered. Sol reluctantly stripped various articles of clothing from several of the corpses. By now, Sol had learned that disobedience was impossible. Outwardly submissive but inwardly furious, he did as he was told and grudgingly put on some of the clothes. Later that day, after his return to the warehouse, Sol removed these items of clothing, selling the jacket and pants to Poles. He quickly replaced them with pants and a shirt from one of the barrels, although these clothes were worn through.

A few days later, while Sol was working in the warehouse, a young German Wehrmacht officer named Schneider called Neumann and Sol into his office. Sol had spoken with Schneider several times as the German made his daily inspection tour through the warehouse. Schneider enjoyed Sol's company because Sol could converse in German. He ordered Neumann to give Sol some decent clothing. Neumann looked skeptically at Sol, and noting that he had given Sol replacement clothing just a few days earlier, he replied: "He is doing something with his clothes." His face flushed, he pointed at Sol, and began to threaten him, "You are going to get me into trouble," he shouted, striking Sol several times.

Schneider ordered Neumann to stop immediately. "Enough," he said. "Find him clothes. Do as you are told." Even more irritated, Neumann grunted his assent. Sol and Neumann left the office; this time Sol was given clothes salvaged from a barrel.

In spite of the attack and Neumann's daily scrutiny, Sol did not alter his routine. He continued to change clothes and clandestinely trade clothing for food on the black market. While

Neumann appeared to be too preoccupied with other tasks to notice the frequent changes in Sol's apparel, this finally attracted Schneider's attention.

Mild mannered and less doctrinaire than most German officers, Schneider did not appear to Sol to be as inhumane or sadistic. Sol had heard he was well-educated and had been a chemist or engineer prior to the war. One afternoon Schneider eyed Sol, "You have been getting clothes. What have you been doing with the other clothes?"

Sol shrugged, "They wore out."

"Don't lie to me!" Schneider barked. "I know what you have been doing. You have been swapping them on the black market. I don't want to catch you again!" he threatened. He then turned to Neumann and ordered him to give Sol clothes from the warehouse with some distinctive marking on them so that they could always be recognized. So Sol was marched back to the warehouse where he was given a brand new railroad conductor's uniform with shiny gold buttons. Even though the coat and pants were Several sizes too large for Sol, Neumann ordered him to report to work each morning wearing the uniform so that he could see those gold buttons. In spite of the risk, Sol was so hungry and desperate for food, that he bartered away the conductor's jacket shortly thereafter. However, he wisely cut off the buttons and had to stay up at night sewing them on another jacket.

After less than two weeks in the warehouse, Sol was reassigned to Factory C. The complex was housed in a dirty building covered by camouflage to shield it from allied air strikes. Inside the poorly ventilated structure, the prisoners were engaged in the manufacture of dynamite. The mortality rate suffered by the slave laborers who worked there was so high that the Germans sarcastically referred to the building as "Toneswerk," or "Death House". The factory had been assigned by the Gestapo to a Leipzig firm, Hasag Werke, which was charged with managing the factory and increasing production. Dr. Arthur Rost, the civilian supervisor of Factory C, was responsible for the ongoing reign of terror. Sol was amazed when he first saw the slave laborers who worked there. Most were Sol's age, but they were so worn and tired that they appeared much older. Due to the sulphur used to make the ammunition, all the prisoners had a yellowish hue to their skin and yellow dust on their clothing. For this reason, the Germans scornfully referred to them as "canaries." The air was heavy with sulphur fumes and the heat from the furnaces made the prisoners sweat profusely. Sol had long since lost all track of time, but he guessed that his transfer to Factory C occurred at about the time of his seventeenth birthday; however, this was no reason to celebrate.

After reporting to his foreman, a bigoted pro-Nazi Polish collaborator named Kupetski, Sol was assigned to a five-man work squad. All in the group were Polish teenagers who, like Sol, had been orphaned by the Nazis. Of the five, only one was a girl. Shy and introverted, she was protected by the boys who assumed she had endured much pain.

Sol was given no instructions, nor was it explained to him how dangerous it was to handle the unstable materials. The workers were given no protective clothing, no masks, no gloves. They worked in shifts: twelve hours on and twelve hours off with two short breaks. If they did not meet the daily production quota, there would be severe punishment. Following his first day in Factory C, Sol collapsed on his bunk from weakness, exhaustion, stress, and the effects of the nauseating, sulphur-laden fumes. Each day was a learning process, and Sol was forced to learn his new trade on the job with ultimately tragic results.

Each member of Sol's crew had a specific task. While one worker served as a supervisor, another would carefully measure the dynamite powder; a third poured the powder into a steel mold; a fourth inserted a screw into the mold and then Sol, who acted as the presser, would take over. Because of his strength, he was given the task which was the most critical and delicate part of the process. Sol had to ram the powder into the steel mold until the powder formed a square within the mold, leaving space for the primer. Then Sol would push the armature in the oven, close the security shield, and press three times in rapid succession until he heard a click, which meant the cylinder-like screw was in place. He then opened the oven door and quickly pulled out the mold, removed the dynamite, and placed it in a box. If the dynamite powder was overheated at all, even for an instant, it could ignite and explode. Moreover, even the slightest vibration could trigger an explosion.

Later, ignition wires were attached to the screws of each dynamite stick by another worker and the sticks were placed back in the box. After that, random testing of the dynamite was conducted. Finally, the boxes were carried to a loading dock. There they were placed on trucks which took them to the railway station for transport to the eastern front.

One night, after several weeks on the job, all the members of Sol's work team were especially tired due to the excessive heat which sapped their energy. Unfortunately, they unknowingly permitted the powder to reach its threshold temperature; it ignited, causing a small explosive flash and a bluish-white fire. Though the fire was quickly extinguished and no one was hurt, the loud noise attracted the attention of the guards. They rushed over yelling "sabotage," and demanded an explanation.

The frightened workers tried to explain what had happened, but the Germans remained unimpressed. Sol froze, his heart beating wildly. When it was his turn to speak, he pleaded "I am a good worker. I try to do everything right. I have worked a long time for Germany and do what I am told." The Germans angrily rejected the explanations of the others, but for some unexplained reason, they decided to spare Sol. The other four members of the work team were ordered out of the factory and lined up against a wall. All the other workers were ordered to stop what they were doing and file out to watch as the four children were shot.

Sol had been hardened by his life in the camps; still this entire episode disturbed him deeply. He felt a tremendous sense of loss. He had grown close to the members of his work team and now they were gone. He also felt guilty that he had been the only one to survive; at the same time he was thankful that once more he had cheated death. At least, he thought, his friends would not have to endure any more suffering. These murders over such a minor incident left him angry, and again demonstrated the precariousness of his situation. Once again, as so many times before, he withdrew from reality in order to survive.

Shortly thereafter, while still working in Factory C with a new crew, another act of senseless violence occurred. Without warning, whistles screeched and the workers were ordered immediately out into the yard. Sol didn't know what was happening, but he sensed trouble whenever the Germans altered the routine. Once outside, the prisoners were shoved together by the guards. Then Sol saw why they were there. A gallows had been hastily erected in front of the factory. A boy younger than Sol was pleading not to be separated from his father. One of the German soldiers laughed and snarled that he would get his wish if he didn't leave his father and go to another workstation. When the boy refused, a guard, shouting "Haizel" (swine), placed a noose around the necks of both father and son. Both were then hanged together in front of the horrified onlookers. The youngster struggled for a long time before he became still. The spectacle almost proved too much for Sol, who had recognized both victims from his shift in the factory. He became momentarily weak and felt his legs begin to buckle. Quickly he composed himself and stood rigid, teeth clenched, throughout the remainder of the incident. That night Sol lay on his bunk in the barrack staring at the ceiling. As tired as he was, sleep wouldn't come. He was plunged into utter despair. His mind was filled with terrifying images he could not escape. Although he still had heard no news of the war, Sol prayed that there would be an allied victory before the Germans killed all of them; there had to be someone left alive to tell the world what the Germans had done.

The next morning, as Sol trudged to the factory, he saw the two bodies still dangling there, their faces frozen in pain. Sol was reminded of Majdanek; he knew that this was the German way of instilling fear and reminding the prisoners how little their lives were worth. When Sol left the factory at the end of his shift, the bodies were gone, but Sol knew the public executions would continue.

Not a day passed without death. Those "canaries," weakened by sickness who could no longer perform their jobs, were ordered out of the lines at the morning roll calls. They were piled into overloaded trucks and driven to a field called Sczelnice a few miles away. There they were lined up and shot by firing squads. Several hours later other prisoners were taken to the killing fields and given spades and shovels to dig mass graves. Then they too were shot, their bodies also thrown into the trenches.

Sol was all too familiar with the selection process. Therefore, when the guards unlocked the doors in the morning, Sol would run to the rear of the barrack. There he would take a red brick, rub it with a rag, and then brush the rag over his face and body to remove the yellow hue and give himself a ruddy, healthy appearance. Sol did this so often, he rubbed the skin off his nose, but the procedure served its purpose. He continued to cheat death.

In spite of the atrocities and danger, Sol still took risks in order to satisfy his hunger. He worked out a simple barter system with the sparse materials to which he now had access: coal, which was stored for use in the furnace, and sulphur. At the end of his shift, he would hide several pieces of coal in his clothing. Later he would trade the coal to other prisoners in exchange for potatoes. To some prisoners, the coal was more important than was food, as it provided warmth during the bitterly cold winter. The coal, however, was covered by a thin veneer of sulphur; one time, when the prisoners placed the coal in a small stove, there was a minuscule explosion. No one but Sol ever understood the cause. Sol also stole sulphur, wrapping the powder in bags, and stashing the bags in his pants.

After his shift, he walked over to the women's barrack and traded sulphur for potatoes. Since the sulphur killed lice, it was a valuable commodity which the women dusted on their bodies.

On his frequent trips to the women's barrack, he became friendly with several of the prisoners. Gradually, over time, Sol established a warm relationship with a few of the women. He discovered that one inmate from Warsaw had by coincidence been at Majdanek at the same time as Sol. Anxiously, he asked her if she remembered Bella. The woman had known Bella, but did not know what had happened to her; she did indicate, however, that Bella had always received ample rations, at least compared to the others. Sol understood this favoritism immediately; he assumed that the gold coins hidden in the hollowed-out heels of Bella's shoes had served their purpose.

One evening, after an especially exhausting day during which Sol had had nothing to eat, he decided to go directly to the infirmary rather than return to the barrack. Sol hoped that Julek would be working late and be able to get him some of the food stored in the clinic for German patients. The night was pitch black; he looked around carefully to avoid detection. He climbed to the roof and began to stealthily cross it, planning to lower himself through a small opening beneath the roof line on the far side of the building. Suddenly, without warning, a portion of the roof gave way. With a loud crash, Sol fell through the ceiling into the clinic.

A startled doctor, sitting alone reading a book, jumped up in shock. He rushed over to Sol, who was somewhat dazed; fortunately, Sol had only a few superficial cuts. The doctor began to treat Sol, asking him what he was doing up on the roof. Sol explained that he was scavenging for food; he begged the doctor not to turn him in. Seemingly sympathetic, the doctor told Sol that he, too, was a prisoner. He had been separated from his wife and children in the early stages of the deportations and then transported from Germany. While Sol was having his cuts dressed, he asked about Julek. He was relieved to hear that Julek was well.

Sol asked the doctor to tell Julek he had inquired about him. The doctor assured him he would, and then left the room to get Sol something to eat. As Sol ate, the doctor told Sol he had to repair the roof and ceiling so that the Germans wouldn't be suspicious. He told Sol to climb up into the attic where he would find extra tiles, sheet rock, and tools. "Do the best you can," he said, "and then disappear. Your secret will be safe with me. I will cover for you." Sol worked feverishly for over two hours. Except for the medic, the building was deserted, so Sol did not have to worry about the noise. Although Sol lacked carpentry skills, the break in the roof and ceiling required only two pieces of plywood, so it was relatively easy to fix. After sweeping the floor of all debris, Sol left quickly, this time by the door.

One day Sol was summoned by Kupetski, his foreman in Factory C, to what appeared to be a hastily arranged meeting. Kupetski told him he was being reassigned from the factory to an inspection job in the fields. Sol assumed he was replacing someone who had been killed during the testing process. Nevertheless, Sol didn't care: he was glad to have the opportunity to get out of the factory and breathe fresh air. He wanted to get away from the sulphur which continually burned his nasal passages and constantly made him sneeze. Moreover, Sol reasoned, no matter how dangerous the testing, it could not be worse than Factory C.

In fact, the work, while less demanding, was still extremely hazardous. Sol was ordered to take a small railway push car from the station to the factory loading platform. He was then to load boxes of the finished dynamite onto the car, and push it to a nearby field. There, he was to test the newly-made explosives. One hundred and twenty sticks of dynamite were packed in each box; Sol was directed to randomly select several sticks from each box for testing. He was given a cursory lesson and a special tool. If flaws were found in the wiring, charge, fuse setting, or weight, the dynamite was to be discarded. He was accompanied by a German officer who supervised him from a safe distance. Sometimes the Polish foreman, Kupetski, and more often, Schneider, would also observe him. However, because they stood several hundred feet away, they had difficulty seeing exactly what was happening. Sol saw this as an opportunity to gain revenge for all he had suffered by sabotaging the Nazi war effort.

Daily, Sol approved flawed dynamite for shipment to the front. He examined the sticks, making certain that the ignition wires in the primers were faulty. Sol felt that this was his contribution to the war effort: "I made sure most of the explosives were no good," Sol said. "In my own mind, I believe I made a contribution to the allies." He packed and sealed half empty boxes, but labeled them full. Sol knew the consequences if he were caught, but in order to inflict harm on the Nazis he was willing to take the risk.

When Sol told several of his friends what he was doing, they warned him of the repercussions if he were discovered. "The Germans will not even bother shooting you," one said, "rather they will cut you into little pieces, Salik. You are taking too great a chance."

But Sol never wavered; this was his way of exacting retribution. Every time he approved a faulty shipment, he secretly congratulated himself: "Good." he told himself.

One afternoon, Commandant Walthers, Schneider's immediate superior, came by the field and randomly chose a stick of dynamite from one of the boxes Sol had approved. Walthers indicated that he personally wanted to test the dynamite. Whenever possible, Sol tried to avoid Walthers, who had a reputation as a brutal and sadistic man. Walthers motioned Sol to the side. Certain the dynamite was flawed, Sol was afraid his luck had run out. However, by some miracle, the dynamite exploded. Once again, Sol had narrowly escaped. However, this was not the last time Sol was to encounter Commandant Walthers.

When Sol had finished "testing" in the field, he would push the minicar loaded with the sealed dynamite boxes from the field to the main warehouse for storage and later shipping. On the way to the warehouse, Sol noticed that the Polish workers temporarily placed their lunches on the window sills of their factory building. Sol would always slow down when he passed this building; when he thought no one was looking, he would jump off the rail car and steal one or two bags of food, together with any cutlery. Then he would dash back to the still moving car and jump on, ravenously devouring the food. He buried the lunch containers in hidden caches in the forest; then he headed back to the warehouse as if nothing had happened. Later he traded the spoons and forks to other prisoners for a piece of bread or half a potato.

There was something else that captured Sol's attention as he moved the explosives from the testing field to the warehouse. Sol noticed a Polish farmer who passed by in a wagon at approximately the same time every afternoon. Sol guessed that the farmer was en route home after a long day in the fields. In the back of the wagon Sol could see a cauldron of soup and other food. Finally, the temptation was too great to ignore. Sol retrieved an empty ammunition can, which he washed thoroughly. One afternoon, after leaving the warehouse, he made his way to the edge of the woods; there he waited. As the farmer passed by, Sol jumped quietly on the back of the wagon. As silently as possible, Sol lifted the lid and smelled the soup. He had almost forgotten how good food could smell. He quickly filled the ammunition can with soup; then he jumped off the wagon, trying not to spill a drop.

Hurrying to a secluded spot in the forest, Sol drank greedily from the awkward container. The lukewarm soup was bland, but to Sol it was delicious. He drank all of it, about three to five gallons, gulping so quickly that his stomach became distended. When the hunger pangs subsided, he immediately became nauseous. Sol vomited and sat leaning against a tree to catch his breath. He remained alone in the woods for perhaps an hour. When he felt a little better, he cautiously returned to the barrack. There he fainted. Later, he felt someone lifting him to his feet and hitting his stomach. Again, he regurgitated. He learned later Neumann had resuscitated him. Fortunately for Sol, Neumann did not report him to the Germans and Sol suffered no repercussions.

Eventually, Sol's ever-present hunger pangs forced him to do something he had promised himself he would never do. Sol resorted to stealing food the Germans had thrown on the ground to feed the rabbits. One day he was caught. Officer Walthers, who happened to observe Sol, forced him to eat a bar of soap and then beat him severely. "Ungeziefer! (Vermin!) You are a thief," he screamed. In a bullying tone, he warned Sol: "Anyone can do the same job you are doing. My patience is running out." Sol fled. His bruises were so pronounced, it took him a week before the swelling subsided and the discoloration disappeared.

Fortunately for Sol, before he could blow himself up testing dynamite, he got another lucky break. Because of his quick mind, fluency in German, and mathematical skills, Schneider made Sol his bookkeeper. Sol was given a small office in the big warehouse where ammunition was stored.

Over time, an amicable relationship developed between the older German and young Sol; gradually this deepened into mutual respect. Schneider's tone of voice and treatment of Sol became friendly and polite. The master-serf relationship which existed between German and Jew disappeared. Sol admired Schneider's bureaucratic skills, and Schneider complimented Sol on how quickly he learned bookkeeping. As Schneider became more comfortable in Sol's presence, he gave Sol unexpected latitude. For example, Sol was allowed to use the latrine in the warehouse; for the first time, Sol could enjoy a few moments of privacy. He even appreciated the simple pleasures of toilet paper and soap. These privileges helped him regain a small measure of dignity and contend with the stress which had become so much a part of his life.

Sol's days were now less structured and strenuous. He was not constantly observed. Nor was there the ever-present fear of punishment. Some evenings he would stop for a few minutes by the outdoor stage where a band played Polish folk music for the guards. The upbeat music reminded him of another life and momentarily helped him escape reality. Moreover, he was freed from the time warp in which he had been imprisoned. The wall calendar behind Schneider's desk gave Sol his first precise indication of the passage of time and the length of his imprisonment. It was now September 1944, over a year since his deportation from Warsaw. There was only one aspect of his daily existence that had not improved: the discomfort he felt caused by his constant nagging hunger.

One day Sol asked Schneider if he could go into the woods to pick wild blackberries. "Ja, ja," came the reply. As Sol was picking the berries, he heard the voice of a Ukrainian camp guard. Sol remembered enough of the Ukrainian he had learned from Olesza, his family's maid, to know that the guard was ordering him to return to the camp.

As Sol turned around, he saw that the guard had lowered his rifle and was pointing it at him. He froze, staring at the rifle; finally, he managed to shake off his paralysis and began to run. The guard opened fire, stopping Sol in his tracks. The Ukrainian then came up to him, grabbed him, and took him back to Schneider's office.

The Ukrainian spoke no German, so when Schneider asked what had happened, Sol replied that the guard had shot at him and grabbed him. The Ukrainian blurted out that Sol did not have the right to pick berries in the woods, but no one understood him except Sol. The heated words of the guard caused Schneider to react. He rose from his chair and the two men started arguing with each other in different languages, neither understanding what the other had said. Before long, fists were flying. The burly Ukrainian appeared to have the upper hand as he wrestled Schneider to the floor. Sol intervened, kicking the guard hard in the face, temporarily stunning him and giving him a split and bleeding lip. Sol then picked up the telephone to call for help, and rushed over to separate the two men. Finally, a German officer arrived on a motorcycle. He wrestled the guard to the floor, disarmed him, and began to beat him with his own gun. The Ukrainian was then taken away.

Following the fracas, Sol returned to his desk. Shortly afterwards, Schneider, who had received the worst of the blows, called Sol into his office, where the brutal Walthers was waiting. "I heard what you did," Walthers said. "You kicked him pretty good."

Sol replied that he had merely been trying to help his superior. Then Walthers did the unthinkable. Previously austere and unapproachable, like most junior officers with whom Sol came in contact, Walthers displayed the first hint of human kindness. He grinned approvingly and reached out to shake Sol's hand. "What was in the past, is the past. I forced you to eat a bar of soap. For that I am sorry. You are a good person. I was forced to punish you for violating regulations." Sol had won an important ally. Thereafter, Walthers' change in attitude, together with Schneider's friendship, served to somewhat moderate the harsh conditions under which he was forced to live.

Word of the incident spread quickly throughout the camp. When Sol returned to his barrack, one of his new friends, Max Kornhauser, who had recently arrived by transport from the Cracow ghetto, was waiting for him. "You must watch yourself," he warned. "The Ukrainian guards call you the 'Warsaw Thief.' If anything is missing they will blame you. You must be careful. Don't let down your guard. The Ukrainians may try to get even with you." His words alarmed Sol so much that he went to Schneider's office to express his concern. He told Schneider he had been warned to be careful of the Ukrainians.

Schneider replied, "No one will touch you. I am in charge, not the Ukrainians. Don't worry about it. I am going to speak to the Ukrainians." Schneider then turned to the kapo, Neumann.

"Sol had nothing to do with what happened between the Ukrainian and myself. Do you understand?"

"Jawohl!" replied Neumann.

"Tell the Ukrainians that if Sol is harmed they will be held responsible," Schneider continued. The incident was effectively closed. The Ukrainians never retaliated against Sol.

Sol continued to try to ingratiate himself with Schneider. As the German was having an affair with a young Polish girl, Sol asked the officer if he wanted him to give the girl lessons in German. He further volunteered to teach the German some Polish so that they could communicate. The officer enthusiastically accepted Sol's offer. After that, Sol and Schneider huddled over Schneider's desk for forty-five minutes each day while Sol tried to teach the German officer basic Polish vocabulary.

In spite of the good working relationship with Schneider, the German never helped Sol get any extra food rations. Sol never knew whether Schneider simply didn't care or whether, being a stubborn bureaucrat, he just wanted to keep Sol on a short leash. But the hunger caused Sol to continue to take risks scavenging for food. The Germans kept huge barrels of jam in the kitchen. The barrels were then removed when they were empty. One day Sol offered to help with this task. He was so hungry, he dove right into one of the barrels to lick the last remains of marmalade from the barrel staves. When other prisoners in the room tried to jump into the barrel with him, it broke under their combined weight. The boys were so hungry, they even began to lick Sol.

While working in Skarzysko, Sol had noticed that many of the Poles who worked in the ammunition factory were paid wages. In prewar Warsaw, a distant cousin, who was a dentist, had placed two gold crowns on Sol's teeth. Sol reasoned that he could sell the gold to the Poles for something to eat. He approached several of the workers, offering them gold for food. "What will you give me for the gold?" he asked.

"Bread, cake, cigarettes," was the response. Eventually Sol made a deal. He had been giving serious thought to removing the crowns anyhow, but for a different reason. Herman Kornhauser, Max's brother, had warned him that the Ukrainian guards had been eyeing Sol ominously. Herman reasoned that the guards wanted the gold and if so, Sol's life was in danger as long as he still had the crowns. Now Sol was faced with the task of actually removing the crowns. He did so with a pair of pliers, and then carried out the deal. Since the crowns were tin gold which was virtually worthless, Sol had no qualms about trading it away for the food he needed to survive.

A short time afterwards, Sol, along with hundreds of other inmates, was ordered to prepare to march to an unknown destination. Again, alarm bells sounded for Sol. He noticed the guards were separating those prisoners who worked in the dynamite factory and whose faces had a sickly yellow pallor from the main group. Sol knew what to do: he ran behind the camp barbershop where he had seen several loose bricks on the ground. Feverishly, he rubbed a brick over his face to improve his appearance and remove any trace of pallor. He then ran back to the front of the barbershop; there the guards pointed him toward the group preparing to leave the camp.

The inmates were anxious, as they had no idea what awaited them. As harsh as their circumstances had been, the unknown could still be worse. Sol's friendship with Schneider had served to shield him from the worst of the abuses and given him some sense of security. Yet Sol welcomed the opportunity to leave the hated camp in spite of the unknown dangers that lay ahead. It was now October 1944, and Sol was willing to confront new risks.

At the end of the first day's march, the prisoners arrived in Piotrkow, Poland. There Sol and many others were crammed into the town's small jail. After an uncomfortable night in the overcrowded cell and a weak, watery cup of coffee in the morning, the inmates renewed their march. Early that afternoon, they arrived at an enormous field near Sulejow.

Here, under the watchful eye of the guards, the prisoners were ordered to dig huge ditches. Initially Sol feared that the trenches were to be used as an enormous burial ground for the inmates. However, as the days stretched into two weeks and the pits took shape, Sol's apprehension lessened. The German guards did not seem intent on killing them. They were not especially cruel and seemed more indifferent than anything else. When the digging was completed, the workers removed the debris, and painstakingly covered the ditches with branches and shrubbery so that they blended in with the landscape. From eavesdropping on the guards, Sol learned that these were intended to be antitank traps and artillery dugouts. They were to serve as a fallback defense to slow an anticipated Russian push west.

The labor was hard and the workdays long, but for Sol it was a refreshing change. The cold, fresh air was exhilarating after being confined indoors for so long. Sol even preferred sleeping outside on the hard pavement of a large courtyard to the dirty lice-ridden bunks on which he had slept for so long. Moreover, being outside afforded Sol more opportunity to scavenge for food. Sol's spirits were also lifted by the conversations that he was able to overhear among the guards. Since they were not aware that Sol understood German, they discussed the German defeats and Soviet advances on the Eastern front openly. Perhaps his long nightmare was nearing an end. It was reason enough to hope.

When the work was completed, the prisoners were marched to a railway siding. There they were told to sit and wait. Within a few hours a train with a long line of boxcars appeared and the prisoners were shuffled aboard. Sol tried to prepare himself for yet another long, agonizing journey. This time, however, the trip lasted only a few hours. The train halted at the Nazi labor camp at Czestochowa, 136 miles southwest of Warsaw. The city housed Poland's holiest shrine, the famous

"Black Madonna," a painting of a dark-skinned Madonna and child. It also contained numerous industrial plants, including foundries and ammunition factories, whose workers included slave laborers from the nearby concentration camp.

The prisoners were ordered off the railcars and marched to barns outside the city. The barns were to be their new living quarters. While drafty, the old wooden buildings were large enough so as not to be overcrowded. Moreover, Sol found the ample supplies of hay were much more comfortable to sleep on than the bunks in the camps. In addition, one nearby building contained showers, a luxury unknown to Sol in previous camps.

Sol's survey of the camp was interrupted by the screech of whistles. The prisoners were then ordered to line up for roll call. Soon afterwards, three men appeared: the camp commander and two kapos, Weinberg and Fragner. The commander stepped forward and introduced himself in German with a strong Polish accent. "My name is Rosensweig," he said, "I command this camp. It is a labor camp and you will be expected to do as you are told. We want no problems so perform your jobs as you are instructed." Sol eyed him closely. He was short, bulky, and in his early thirties. His eyes looked tired, his face worn and weathered. His voice was soft and his tone lacked the cruelty and arrogance Sol had come to expect from the officers he encountered. It was almost as if the Pole was tired of the war and his part in it. Sol's intuition told him Rosensweig identified with the prisoners and could be trusted.

At Czestochowa, Sol worked two jobs: one in a munitions factory manufacturing artillery shells, and later with a railroad crew, repairing rails. In both jobs, he tried to make himself indispensable to the Germans. "Everything they wanted me to be, I was," he later recalled.

A month after his arrival, Sol was filing through the line to receive his meager ration of soup at dinner time. For some reason, he was served less than half of the usual amount. Famished, Sol temporarily forgot the beating he had received at Majdanek under similar circumstances. He asked the kapo why he had given him so little soup. Sol saw the kapo's expression harden. The kapo raised the soup ladle to strike Sol, but this time Sol was ready. He reacted quickly, wrestling the ladle from the kapo's hand and smashing it to the ground. Sol was prepared to punch the kapo in the face, but Rosensweig, who was standing nearby, rushed over to restrain Sol. He then pulled him aside. Bluntly, he cautioned Sol: "Be careful, Salik. You are not in Warsaw now. If you want to survive this war, don't cause any trouble. I may not be around next time."

Sol nodded and walked away with his small portion of soup. He knew Rosensweig was right and appreciated his intervention. When he thought about it later, he realized that without Rosensweig, the situation might have been far worse. He was thankful that his intuition about Rosenwzeig had been correct.

During the next few weeks, Sol got to know the two kapos, Fragner and Weinberg. Sol estimated that Fragner was in his late thirties and had a university background because he was so well-spoken. He was tall, thin, not very physically imposing, and of light complexion. Like Rosensweig, he showed concern for the welfare of the prisoners and tried to protect them as much as possible. He befriended Sol and he, too, cautioned him to exercise prudence: "This is a dangerous place, Salik. Don't take any chances and don't step out of line. If you want to survive here, do what you are told and don't anger the authorities." Sol knew he could trust Fragner and tried to heed his advice.

Sol was fortunate to have the protection of men who had not lost their humanity, for the other kapo assigned to Sol's barrack, Chaim Weinberg, was devious and authoritarian. One evening following an extremely demanding work day at the ammunition factory, Weinberg strode into the barrack where Sol was resting on his bunk. He ordered Sol to hurry over to the loading platform; workers were needed to load munitions aboard a railcar. Weinberg promised Sol extra rations of bread for his effort. Though exhausted, the prospect of additional food was too good to refuse. Several hours later, Sol returned to the barrack, where he found Weinberg sitting on his bunk. When Sol asked him for his bread, Weinberg answered that there had been no bread to begin with: "You wouldn't have worked had I not made the offer and I was ordered to find workers. As you can see my subterfuge worked."

Infuriated, Sol raised his fist to strike Weinberg, but the kapo struck first. He lashed out at Sol with his whip, slashing the top of Sol's head twice. Sol backed away in agony. Sol's friends, knowing that a fight with a kapo would bring the SS running, intervened. Grabbing Sol, they forcefully restrained him. Defiantly, Sol yelled, "You no good kapo. Your time will come. Someday you will get what you deserve." Sol's friends then helped him from the barrack. Outside, they did their best to cleanse his wounds and cautioned him to stay away from Weinberg, who did not forgive or forget easily.

By now the weather was turning much colder. Since the Germans supplied no cold-weather clothing, Sol created his own winter wardrobe. To augment his shabby and worn garments, he took the thick sacks that had held cement mix and fashioned them into coverings for his chest and legs by tying the assorted pieces together with string. The added layers, while not exactly fashionable, did supply much needed protection from the sub-zero temperatures he would have to endure.

Throughout the war, the Nazis made good use of local collaborators. In the rail yards, Sol was supervised by an enormous Polish foreman by the name of Malinowski. A physically imposing man over six feet four inches in height, Malinowski was known for his cruelty; he enjoyed deliberately humiliating the Jews. Everywhere he went, he carried a whip in his right hand, never hesitating to use it. He would constantly scream, "Schnell, Juden!" ("Faster, Jews!"), the only German words he knew. The prisoners disliked him intensely.

One day, while they were laying rocks for a railroad bed, a German officer told Malinowski that he was using too many rocks on the roadway. Malinowski did not understand anything the German said, but still he replied, "Ja, ja, ja".

The exasperated German shouted, "If you don't understand, don't say ja, ja, ja."

Overhearing the conversation, Sol volunteered, "I don't think he understands. May I translate into Polish?" The German officer cast a surprised look at Sol and then finally agreed. Sol carefully translated the German's orders word for word. From that time on, Malinowski came to rely on Sol as his interpreter.

On another occasion, when a couple of his friends came back into the barrack with lash marks on their faces and on the back of their heads, Sol asked them what had happened. They replied that Malinowski had beaten them. Sol lay awake in his bunk that night, angered over the incident. He resolved to confront Malinowski the next morning, but thought better of it in the light of day. The time was not yet right, he reasoned.

But it was not long before the right time did arrive. Once a month, the Germans provided Malinowski with a small truck on which to load coal. Unknown to the Germans, Malinowski would always stop at a warehouse where he would have the inmates load electric motors and pumps in an elongated box; he then had the prisoners place the box in a compartment on the truck bed. Next Malinowski would drive the truck to the coal yard, and load the coal over the container to conceal it. Sol was aware of the theft, as he did much of the loading for Malinowski, but he said nothing. However, one very cold morning, Sol and the other inmates lit a fire to warm themselves before beginning their work. Furious, Malinowski began screaming at them, calling them all kinds of derogatory names. Most of Sol's friends got up quickly to return to work, but not Sol. "What the hell are you staying here for? Go with the rest of the Jews," Malinowski yelled.

Sol stood his ground: "I will remain here and warm myself." Malinowski picked up his whip to lash Sol, but Sol caught the whip and pulled it to him, shaking the giant Pole with all his might.

"I know what you have been doing, and if I tell the Germans you and your family will end up as slave laborers like the rest of us," he warned the collaborator.

A look of shock and fear crossed Malinowski's face. A complete role reversal had taken place. Fearful, Malinowski pleaded that the motors and pumps were going to the Polish underground to help fight the Germans. "You, Salik, are a good Polish Jew. You would not want to do this to the Polish nation."

Sol knew Malinowski was lying to cover up his actions, but he offered him a compromise. Sol would not report the theft to the Germans, but in return, Malinowski had to promise never to strike him or his friends again. "When the Germans come around," said Sol, "you can say, 'Schnell, Juden!' all you want, but you must never use the whip."

Malinowski hastily agreed, but from that time on he was always worried that the Germans would find out about his thievery. He promised Sol he would keep his word. Indeed, after that incident there was an obvious change for the better in his treatment of Sol and the other prisoners. He even began to bring Sol extra rations of food and cigarettes. Never again, to Sol's knowledge, did Malinowski ever use his whip on any of the them.

Chapter VII

Buchenwald

In late December 1944, Sol was ordered to board yet another train. This time the train, which consisted of freight and cattle cars, was heading for the largest concentration-extermination camp in the entire Reich, the dreaded Buchenwald. The trip was supposed to last several days; Sol prepared for the worst. The train happened to approach the city of Dresden in the midst of a British air raid on the rail yards. Halting in some deep woods outside the city, they waited for the all-clear to sound. But even after the raid ended, the train still could not move because the destroyed section of track had to be repaired.

The discomfort on the train was acute. Finally, the guards unlocked the doors of the boxcars to allow in fresh cold air. They also brought in some food; it was little more than the hay fed to horses and didn't satisfy Sol. Hunger and thirst continued to gnaw at him. Moreover, his body ached from the crowded conditions.

Watching the guards from the open doors, Sol saw that they were not alert; they were too occupied relaxing and playing cards some distance from the train. Impulsively, Sol decided to flee. He took a deep breath, ran to the door, and dropped to the ground. Undetected, he ran deep into the woods. He found a hiding place beneath a pile of branches and dense undergrowth. When the rapid beat of his heart returned to normal, he noticed how good everything smelled. The countryside was so fresh and clean from the snow. The air was moist and heavy with the scents of the earth and trees. It was like another world from the foul smell of the camps and boxcars. He was also awed by the silence and tranquility of the woods. Sol lay quiet for a long time. Then, with a shock, he came to the sudden realization that he had not been missed: he was free. On the other side of the woods, he paused in a clump of trees on top of a hill. For a brief time he allowed himself to fantasize about what a normal like would be like. Snapping back to reality, he realized he needed to find shelter. From his hiding place he saw several seemingly deserted homes about two hundred yards away. Singling out a small house, he ran to it, hoping to seek refuge. He knew that Germans who sheltered Jews were taking a mortal risk, but he felt he had to take that chance. Slowly he opened the door, startling a young nurse, 18 or 19. Sol wasn't sure what alarmed her more: his disheveled appearance or the fact that an uninvited stranger had entered her home.

The girl was wearing a uniform with a little cape on the back and a white hat with a red cross. She was slightly taller than Sol, and very attractive. Afraid, she backed off. However, Sol introduced himself, telling her not to worry. He said he would not harm her; he only wanted help. "I ran away from the prison train which is not too far from here," he told her. "The train is going to Buchenwald, but halted because of the air attack." Apparently she believed Sol, as she indicated that she had heard the explosions from the bombing raid. Relieved and calmed by the tone of his voice, she invited Sol in and offered him food and water. She went into the kitchen and prepared a plate of sliced ham, cheese, and black bread and carried it to the table with hot tea and a chocolate bar. The sight and smell overwhelmed Sol. Apparently the girl could sense this. She told him her name was Marta; then she cautioned him not to eat too fast, and to chew his food carefully. Sol savored his first good meal in months. He was thankful to finally be rid of his terrible pangs of hunger.

Marta asked him if he wanted to bathe. Sol could not remember the last time he had taken a bath, perhaps two years before, he thought. He accepted eagerly. She showed him to the bathroom and, as they walked, he glanced around. The appearance of the little house was reassuring. It was quiet and cozy and had a clean smell about it.

After taking off his clothes, Sol examined himself in the mirror. He hardly recognized himself. "Could I really be this filthy and unkempt?," he wondered. His hair was matted and overgrown; his skin had an unhealthy yellowish-white pallor; his rib cage jutted out and his thighs and buttocks were much thinner than he remembered. His ankles were swollen and sores covered his entire body. Sol lay in the hot bath for what seemed an eternity. When he was through, Marta gave him a pair of shoes and some men's clothes to replace his soiled smelly rags. She explained that the clothes belonged to her brother, but that she was currently living there alone. She then said she had to make a telephone call. Sol was alarmed, and asked who she was calling.

Sensing his worry, she reassured him that she only wanted to call the hospital to let them know she would be late for work. "I want to spend a little time with you." Sol nodded his appreciation. He listened, relieved, as she explained to her supervisor that she wasn't feeling well and would be late for work, but she nevertheless promised to come in. Turning from the phone, Marta handed Sol a comb. He had not used one in months. It felt good to run it through his hair, which was now smooth and clean.

Then Marta asked Sol if he minded if she shaved him. Sol was momentarily anxious, but she smiled and assured him that she had shaved her father many times; Sol relaxed and gave his consent. Marta pulled up a chair, sat down and began to soap up his face. Sensing his hesitancy, Marta said, "I will be careful. Don't worry. It's a shame you have to go through the agonies you are enduring."

When she had finished shaving him, Marta and Sol sat and talked. She asked no indiscreet questions, but did want to know more about him. When he told her he was Jewish, Marta didn't flinch. "What did you do wrong?" she asked.

"I did nothing wrong," Sol answered. "The only thing wrong is that I am Jewish."

"That doesn't make sense," Marta replied. "I have never been around Jews but I have heard Himmler and Hitler talk about the Jews and how they wrecked Germany." She continued by saying that she thought it was all propaganda. Although she had never attended school with any Jews, she knew from her readings that there were many highly educated Jewish people who were artists and scientists. She had been led to believe that all Jewish people were evil, but since she had met Sol she could see that this was not so.

"You look as good as anyone else to me, maybe better. Some of my boyfriends don't look as good as you. You shave, you put on some shoes, and you wouldn't look at all different from anyone else," Marta said. She became more animated as she continued and asked Sol if he would like to stay. She offered to care for him and nurse him back to health. Sol felt somewhat apprehensive as their conversation continued; he was not sure where all this was leading.

Marta then turned the conversation to Sol's background and family. She inquired about his parents. Sol told her what had happened to them. He assured her they had never done anything wrong. They had never harmed anyone, and neither had he. "The only thing I believe in is God. I am Jewish, and because of this I am a criminal."

Sol also told her of the extermination-concentration camps in Poland. She denied knowing of their existence, although she said she had heard about the prisons at Buchenwald and Dachau and thought they existed to punish people who were against the German government. She expressed surprise to learn what was happening at the camps in the East; Sol felt from her look of genuine concern and from the tone of her voice that she was sincere.

Rising, Marta told Sol she would show him the cellar where he would be safe in case of stray bombs from the almost daily raids. As they stepped down into the basement, Sol asked Marta about her family. She explained that her mother was dead and that her father and brother were serving on the Eastern Front with the Wehrmacht. She lived alone, and since her home was so isolated, she seldom had visitors. Mail was not even delivered to her house. If she wanted to meet people, she had to go to the dance halls in Dresden. She paused, and seemed to reflect: "The war will soon be over. We are not doing well. Everything has fallen apart. I want to do something to help. I am a good person. Please, stay here."

Sol replied that he would think about her offer. He did not want to jeopardize her safety, but secretly he was tempted to accept. Anxious to know more about the course of the war, he asked Marta to tell him what she knew of recent events. She replied that all news was government-controlled, but nevertheless the latest information was not good for the Germans. Anglo-American forces had landed in France that summer and already wrested that country from German control. To the East, Russian spearheads had ousted the German Army from the Soviet Union and were now in Eastern Poland. In the air, as Sol had observed, the Allies had won mastery. Sol was both surprised at her honest appraisal of the unfolding events and elated. There was no bitterness in her voice, only sadness for what Germany was enduring. Whatever the outcome, she hoped the war would end soon and her father and brother would return safely. She rose from her chair, hugged Sol, and told him she was leaving for work, but hoped he would be there when she returned. She put on her coat, walked to the door, turned and saying *"Auf Wiedersehen,"* rode away on her bicycle.

Sol sat in the stillness of the empty house. He began to pull his fingers, a nervous habit he had acquired at the time of the German invasion of Poland. He then began to consider the pros and cons of staying. He had learned through bitter experience never to trust anyone. His fellow Poles had discriminated against Jews before the war, and had collaborated with the Germans in their plans to exterminate the Jews during the war. The Germans were even worse, systematically enslaving and then murdering all who were Jewish. While Marta appeared to be sincere and compassionate, he was afraid that at any moment she might turn against him and call the Gestapo. He feared she might be like the Poles, sweet on the outside, but a turncoat on the inside. He decided he was too afraid to trust her; he did not want his life to be over so near the end of the war. Was he making a mistake? He knew that he could not afford to make the wrong choice. Yet life in the forests all alone would be dangerous and difficult. He would have to face the constant threat of death from exposure, betrayal by German civilians, or the fear of being hunted down by the Army or Gestapo. He would also have to worry about food. Escape from the camps did not guarantee survival, especially in a country that had condemned all Jews to death. He could not risk the unknown; he would not chance life on the run. Better to return to the railway car where he could be with his own people until the war's end. At least by going back, Sol reasoned, he would have a chance.

While Sol was too frightened to even think of a relationship with Marta, he enjoyed the feeling of being around a girl again. Due to the horrors of the war, Sol had had virtually no opportunity for a normal adolescence. Sexual relationships in the camps were practically unthinkable, although not entirely unknown. Although young, Sol was old enough to realize that sexual experience had been denied him. Another reason, he thought, to resent the Nazis.

Sol vacillated a while longer. He wished he didn't have to decide one way or the other. But finally he convinced himself that it was a delusion to think he could find safety and security in the home of a German. There were just too many uncertainties.

Leaving the comfort of the house behind, Sol raced back to the railway car. He stopped in a clump of trees near the tracks, on the lookout for the guards. All of them were still huddled together, laughing and smoking in front of the car at least two hundred yards down the track. Miraculously, the door to his railcar was still partly open. He took a deep breath and ran the few yards to the car, climbing back in undetected.

A short time later, the doors were sealed and the train resumed its journey. The boxcar was gloomy, with the darkness penetrated only by narrow shafts of light that came through holes in the walls of the car. The trip, like the others Sol had experienced previously, was a test of his capacity to endure. Sol tried to ignore the stench of human waste, the cries for water, and the periodic rifle shots. From prior experience, Sol knew he should remain as motionless as possible to conserve energy. However, this time he was sustained by the nourishment and relief provided by his brief stay with Marta.

Though Sol lost all track of time, it did not seem long before the train arrived at Buchenwald, one of the earliest of the Nazi extermination camps. Ironically, Buchenwald was located just outside Weimar, the German city where the short-lived democratic republic had been born following Germany's defeat in World War I. Weimar, the home of German cultural giants, men like Schiller, Liszt, and Goethe, had now become the center of the vast killing machine. More than 56,000 prisoners had been murdered there since the camp had begun operations in 1938.

Sol arrived in Buchenwald in the closing stages of the war. As the allied forces closed in on the Reich, the Germans accelerated the pace of the evacuations and killings of the last remnants of European Jewry. Their hope was to eradicate all traces of their atrocities. The Germans, therefore, shipped tens of thousands of slave laborers from the labor and death camps throughout the East, funneling them to Buchenwald. Sol was part of this huge mass movement.

As Sol was hurried off the train by the guards, he heard the strains of soft music. After passing through the gate, he saw a small orchestra composed of internees, all female, mostly young, dressed in white blouses and navy blue skirts. They were playing songs Sol recognized from the pre-war days in Warsaw, soft, classical harmonies that belied the harsh circumstances and cruel environment of the camp. Everything seemed surreal. Before Sol could grasp what was happening, the music ended and a gruff SS officer barked at the deportees, "This is a labor camp. All able-bodied men are expected to serve the Reich in whatever capacity is asked of them." Then he continued ominously, "Anything less than everyone's full effort will result in dire consequences." Since they were at the entrance to the camp, the prisoners could see only the raised platform surrounded by well-kept shrubbery. There was no hint of what awaited them.

The camp itself was overflowing with 50,000 sick and starving prisoners. The crowding had caused the camp to spill over into a lower camp as well as more than one hundred sub-camps. The lower camp contained crudely-built barracks, reserved solely for those at the very bottom of Germany's social order: Jews, Gypsies, and those prisoners from the upper camp near death from overwork, malnutrition, or medical experiments. The two camps were separated by barbed wire fences. The level of health and sanitation in the lower camp was even more inadequate than in the upper camp, where conditions were minimal.

Sol was ordered to the showers. Terrified, he reluctantly plodded forward. An intimidating kapo barked at the prisoners to disrobe. Slowly Sol removed his clean clothes which he had hoped to wear considerably longer. The prisoners were lined up and filed through a room where other prisoners cut their hair. At least, Sol thought, they weren't being hurt when they were shaved as at Majdanek. All types of thoughts raced through Sol's mind: he wondered if his life had finally come to an end; he thought about how he could avoid the showers, what he could do to escape. But there was no more time to think. Certain he was about to be murdered, he was herded with the other prisoners into a forbidding enclosed room of gray concrete. Sol stared at the shower heads in the ceilings. He inhaled, trying to detect the odor of gas. He edged closer to the front of the room, trying to get as far away from the showers as possible. He had worked himself into a state of near panic. Then the showers came on and rushing water poured out. Sol was so relieved his knees almost buckled and his body began to tremble; he grew momentarily weak and light-headed. Soon the showers were shut off and the doors opened. The prisoners were directed next to another building where they were given a blanket, clothes, and shoes. Sol assumed that these came from dead people, but at this point he did not care. He was just glad to be alive.

Sol was then marched to Barrack Number 65 in the lower camp. It was a dark, dismal, barn-like structure meant to sleep perhaps 450, but at that time it contained approximately 1000 to 1200 inmates. The prisoners were stacked on shelves with nothing but lice-infected straw for mattresses. Lying there in the dark were both the dying and the dead. Indeed, every morning the bodies of roughly two dozen prisoners were carried from the barrack, and piled up for later removal.

Adjacent to the stack of dead bodies were the latrines; they consisted of an open concrete-lined ditch which ran between the barracks. The ditch was roughly twenty-five feet long, and twelve feet wide. There were railings along the side that the inmates used to squat on. The latrines were overflowing; Sol never did observe any attempt to empty them. As in the other camps, there was no toilet paper. The barracks reeked from the indescribably putrid stench of the latrines.

Shortly after Sol's arrival, the barrack kapo came in, screaming for silence. He then proceeded to introduce himself. Gustav was a stocky Pole, about six feet tall with red hair and a fair complexion. He looked quite unassuming, but proved to be a cruel taskmaster. He appeared well-dressed in clean freshly pressed clothes, and his trademark officer's boots had a highly polished shine. But he was verbose and domineering, and it was not long before he revealed his true character. First, like the other kapos at previous camps, Gustav demanded that the newly-arrived prisoners turn their valuables over to him. Sol knew that he used the jewelry and gold he collected to bribe and ingratiate himself with the SS. It was no surprise to Sol, therefore, that his relationship with the SS officers appeared to be friendly. Sol also noted that Gustav ate his meals with the Germans and socialized with them at every opportunity. But he was somewhat surprised to note that the SS men always returned Gustav's salute. They gave him a wide latitude to run the barrack and allowed him to treat the prisoners any way he wanted. Gustav always smelled of liquor, but it rarely seemed to affect his behavior. Like the kapos at other camps who seemed accustomed to drinking a lot, Gustav had developed a high tolerance for alcohol.

Gustav determined who would live and who would die. Life had little meaning for him. He murdered many prisoners for seemingly little or no reason at all. Describing himself as the "King of Barrack Number 65," Gustav met all transfers to the barracks and interrogated them. He made it a point to learn each new prisoner's name, including Sol's. He was particularly interested in knowing whether any of them had been kapos, foremen, policemen, or in any other position of authority at other camps. He would tolerate no opposition; he was the sole ruler. If any prisoner answered affirmatively, that was reason enough for Gustav to have him murdered. One day Gustav came into the barrack and seized two of Sol's friends, the Katz brothers, with whom Sol had grown very close. They were dragged outside and killed. Sol knew that they had previously been policemen at Skarzysko and thus they represented a perceived threat to Gustav. Gustav inspected the barrack daily, always accompanied by SS guards. Sol often saw Gustav enter the barracks and pull sick and malnourished prisoners outside, where they were turned over to the SS and shot.

In addition to Sol's barrack, Gustav had sole authority over the children's barrack. For some reason, these particular youths had been spared the gas chambers. Some served as messengers, "Laufer," spending their days running throughout the camp delivering messages. Most were only a few years younger than Sol. This enormous block housed almost 1,000 children, some of whom had parents who were still alive elsewhere in the camp. Sol was not surprised to hear whispered rumors that Gustav was a pedophile, which explained why he spent so much time with the children.

At night, Gustav would frequently order special trials of inmates he had singled out as victims. The trials had a foregone conclusion. Then Gustav ordered all the prisoners outside to watch the punishment. Sticks with nails hammered into them were distributed to the children, who were ordered to beat the unfortunate victim to death. Those children who did not take part in the killing nevertheless had to stand and watch the grisly scene.

One night a loud and boisterous man called Pantel, who lived in Sol's barrack, was selected for the ritual sacrifice. Sol knew he had been a policeman in the Cracow Ghetto before being transported to Buchenwald and suspected that was why he was targeted. After Pantel's murder, a blanket was thrown over the corpse, and the next morning Gustav reported to the SS that another of the prisoners had died. To Sol's knowledge, the SS never questioned the cause of death of any of the prisoners. Moreover, Sol could only imagine the kind of deep-seated scars the children would have to bear.

Theoretically, Sol's barrack, like others at Buchenwald, was organized by nationality. Each barrack in the camp, except the children's, had a kapo in charge who was supposed to be the same nationality as the inmates. However, because of the influx of so many deportees, men of many nationalities as well as quite a few German communists and political dissenters were housed in Sol's barrack. There were also numerous Gypsies, Seventh

Day Adventists, and homosexuals. The German prisoners were the only ones who were given CARE packages containing sweets and cigarettes. Several of the homosexuals, who placed makeshift curtains around their bunks to give themselves some privacy, seemed to have more privileges than most of the other prisoners in terms of extra food, blankets, and work assignments. This caused Sol to question their relationship to Gustav. Some of the homosexuals invited several of the new arrivals, including Sol, to their bunks with offers of candy or cigarettes, but Sol always managed to find an excuse. When they threatened him, Sol brushed off their warnings, saying, "I will come tomorrow or the next day," or "I worked too hard today. I need to rest." For the homosexuals, tomorrow never came.

Sol had learned his lessons well at the other death camps. He did what he had to do to survive in Buchenwald. He became an instant expert at whatever the Germans needed at the moment; at the very least, it limited his contact with Gustav. Sol had believed at one time that his compliance and contributions to the German war effort would spare him. Now, although he seriously questioned this assumption, he saw no other alternative if he wanted to survive.

Initially Gustav ordered Sol to go on work details. Sol left the camp early every morning to be trucked into Weimar. There he was part of a huge number of slave laborers who cleared debris from the constant Allied bombing raids. He was also ordered to locate and dig up bodies of civilians killed in the raids. Sol didn't mind this work because it took him outside the camp and gave him an opportunity to scavenge for food.

One day as he was clearing out a cellar, he discovered some blackberry preserves. Breaking open the bottle, he devoured the contents. A German woman saw him and complained to the guards that one of the prisoners was stealing her food. A guard demanded to know who was responsible. When no one came forward, he ordered the prisoners to stick out their tongues. Sol was easily identified; in retribution the guard smashed his rifle butt into Sol's shoulder, knocking him to the ground. "This is your last warning," he threatened. Although the pain was intense, Sol's hunger pangs soon caused him to ignore the warning.

Shortly thereafter, while clearing a bombed-out kitchen in Weimar, Sol found a bunch of onions which he hid in his clothing. When he returned to the camp entrance that evening, he and the other workers were stopped at the gate and ordered to jump up and down to see whether they were smuggling anything into the camp. When the onions fell out, the SS officer began to whip Sol fervently, accusing him of theft. Sol argued, "No, I found them in the garbage." The SS officer gave the onions to a Russian prisoner, but when they were away from the sentry, the Russian quietly returned them to Sol.

Several days later, Sol came across an acquaintance from his recent past. While clearing away rubble in Weimar, Sol recognized one of the prisoners in his work detail; it was Rosensweig, his former commandant at Czectochowa. Since Rosensweig had had his position and perks stripped away, the two were now both ordinary slave laborers. They talked as they cleared a basement of debris from a recent bombing. Sol had a genuine affection and grudging respect for the man. He had walked a tightrope between German authority and his own conscience, and treated the prisoners with a degree of humanity seldom seen in the camps.

Discovering several potatoes in a barrel, Sol scooped them up and put them in the pockets of his pants and shirt. When Rosensweig offered to give Sol bread in exchange for the potatoes, Sol agreed. He gave the potatoes to Rosensweig; but before Rosensweig could go and get the bread for him, another British air strike began and everyone had to flee for cover. When the raid ended, Sol looked for Rosensweig, but he was nowhere to be found. When Sol returned to the barrack that evening, he asked about Rosensweig. He learned that the former kapo had been shipped by transport to another slave labor camp that afternoon.

Sol was disappointed, but promised himself that if by chance he and Rosensweig ever met again, he would remind him of his debt.

Sol's work took him to many locations in the city. The slave laborers worked under the watchful eyes of civilian guards who held whips or rifles. Sol said nothing, but learned a great deal by listening to the conversations going on around him. The talk reflected the breakdown in order and discipline that was plaguing the civilian sector in the wake of military disasters. Sol overheard the Germans bitterly condemning the conduct of the war. He also listened to many complaints about husbands and sons serving on the front lines while their homes and cities were being destroyed by storms of death raining down from the skies. He learned that Russian and American troops were making rapid advances; the German army was reeling under Allied assaults. The people no longer believed the government's promises; morale was crumbling. Sol sensed an overwhelming fatalism. Defeat and surrender, while still unspoken, were no longer unthinkable.

Sol was caught up in several more Allied air attacks while he was working. Together with the civilian population, he fled to underground cellars until the all-clear siren sounded. The damage in human and physical terms was devastating. Sol was convinced that the war was drawing to a close. If he could just survive a little longer, he thought, perhaps, with a little luck, he could outlast the war.

One day a call went out for plumbers. Sol had never even held a wrench in his life, let alone worked as a plumber. Nevertheless, he volunteered. He was ordered to fix a stopped up sink. In attempting to make the repairs, he accidentally pulled the sink off its mountings. Furious, the guard slammed his fist into Sol's face, knocking Sol to the ground.

As Sol was recovering from that attack, the Germans requested volunteer groomsmen for the stables. This was one job for which he really did feel he was qualified, as Sol's early years had been spent around horses; again, he volunteered. Compared to his heavy labor jobs, this was child's play. The stables were located at the camp's southern perimeter, away from the filth and congestion of the barrack. The area was well-kept and in all respects superior to the facilities provided for the camp's human inhabitants. Sol looked forward to grooming the horses. Moreover, he could partially satisfy his hunger by eating the bread meant for the horses.

One day, while helping the daughter of a German officer, he happened to place his hand on her buttocks to help her mount her horse. She immediately scolded him and accused him of evil thoughts. "Never do that again!" she shrieked.

Sol protested, pleading, "No, no. I did not have anything in mind. I only meant to help you." He was frightened he would be reported; fortunately, however, there were no repercussions.

A short time later, Sol was forced to leave the peace and security of the stables. He and hundreds of other slave laborers were ordered into the countryside to dig huge tank traps and ditches. The workers were given daily quotas to fill. If their quotas were not met, they were whipped severely. The heavy labor and fresh air made Sol even hungrier than usual. Sol could not help noticing some salami sausages hanging from small cords in the field kitchens of the German guards. One night the temptation was too much to resist. Sol sneaked out, managing to avoid detection, and stole several sausages. Back in camp, he and his friends devoured all the salami.

However, several days later, Sol was again so driven by hunger that he made a pact with a friend that would have been unthinkable before the war. Sol had known Herman Kornhauser and his older brother, Max, since Skarzysko. The Kornhausers had been deported there directly from the Cracow Ghetto; later they were also shipped to Buchenwald with Sol. Herman was about twenty-eight and Max a year older, but in spite of the age difference, a singularly close relationship had developed between Sol and the two brothers. At Skarzysko, the Kornhausers had worked in a factory not far from where Sol had manufactured dynamite. At night, in the barrack, the two brothers and Sol would unwind by sharing the details of the horrors they had endured and by imagining how they would someday retaliate against their captors.

Herman had been digging ditches at Buchenwald as part of a work detail; at the end of a particularly exhausting day, his party was told that they had not fulfilled their quota. Therefore, they would each be subject to twenty-five lashes. Herman dejectedly told Sol that he did not think he could survive such a beating. Sol offered to take the whipping for Herman in exchange for one day's supply of soup and bread. Herman readily agreed.

They approached the guard and asked to switch places. Apparently amused by this novel idea, the guard consented. Sol was escorted to the field, ordered to remove his shirt, drop his pants, and get down on his hands and knees. He knew what to expect. Every muscle tensed. He closed his eyes, gritted his teeth, and waited for the sting of the first lash. The whip, fashioned from an old belt, tore into his flesh, from his neck to his thighs. Old wounds were reopened and new ones appeared as his blood ran profusely. But Sol never lost consciousness nor did he cry out. He was determined to maintain his dignity. Silently he counted the blows. When the ordeal was over, he was helped by the other prisoners back to his barrack. There he collapsed, while his friends did their best to tend to his wounds. Herman kept his promise; he turned over his food to Sol, grateful to him for saving his life. Sol continued his daily digging in spite of the sharp pain. His latest wounds healed slowly. But his ordeal was far from over.

Sol was constantly trying to get work outside of Buchenwald. He knew he had a better chance of getting food outside the camp than within. One day the Germans announced they were looking for workers with technical backgrounds in engineering or radios. Again, Sol volunteered, telling the Germans he had worked in a radio repair shop before the war and later in an ammunition plant at Skarzysko. While this was only partially true, it did get him the assignment. However, Sol got more than he bargained for. He was given rudimentary lessons in deactivating and detonating bombs, and given a scope and other assorted tools. He was then assigned to a truck with the task of picking up unexploded bombs. A guard escorted him to the nearby truck, where two other slave laborers, a Hungarian and a Belgian, were standing at attention. Sol was told that the three of them were to locate and pick up unexploded bombs in the area. A hand-cranked ancient-looking winch in the rear of the truck was to be used to hoist the bombs off the ground to the flatbed of the truck.

In spite of language barriers, all three prisoners worked well together. With the help of hand signals and grunts, they spent the next several days excavating bombs and gently lifting them aboard the truck. Then the truck slowly made its way to a nearby military airfield where the bombs were gingerly placed on the ground for deactivation or detonation by other prisoners. Although bewildered by the whole process, Sol soon became adept at the work. The slightest mistake would have meant instant death. It was on the job training in its purest sense, frightening and stressful to the extreme.

While working at the airfield, Sol observed the planes and pilots closely. He talked with the pilots and tried to learn as much as possible by asking seemingly innocent questions about the planes'operations. Knowing Russian forces were in the area, he even conceived a plan to hijack a plane and fly to freedom behind the Russian lines. When he told some of his fellow inmates about this scheme, they pointed out one major drawback: Sol didn't know how to fly a plane. This was one plan that never came to fruition.

One day, in February 1945, Sol and the other inmates in his work section were taken into the air force dining hall on the base. The prisoners sat down at a table to eat. Seated at a nearby table, a young Luftwaffe officer began singing a song Sol would never forget: it was a vicious anti-Semitic diatribe. Soon other pilots eagerly joined in. The pilots were young and were not S.S. The Germans had lost the war, yet they were still singing songs of hate. Sol was stunned by the deep-seated anti-Semitism harbored by these typical German airmen. Even as the war turned against Germany, hatred of the Jews continued to rage. Whatever the outcome of the war, thought Sol, anti-Semitism was too intense to allow the Jews to lead a normal life in postwar Europe.

Yet, Sol also encountered isolated instances of civilized behavior. On one occasion, while Sol was clearing away rubble from a bombing raid in Weimar, a lieutenant asked Sol where he was from. Sol replied that his family had originally come from Germany. The lieutenant surprised Sol by saying that what the Germans had done to the Jews was shameful. He said he had once had Jewish friends before they were taken away. He believed they were good, cultured people, and he was sorry to see them expelled from Germany; nor could he understand why they were forced out. Nowhere in his conversation did he mention the subject of mass extermination. How could he not know, thought Sol, being stationed so close to Buchenwald. But incidents such as this demonstrated to Sol that there were at least some decent Germans who had misgivings about German policy.

Another incident occurred while Sol, along with hundreds of other slave laborers, was digging antitank ditches and artillery dugouts outside Weimar. Suddenly a British bombing raid began. The laborers and their guards fled for the security of the tree line where they could not be seen from the air. While they were waiting for the all-clear to sound, one guard, a Waffen SS officer, began to talk with Sol. He told Sol he was forced to take this job for which he didn't volunteer. He said he was disturbed by the mistreatment of the prisoners. He pulled out a pack of cigarettes, offering one to Sol. When Sol said he did not smoke, the German nevertheless insisted that Sol take the entire pack and use it to trade for food when he returned to the camp. After the all-clear sounded, the guard helped Sol up and wished him well.

On yet another occasion, while Sol was working in Weimar, the Allies launched another of their almost daily devastating raids on the city. Fire, smoke, and death were everywhere. The guards hurriedly rounded up the inmates and took them to an underground infirmary located in a tunnel. The odor of antiseptics and damp mold permeated the air. The walls were lined with cots, all of which were filled with injured military personnel and civilians. Nurses rushed about frantically, as soldiers continued to carry in newly wounded patients on stretchers. The prisoners were ordered to remain still while the German doctors on call stuck their fingers with needles to check their blood types.

Sol, the only Jewish prisoner in the group, was told that his blood would be needed to save the life of a seriously wounded high-ranking German officer. A middle-aged doctor wearing a stained and wrinkled white lab coat walked up and in a low but tired voice introduced himself as Dr. Roth. He instructed Sol to relax and began to draw his blood. At that moment, the doctor's young assistant shouted angrily, "You can't give Jewish blood to a German officer!" He shrieked some other words, many of which were unintelligible, but Sol got the idea. The soldier made clear he despised Jewish blood, which he considered polluted and evil.

The older physician replied, "The boy has good blood and it will save a human life."

"The officer will eventually find out that you gave him Jewish blood and he won't be happy," argued the young assistant. The doctor responded that, on the contrary, the officer would someday be thankful to this boy for saving his life. He then turned to Sol and channeled the conversation in a different direction, asking him questions about his background and family.

"Did anyone in your family have a mental illness?"

"No," said Sol.

"Have you ever had sex?"

"Yes." Sol answered,

The young assistant said, "I bet you had sex with German girls."

"Yes," Sol replied, smiling for the first time in a long time.

The doctor looked at his assistant and said, "I like this boy." He then asked his assistant if he had ever engaged in sex.

"No, no," he replied. "I am engaged. I will wait until I am married." The physician then turned to Sol and told him he hoped he would survive the war. He finished drawing his blood, and then took a small bar of chocolate and a ham sandwich from a satchel and handed them to Sol. Sol had not experienced such kindness in a long time. He was so nervous, he almost forgot to thank the doctor. As he rose to leave, the doctor shook Sol's hand and wished him good luck.

At one time during the war such an act of compassion would have been unthinkable. Perhaps, Sol reasoned, as the Germans realized there was no longer any hope of victory, they were not quite as arrogant.

When Sol returned to the camp that evening, Gustav, the barrack kapo, was waiting for him. He had already heard that Sol had given blood. As Sol jumped off the truck with the other workers, he called him aside. "How much blood were you required to give?" he asked Sol. "How do you feel now?"

Inwardly Sol was alarmed, but outwardly he tried to appear calm. "I do not know how much blood they took from me, but I feel fine, very healthy," Sol responded. Gustav scowled at him and then told him to leave. Sol felt a sense of relief. He feared that if he admitted anything negative about his health, he might be put to death.

A short time later, Sol's world was once again turned upside down. The loudspeakers announced that all Jews must meet on the roll call square, prepared for immediate evacuation.

This had to be yet another selection procedure, Sol reasoned. He was standing next to the Kornhauser brothers when he heard the announcement. Turning, he exchanged glances with them; all three had the same startled look. Fearing the worst, Sol refused to go. "If we obey the command," he said, "we will be sent to the gas chambers." The brothers agreed. Sol told them to follow him. In the swirl of prisoners moving across the square, they blended in and ran under a barrack used as a whorehouse where women prisoners were forced to prostitute themselves with SS guards and special prisoners. Sol and the two brothers lay quietly on the ground for several hours until night fell. After all was quiet, they came out of their hiding place. Seeing that the square was clear, they made their way to a nearby Gypsy barrack. All three were welcomed by the understanding Gypsies and given new Polish identities.

One Gypsy, seeing how frightened Sol was, gave him a work jacket with the letters "U P" on it. Instantly Sol became a Pole rather than a Jew. To make his new identity more believable, Sol assumed a Polish name, Stash Yashinsky. He took an empty bunk and for the next several days followed the daily work routine of the Gypsies. Fortunately, deaths and transfers into the barracks made names and numbers needed for roll calls virtually meaningless. With his newly acquired identity as a Pole and his fluency in German, Sol once more was able to cheat death. Thus he was spared the fate of most of his fellow Jews at Buchenwald, who were murdered shortly thereafter.

Less than a week later, on April 8, 1945, with American forces fast approaching Buchenwald, the Germans ordered all remaining prisoners to prepare for evacuation. Determined to hide all evidence of their atrocities from the advancing Allies, the Nazis were intent on force marching the survivors to areas still under secure German control. Again, Sol did not want to leave, but the guards seemed to be everywhere and this time there was no place to hide. But Sol had survived yet another internment, and the war was almost over. He knew the Germans were becoming discouraged as their chances of winning the war diminished. He believed he would finally be liberated if only he could summon the strength to continue a little longer. He resolved not to give up, not to abandon his personal battle to survive.

Chapter VIII

Dachau Death March

It was bitterly cold. Sol and the other prisoners guarded by SS troops were marched in a southerly direction toward the Czech border. Sol had no idea of their final destination, but he knew they were heading away from the advancing Allied forces. Of the roughly seven thousand detainees in the march, very few were Jews; those who were Jewish, like Sol, had hidden their true identities to avoid execution. There were many nationalities among the prisoners, but most appeared to be Poles, Czechoslovaks, a few Hungarians, and Russian prisoners of war captured on the Eastern front. The others were either civilians who had opposed fascism or clergymen who had aroused the mistrust of the Nazis.

As they marched, all the prisoners were expected to keep up at a brisk pace. Because of SS threats that all stragglers would be shot, the prisoners managed to stay together during the first few hours of the march. Nevertheless, many emaciated and exhausted prisoners had to be coaxed and bullied by their friends not to fall behind; those who faltered were shot or clubbed to death with rifle butts. Sol helped support several prisoners who were so wretched that they were ready to give up. He told them that they couldn't quit after all they had been through.

As the first day wore on, progress through wooded and hilly areas slowed. Very soon the rapid pace of the march began to take its toll. Meanwhile, the guards, walking on both sides of the column, forced the prisoners to keep going. The area was sparsely populated. For the most part, the few inhabitants of the German villages ignored the prisoners except for some children who threw stones at them. Sol noticed several adults staring at them from behind closed windows.

Due to the extreme cold, the guards finally permitted them to slow down. Sometimes this gave the prisoners a chance to forage for food. In one village, Sol noticed a freshly-baked loaf of bread cooling on a window sill. The smell alone was more than he could resist. He slipped out of the line to steal the loaf, quickly jamming it inside his shirt. Unfortunately, though, some Russians had seen him; he had no sooner sneaked back into the line, when they jumped him. Sol was knocked to the ground, kicked and beaten. Even worse, the bread was wrenched away from him; Sol did, however, manage to hold onto a small piece of crust. Nearby guards, seeing the commotion, fired warning shots into the air. Sol got up from the ground, wiping off the mud and snow. He saw that his shirt had been ripped, but at least he had kept a piece of the bread to show for his efforts.

The afternoon of the first day, several prisoners halted in front of a cross by the roadside to pray. SS guards ran up to them, shrieking orders. Since the Polish prisoners understood no German, they hesitated. The guards began to shoot them. Sol was terrified. He tried to concentrate on staying in the column and keeping up. However, it wasn't easy to maintain the pace. The uphill climbs were especially exhausting, and the ground was slippery from the accumulated snow. Sol had wrapped one thin blanket over his head and shoulders to keep warm, yet in spite of the bitter cold, he became overheated and began to perspire.

By mid afternoon, what had at first been a tight column had slackened and now stretched for several miles. Even some of the guards looked exhausted. This gave Sol an idea. He saw an older guard, in obvious distress, weighted down by a heavy knapsack on his back, trudging up a steep hill a short distance ahead. In spite of his own weakened condition, Sol quickened his pace, soon catching up with the guard; Sol then offered to help him with his knapsack. The guard, surprised by Sol's fluent German, looked at him carefully. Sol assured him that he was a Pole, promising he would take good care of the knapsack and would give it back to him whenever he wished. Actually, Sol hoped that it would contain some food that he could steal. The German eyed him suspiciously, but reluctantly agreed. Sol placed the knapsack on his back and quickly fell back in with the throng of prisoners. When he was sure the German had lost sight of him, Sol removed the knapsack, cradling it protectively in his arms, and covered himself with the blanket so that the knapsack was hidden. Now he blended in with the thousands of other prisoners. Then, as he moved along in the throng, he opened the knapsack. He found exactly what he had hoped for: candies, sausages, hard bread, canned food, and some perishables. Excitedly, Sol wolfed down as much as he could eat. What he couldn't finish, he stuffed into his pockets. The food not only eased his nagging hunger, but it gave him energy and lifted his spirits. Now Sol knew he could make it through one more day. More importantly, he felt better knowing that he had some small reserves of bread and candy which he knew he would need later. Sol then discarded the sack along with its razor blades, soap, and shoe brush. By then, Sol could see the guard walking up and down the column, angrily examining the prisoners. Sol just hunched down under his blanket; as Sol had hoped, the guard never did recognize him.

On the first night of the march, the prisoners were led to the edge of a forest where they were to sleep. A freezing wind howled across the field. Sol found a high snowdrift to use for protection. He dug in the soft snow, creating a small crater. He then crawled into the snow, pulled his knees up to his chest into a fetal position, and massaged his body to maintain circulation. He was soon joined by the Kornhausers who gingerly got into the crater and lay down on either side of him, sharing his thin blanket as their only protection from the cold. That night the three tried to absorb each other's body heat, as they lay shivering and exhausted on the frozen ground. Their rest was interrupted several times by a number of fights between Russian and Polish prisoners feuding over blankets. Ironically, while hiding his religion from the Germans, Sol told the Russians he was a Jew and not a Pole. Sol knew the Russians hated the Poles; in this way, he hoped to ingratiate himself with the Russians, protecting himself from Russian abuse. To survive, he would do anything.

The next morning he woke up shivering and stiff from the cold. When he arose and looked around, he saw most of the prisoners were up, walking around and rubbing their hands together for warmth. But for some it was too late. Sol saw the corpses of over a dozen men covered with frost. All had apparently died in their sleep. They appeared to be little more than skeletons in tattered clothes. Some bodies were still twitching, but they were too far gone to be saved. They would die, thought Sol, and many other weakened prisoners would follow. The cold was aiding the Germans. The inadequately clothed prisoners, many with no coats or shoes, were dying, and the Germans didn't even have to bother killing them. This thought only increased Sol's resentment because it all seemed so senseless. The war was almost over but the Germans were still claiming victims.

Sharp pain in his feet caused Sol to consider his own situation. He knew if he were to get through another day, he would have to do something. He sat down and began to vigorously massage his feet until there was renewed feeling; then, since his shoes were worn through, he wrapped rags and paper bags around his blistered feet. When he tried to walk, each step was still painful. He just hoped they were not far from their destination.

While the prisoners were waiting for the order to march, Sol considered trying to escape; he soon realized how foolish that would be. Even if he did manage to elude the guards, he would still be in Germany, enemy territory. The activities of the *Volksturm*, the German home defense army, were well known to Sol. Escaped prisoners were ruthlessly hunted down and shot. He knew that the soldiers would comb the countryside until they found him and that a captured escapee faced immediate death. Nor could he get very far with a shaved head and in prison garb. Although he knew the situation for Germany was deteriorating, he could not count on the German civilians for support or refuge. He had seen their callous expressions and total disdain for the prisoners. Without help, without a hiding place or food, without the means to resist, he reasoned that it was hopeless to flee.

The second day dawned gray and dismal. A cold drizzle was falling, trickling down his neck and soaking his mud-covered clothes, thus adding to the misery. Even the guards were grumbling and complaining as they ordered the men to move out. Sol tried to overhear their conversations; he wanted to know where they were going and what was happening in the war effort. The guards spoke grimly of an American general named Patton and of his successes in the West. This was the first time Sol had heard the name. He did not know exactly what role he had played in rolling back the Germans, but Sol was pleased.

By late morning, the guards appeared to be losing control over discipline as well as their tempers. The physical strain of the march was beginning to tell. The long columns of marchers became more ragged and the ranks began to thin. The guards took out their frustrations on the prisoners. Sol heard pleas for mercy in several languages, followed by the staccato bursts of submachine guns. He purposefully slipped into the middle of the throng to make himself even more inconspicuous.

The prisoners continued to scavenge for any nourishment they could find. In spite of all he had eaten the day before, Sol was once again starving; his gnawing hunger pangs got the best of him. Since most Poles could not speak German, Sol slid up to a guard and, pretending to be German, he begged the guard for something to eat. The guard looked at him with some compassion and handed Sol a loaf of bread. Sol quickly hid the bread under his shirt; after the incident of the day before, he knew better than to let any of the other prisoners know he had any food. Later he shared his windfall with the Kornhausers.

As the day dragged on, the march became even more difficult. The snow and rain continued intermittently, and the ground remained slippery. All of Sol's energy was focused on placing one foot in front of the other. Every muscle seemed to ache. Sol was grateful for every patch of dry or level ground. No one spoke, not even the guards; all were trying to conserve energy. Since no stops or rest periods were allowed, the prisoners were forced to relieve themselves while they walked. Nor were there any rags they could use to clean themselves; by dusk the waste had frozen to their legs.

There was, however, one unanticipated interruption. Without warning, British warplanes suddenly appeared overhead. Bullets seemed to ricochet everywhere, causing many casualties. The column scattered, amidst cries of anguish, as the prisoners took shelter in the forest. Sol lay down near some underbrush. His heart went out to the wounded and dead prisoners, but, nevertheless, the sight of the British energized him. With Allied forces so close, Sol felt the end of the war couldn't be that much longer. While hiding in the forest, as the British planes circled overhead, Sol used the few available moments to try to pick off the lice which covered his body. He also scooped up handfuls of snow to drink and to wash the accumulated grime off his body.

When the all-clear sounded, the march resumed. Sol had noticed a black Mercedes, presumably carrying high ranking SS officers. It moved slowly toward the front of the column. Burlap sacks filled with wood chips were tied to the roof of the car. The car was powered by a makeshift boiler which converted the wood chips into ethyl alcohol. In an effort to save fuel, the car halted at the bottom of each steep uphill incline and prisoners struggling alongside the car were ordered to push the car to the top. Sol trudged over, and when a dozen or so other prisoners began pushing the car, Sol jumped on a bumper to hitch a ride in order to conserve strength. Instantly Sol knew he had made a big mistake. Through the rear window, he saw a soldier turn around to stare at him, his face twisted in an ugly scowl. Sol could see the fury in his eyes as he began screaming obscenities at him. The prisoners stopped pushing and the car came to a halt. Immediately the door to the Mercedes flew open and an angry SS officer leaped out. Before Sol could move, he was yanked roughly off the car. Without warning, the officer struck him hard across the face. He then grabbed Sol by the front of his tattered shirt, lifted him up and slammed him against the car. Sol froze, clenching his fists to his sides. Past experience had taught him the futility of resisting.

"Don't fight back," he told himself. "It will only make matters worse."

The officer hit Sol hard again and again in the face and upper body and then ordered him to the rear of the car to help push. Shaken and hurt from the pummeling, Sol joined the other prisoners behind the car. The incline was steep and slippery and the going was slow and laborious. Two Russians fell down; when they told the guards they could not help any longer, they were beaten viciously until they fell by the wayside unconscious, more dead than alive. By the time the car reached the summit, all of the prisoners had virtually used up every ounce of their strength. Sol was totally exhausted, but the SS officer was still not through with him. He ordered Sol to put the wooden chips into the boiler in order to restart the car. As Sol was given no gloves, his hands were badly scalded. At the first opportunity, he rubbed snow over his peeling skin to soothe the sting and cleanse his wounds. He then removed some clothes from a dead prisoner who was lying along the roadside and tore them into rags; next he wrapped the rags around his hands to protect them from the dirt and cold.

The march continued throughout the afternoon. No food had been distributed since their departure; as the starving prisoners continued to fall, their bodies littered the roadway for miles. Inhabitants of the towns through which they passed eyed them sullenly through their windows, keeping their doors shut. No one offered food or assistance. Desperate, the prisoners grabbed handfuls of snow or stopped to drink water from the same barrels as the farm animals. They raided barns and stole stored potatoes which they ate raw. Some prisoners scavenged for oats, intended for the horses; but the dry, uncooked grain caused serious cases of diarrhea. In one town, Russian prisoners saw a wagon loaded with barley. They were so hungry they ignored SS orders to remain in line. They ran to the wagon, ripping open the sacks, clawing each other to fill their pants' and coat pockets with the grain. Sol joined the other prisoners in looting the wagon, as the guards looked on amused to see the prisoners behaving like animals. Later that night, when the columns stopped for the evening, the prisoners lit fires in the woods to cook the precious barley. As Sol ate, the hard grain was still very hot and burned his tongue. But the taste of hot food more than compensated for the discomfort.

One day blended into another. On many days, the Kornhausers and Sol staggered on alongside Henek, a fellow Jew also disguised as a Pole. While too exhausted to talk except for short grunts, they supported each other and encouraged one another to keep going. Sol wasn't certain how long or how far they walked; but he was in a constant state of exhaustion, hunger, and discomfort from the cold; moreover; the pain from his scalded hands wouldn't go away. Each night they slept outside in freezing temperatures. In spite of all his physical exertion, his body never seemed to get warm. Several nights it rained, and the cold rain made it impossible for him to get any sleep despite his exhaustion. In the morning they set off yet again, the number of dead left lying by the wayside increasing daily. Sol could see the toll that death had taken on the dwindling march and wondered how much more he could take.

Finally, what was left of the Buchenwald survivors straggled into the small town of Flossenburg. Although emaciated and completely drained, Sol was grateful to be alive. The survivors were herded into a square, where they were told to sit and await further orders. For Sol, the rest was welcome; he had been marching nonstop and he felt his legs were about to give out.

As Sol observed the townspeople, he sensed something unusual. They seemed to be quite stirred up and emotional. He wondered what was happening. The answer came a short time later when he saw white flags of surrender being raised. Thinking they were free, the prisoners, overjoyed, began to hug and kiss each other. A collective mood of relief swept over the group. Although the guards continued to keep a wary eye on the prisoners, a tenuous truce seemed to take hold between the two groups. Some of the bolder prisoners even began to leave the square in search of food. Seemingly, there were no recriminations. Observing this, two Polish priests who were sitting with Sol asked him for help. A member of their order was in dire need of medication for his cut and bleeding feet. Moreover, all of them were experiencing severe hunger pangs, but they were too weak to try to find food for themselves. The spokesman for the group, Father Kaminski, asked Sol if he would be willing to take the risk of searching for food and medicines for them. His colleague, Father Jogoda, whom Sol had befriended on the march, told Sol he would understand if Sol refused because no one could be sure how the Germans would react. Sol immediately agreed to try to help. All of the priests were from the Cracow region and had been arrested by the Gestapo for their alleged work with the Polish underground. That was good enough for Sol. Anyone who worked to undermine the Nazis had Sol's full support.

The request reinvigorated Sol. He felt needed and wanted. He headed toward a small hospital that he had noticed previously and which appeared to be unguarded. Finding the door unlocked, he entered the building. A quick inspection indicated that the building was vacant. Sol entered a room which seemed to be a dispensary and walked to the medicine cabinets. The shelves were well stocked with an assortment of pills, tubes, gauzes, and hypodermic needles. Sol stuffed his pockets with medicines which he thought would be useful and quickly departed. Back at the square, Father Kaminski blessed him for his efforts, begging him to return for more medical supplies and any food he could find. Sol agreed, but he said he would have to wait until nightfall, as he had heard that since his foray, the SS had placed guards around the hospital.

In the late afternoon, the prisoners were divided into a number of groups and taken to various locations. Some remained in the square under guard, while others were marched to fenced-in fields or barns or other deserted buildings in the town itself. Sol's group was escorted to an open field, but security was lax and Sol was determined to keep his promise, and at the same time find something to eat for himself. He shared his intentions with some of his friends. They were worried.

"It is too risky," one responded.

"If the Germans catch you, if they don't kill you, they will just make you wish you were dead," exclaimed another. Sol, however, was accustomed to taking risks. He saw that the guards were tired, and while he understood his friends' concern, he believed they were exaggerating the danger. That night, avoiding detection, Sol sneaked back to the hospital which he again found unguarded. He succeeded in bringing out more medical supplies which he turned over to the priests, but he was only able to secure a few cans of food. Through it all, neither the guards nor the local inhabitants made the slightest effort to provide food to the starving prisoners, who still had to brave the elements.

The following day, the white flags of surrender came down and the euphoria the prisoners had experienced came to an abrupt end. The prisoners were reassembled from various locations in the town and ordered to resume the march. The letdown made their despair all the worse. Again, the procession set out for an unknown destination.

Although they did not know it at the time, the prisoners had narrowly escaped a much worse fate: the infamous death camp of Flossenburg was only a few miles away. Begun as a punishment center in 1938, Flossenburg had quickly become one of the most infamous of the death camps. The small crematorium worked twenty-four hours a day. Thus, the prisoners trudged away from almost certain death.

There was still no food or water, so the prisoners had to continue to forage for themselves. Some ate roots and even grass which caused dysentery, weakening them further. Evidence of Allied bombing and strafing attacks along the roadside was visible everywhere. As they headed south, more and more German civilians choked the roads fleeing from the Soviet assaults. But Sol was now beyond any joy these scenes might once have occasioned. His hands were not completely healed, his blistered feet were in constant pain, and his body still ached from the last beating he had received. Plagued by digestive problems and continual hunger pangs, he now weighed less than ninety pounds. He had lost all feeling in his toes and his fingers were frozen and useless. His thin worn blanket provided little real protection from the elements he had been exposed to for more than two weeks. Adding to his discomfort were lice, which infested his entire body, causing constant skin irritation and itching. After years of slave labor, the physical exhaustion and lack of proper care and nourishment were finally taking their toll. Sol knew he was near the end of his endurance. He just prayed that time would be on his side.

The days and nights ran together; Sol lost all sense of time. He concentrated on just getting through one more day. What he did know was that each new morning meant he had gained another reprieve. He tried to block out the sight of men collapsing near him as each day added to the number of dead and dying. It would have been better if the SS had just shot them, thought Sol, and put them out of their misery. Sol had long since overcome his fear of death.

While there is no way to be certain of how many fatalities there were during these last days of Nazi terror, Sol later learned that only about seven hundred prisoners, or roughly ten percent of the original marchers, survived. After more than two weeks, the pitiful remnant arrived at a small, picturesque town nine miles north of Munich in southern Germany. The tranquil scene offered no hint of horror. The prisoners had arrived in Dachau, one of the most notorious of all the death camps.

Dachau, the first camp established in the Nazi system on the grounds of a World War I munitions factory, was built in 1933, just two months after Hitler had seized power. Over the years it became an efficient killing machine, with the murder of Jews as a priority. Indeed, it served as a model for the other death camps in the German penal system. Exploitation and liquidation had been refined into an orderly, businesslike operation. But the influx of thousands of transfers from other camps in Nazi-dominated Europe, together with the survivors of many death marches, proved more than the system could handle. By April 1945, the camp with its one hundred and sixty-seven sub camps had deteriorated into total chaos. For the roughly 30,000 prisoners still alive, this meant widespread misery and often death.

When Sol staggered wearily into Dachau, the first sight he saw was shattering. Passing a railway siding, he saw boxcars full of emaciated corpses, laced with maggots and covered with flies. Close by were additional stacks of bodies in various stages of decomposition piled higher than he was tall. The smell from the corpses hung in the air, causing Sol to choke. The gruesome sight and terrible stench left him in total shock, struggling to maintain control. Sol had thought that after all he had been though, he was beyond such shock. Now he knew he was wrong: he tried vainly to steel himself against the horror. He felt completely drained, both physically and emotionally; only hunger, pain, and an overwhelming numbness remained.

Nonetheless, although his body had become wasted, his mind was clear: he had been designated a Pole and not a Jew and he knew he must cling to this identity if he were to survive. To conserve energy, he would continue to do as little as possible, trying to remain invisible as much as circumstances allowed.

Shortly after his arrival, Sol was marched through a large courtyard to a tightly guarded wooden barrack teeming with Czechs and Poles. Outside the barrack, a German officer sat wearily at a table writing the names of all new inmates in a ledger. As Sol reached the head of the line, the German noted the name on Sol's uniform, "Stash Yashinsky," scribbling it in his book. He then wrote a number by it, #161584. Sol stood silently through the brief formality, hoping that nothing would interfere with his masquerade as a Pole. Fortunately, the German didn't question him. After a cursory glance, he waved Sol into the building.

Inside, it was dark and cold. It took Sol several minutes to get accustomed to the lack of light. The bunks, which consisted of boards joined to the wall in tiers, had no mattresses and were jammed closely together. Conditions were unbelievably filthy: a terrible odor permeated the barracks; the floors were covered with filth and excrement. The regimentation and order of the other camps were absent here. In their place reigned disorder and chaos. Prisoners, scarcely able to move due to starvation and typhus, lay near death. Indeed, it was difficult to distinguish the living from the dead; the inmates lay motionless, their eyes blank and faces expressionless. All were emaciated, broken, and desperate. Most were little more than skeletal figures with sunken eyes and skin hanging loosely over their bones. As Sol shuffled to an empty bunk, several prisoners raised their shaking hands regarding him with vacant stares in a silent plea for help. Some babbled incoherently in strange tongues. Intermittently they were were racked by coughing spells. But Sol, himself exhausted, could do nothing. He only wondered whether he appeared as cadaverous as the others.

Sol found an empty bunk where he collapsed on the hard wooden frame. All he wanted to do was sleep. No food was issued, but there were no roll calls or work details either. The camp seemed to be in a state of suspended animation. Time seemed to pass in a haze. Eventually, the guards opened the doors to announce that CARE packages were being distributed to all Polish prisoners from the Polish Red Cross in London. Sol, eagerly ripped open his package. Inside he found a dry, moldy loaf of bread, crumbled hard cookies, candy, and cigarettes. To Sol, who had lost count of how many days he had gone without eating, this was a gift from heaven. He ate slowly so as not to make himself sick, savoring every morsel. Still, it was difficult for him to chew or swallow. Nevertheless, the food helped lift his spirits and gave him the strength to survive a little longer.

Sol knew the war was almost over, but he could still hear random shots outside the barracks and knew the SS were still murdering Jews. For many inmates, both Jews and non-Jews alike, it was already too late. They were too far gone to be saved, and so the dying continued. Sol still clung to life, although he knew his physical condition was desperate and his appearance was appalling. He could feel his sunken cheeks, swollen ankles, and sunken rib cage. His body was encrusted with a grayish filth and covered with open sores and scabs. His gums were tender, his teeth felt loose, and his nails were brittle. Every muscle and joint ached. Even though Sol had lost so many reasons to go on living, he told himself: "I am only eighteen. I have been through too much to die now. I can't let the Germans win. I am the only one left in my family to carry on our name and memories. I cannot die. I must live to tell my story." Therefore, in spite of his physical condition, Sol willed himself to go on living. He prayed for a miracle to put an end to his three year ordeal.

Roughly two days later, on April 29, 1945, units of the Seventh U.S. Army driving toward nearby Munich detoured unexpectedly to Dachau. The camp was attacked by tanks from the 20th Armored Division and the 42nd Rainbow Division. SS guards, under standing orders to detonate explosives, demolish the camp, and kill all inmates, were caught off guard by the American assault. Only the timing of the American attack prevented the Germans from concealing their crimes. After a brief but bitter firefight, the guards were quickly overcome before they had time to carry out their orders.

At first, none of the prisoners realized what was happening. When Sol heard the bursts of gunfire growing louder, he managed to drag himself to the door of the barrack. He gazed in amazement at a warplane skimming low over the camp. It was at that moment that he and the other prisoners realized they were being liberated. The inmates were overwhelmed by an indescribable wave of excitement. They felt they had been given a miraculous reprieve from certain death.

Initially, since Sol had never seen Americans before, he did not know the nationality of the liberators. However, another prisoner told him they must be Americans because they were chewing gum; others reported that they had seen tanks with large white stars on their sides firing machine guns at the fleeing Germans.

Sol was caught up in the outburst of hysteria. Unsteadily, he struggled toward the perimeter fence as quickly as he could to get a better view. He drew closer, encircled by the crowd of prisoners beginning to congregate in roll call square. As more and more prisoners thronged the square, some, anxious to flee the hated camp, were pushed against the barriers by the crush of humanity. Sol watched in horror as several of those who had been imprisoned with him were electrocuted on the fences. Instantly shock turned to fury. In a frenzy of revenge, Russians, Poles, Czechs, and other survivors of various nationalities attacked the guards. Sol and hundreds of others too weak to join in watched in disbelief as the prisoners' repressed rage erupted in an orgy of beatings and killings. The guards were simply overwhelmed, their mutilated bodies thrown into the ditch which divided the camp area from the crematoria and SS installations. When they had satisfied their hunger for vengeance, the prisoners sang and danced for joy; then they hugged each other, wept, and dropped to their knees in prayer. Sol, however, was beyond elation. To him, it seemed as if they had completely lost their minds.

Sol did, however, join hundreds of other prisoners in slowly making their way across the canal to the SS barrack. While many prisoners rushed in, Sol went to a window and stared at the once formidable guards, now squatting or sitting on the floor, their hands raised in pathetic surrender. Although others continued their attacks on the guards, Sol, unnerved, returned to his barrack. It took several hours until American G.I.'s were able to restore order. Since fighting still continued against pockets of diehard German resistance outside the camp, all inmates were ordered back to their barracks. Guards were stationed at the entrances to the camp and the prisoners were ordered not to leave.

Sol lay down on his bunk, anxious to find out what the new masters of the camp would do. All around him excitement swirled. It wasn't long before the doors to the barrack opened. Soldiers, accompanied by Catholic, Protestant, and Jewish clergy, entered, circulating slowly among the survivors. Several of the G.I.'s , through smiles, gestures, and halting Yiddish, asked if there were any Jews in the barrack. Many inmates answered weakly, but affirmatively. The soldiers told them they too were Jewish, hugging the startled survivors. Three soldiers, who identified themselves as Sergeant Schneider, Sergeant Rosen, and Captain Cahn, helped lift Sol from his bunk and cautiously walked him from the barrack.

Sol, together with many others, was escorted to a nearby truck. The survivors were then asked to disrobe. One after another they were washed from a portable shower and sprinkled with powder as part of a comprehensive delousing procedure. Each prisoner was given a clean German military uniform from the warehouse. Sol, however, refused to wear German clothing; he objected so strenuously that a soldier was dispatched to find clean civilian clothes. In short order, he returned with a clean white shirt and a pair of pants several sizes too large for Sol. A soldier had to give Sol a belt to hold up his pants. Sol stared at the belt which had a buckle; he had never seen a belt like that before and played with the buckle several minutes before he understood how it fastened. The G.I.'s then passed out candy, oranges, and cigarettes. Sol, seeing everyone else lighting up, smoked one of the Camels. He had never smoked before and the nicotine nauseated him and made him dizzy.

A chaplain circulated among the men, passing out yarmulkes. After that the men were directed to a field where army doctors and soup kitchens were waiting. A Jewish physician, Captain Goldstein, examined Sol, gave him several shots, and pronounced him in satisfactory health, considering his ordeal. Since Sol knew no English, Captain Goldstein asked him questions about his health in Yiddish. He warned Sol to eat slowly, stick to soft foods like applesauce, and for the time being not to drink milk. The examination was brief because of the great number of those waiting in line. Nevertheless, Sol was comforted by the captain's reassuring words.

When the examination was over, Sol joined a long line where meals were being served. The smell of the food alone was enough to make Sol hungry. Although there were only normal G.I. rations, to Sol the meal was a banquet. The food was plentiful and good. He tried to follow the doctor's advice to eat slowly, though this took a great deal of will power. When the liberated prisoners had finished eating, Jewish G.I.'s circulated among them, both taking pictures and showing family photos, asking the survivors if they recognized any of those in the snapshots. Others, also hoping to identify a long-lost relative, asked if any of the men were from a certain city or had a specific surname. The soldiers, hoping to meet at least one person who knew their relatives, searched in vain. Sol did not see a single case of recognition; the disappointment of the soldiers was visible.

The mingling of G.I.'s and hundreds of survivors continued for several hours; then a voice came over the loud speakers asking everyone in the square to pause and join together in the singing of Hatikvah. To Sol, the song capped one of the most emotional and extraordinary days of his life, a day he would remember always. He had waited so long for this day to arrive, and so often he had doubted whether he would ever live to see it; but now his dream had come true. When he returned to the barrack that night, he had the most restful night in years.

The following days were intoxicating ones for Sol. As he was dealing with the reality of his new existence, Dachau was visited by such luminaries as Generals Eisenhower and Patton, and Colonel Mickey Marcus, who later lost his life in Israel's War for Independence. The survivors milled around, talking excitedly. They spoke of rebuilding their lives, and finding loved ones. Desperate to establish relationships with others and to restore their self-esteem, they exchanged recollections. However, for some, there were too many scars. Many remained uncommunicative, continuing to hide their innermost thoughts, unable to express the suffering they had endured. Chaplains circulated among the survivors daily, offering counseling and comfort. Care packages from Jewish organizations were distributed, supplementing the plentiful meals. Sol continued to follow the doctor's advice to eat slowly and only those foods which were easily digestible. He took his package back to his barrack where other survivors asked him what he had. He told them he had received gifts from his people. A Pole wanted to know who his people were.

"Jews," responded Sol.

"I thought you were Polish," said another prisoner, puzzled.

"Yesterday I was a Pole. Today I am who I have always

been: a proud Jew!" Sol said defiantly. "If you can't accept this, it is your misfortune." The Poles glared at him with disdain. For Sol, the fear, humiliation, and suffering were over. He no longer had to hide who he was or fear the consequences of revealing the truth. Sol's long ordeal had finally come to an end.

Chapter IX

Buchloe

Within days, Sol's physical condition and mental outlook were much improved, but his joy was mixed with sadness. For many, the liberation had come too late. Many of the inmates had no will left to survive. Thousands died of overeating or because they were too ill to respond to medical treatment. Either their emaciated systems could not digest the rich foods or they succumbed to typhus or other illnesses they had already contracted.

After the initial euphoria of liberation, the inmates found that their lives did indeed begin to change for the better. The victors instituted measures designed to bring about order out of chaos. Gradually they took control of the camp: American forces conducted a registration of all prisoners, improved the process of food and water distribution, and upgraded hygiene. The sick were hospitalized and mass burial of the dead was begun. Furthermore, the prisoners were free to move about the camp. As Sol regained strength, he viewed the administrative skill and acts of human kindness of the Americans with admiration.

At first, Sol could do little more than lie motionless for long hours on his straw mattress. This gave him time to think. The war was over, and he was free, but victory had come at a great cost. He was still haunted by horrible memories. The Germans had robbed him of almost six years of his life. They had taken everything and everyone he loved. Unlike others, however, at least he did not have to face the torment of not knowing; he already knew the fate of his parents and sisters and realized he would have to adjust to a new life on his own. But it would not be in the city of his birth. Warsaw and Poland held too many bitter memories for him. He had no home to which he could return.

Sol was becoming restless and anxious to leave Dachau and the horrors it represented. He wanted to know what was happening in the outside world. When he felt he was strong enough, Sol petitioned the authorities for permission to leave the camp. His request was soon granted and he was authorized to go to a displaced persons' camp in Landsberg, near Munich. That same day he was able to hitch a ride on a U.S. Army vehicle. After being dropped off, he explored the village. Unaccustomed to his newfound freedom, it seemed strange to him to be able to move around freely in a town that just weeks before had loyally supported the Nazi cause. Sol located the camp just outside of the town, and settled in after completing the registration papers. The camp was huge, teeming with refugees. Sol hoped to recognize at least some familiar faces.

Sol was surprised and overjoyed to find Henek, a companion from the infamous death march from Buchenwald to Dachau. Both had horrific tales to share with one another, but they also talked excitedly about their plans for the future. They realized how fortunate they were to be alive. Henek told Sol that he had learned that his girlfriend, Helen, whom he had met at Skarzysko, also had survived and was a short distance away at Buchloe. He was planning to leave Landsberg in a few days and asked if Sol wanted to join him. He said that he understood Helen was living with two other survivors, one of whom was supposed to be a beautiful blond. Sol was intrigued; since he had no other plans, he agreed to go with Henek.

Landsberg had become a site for all kinds of displaced persons from the camps. Many spent hours vainly examining the interminable list of the dead on the Red Cross bulletin board; however, Sol already knew the fate of his family. Looking at the faces of the anxious but somber detainees, Sol reflected on the situation. The whole world was celebrating the defeat of Nazi Germany, but for the Jews the victory was bittersweet. Almost every person in the camp was alone, each one the sole surviving member of his or her family.

Sol spent the time attending movies, small parties, and talking with other survivors. Shortly before he left for Buchloe, as Sol was walking through the camp, he glanced at a man across the field. Sol froze in his tracks and looked again. He gasped; it was Neumann, the kapo from Skarzysko. Sol half ran to him; he saw the blood drain from his face as recognition set in. Before Neumann could react, Sol, out of control, grabbed him and began to assault him. Accusing him of cowardice and murder, Sol continued his attack until Neumann collapsed on the ground, gasping for breath. He pleaded with Sol to stop, delivering a half-hearted apology: "I did what I had to do to survive. I had no choice. I had to do what the Germans ordered or I would have lost my own life. You must understand."

Still incensed, Sol left his hated enemy sobbing and bleeding. Sol was satisfied. He had gained a measure of revenge and, even if justice was not entirely served, his savage attack on Neumann had helped to release a lot of bottled up rage.

The next day, the two boys hitchhiked to Buchloe, catching rides on army vehicles. There they found the small house where the girls were staying. Henek was overjoyed to be with Helen again after so many years. He and Helen embraced tearfully. When introductions were made, Sol was immediately smitten by Tola, a beautiful blond from Lodz, Poland. Like Sol, she had lost her entire family, a brother, a sister, and both parents in the Holocaust. The boys were ushered upstairs to an attic above the girls' room, where they were to stay.

Buchloe was a pleasant little village, less than ten miles from Landsberg; it had been spared the ravages of war. The town was well-maintained, clean, and orderly. In the days that followed, Sol got to know both the town and Tola. He realized that his initial instinct about Tola had been right. She helped him overcome his loneliness, for even though he had freedom, food, housing, and security, there had been something missing from his life. Tola filled that void. He and Tola spent many hours together, strolling through the neighborhoods of Buchloe. Sol discovered that Tola had spent most of the war years at labor camps in Lodz and Czestochowa in Poland and extermination camps in Germany; at Czestochowa, a Nazi guard had brutally beaten her with a rifle butt. The beatings had resulted in severe chronic back pain and permanent scars.

In the latter days of the war, Tola had been among the detainees force-marched to Dachau from Bergen Belsen to escape the advancing Red Army. The march in many ways mirrored the horrors Sol had endured on his trek to Dachau. During their grueling journey Tola was supported by Helen; they had been close friends since meeting at a slave labor camp in Poland in 1943. Outside of Buchloe, due to obstacles blocking the road, the exhausted column was ordered to detour around the obstacles into a ditch. Dusk was falling as the women fell and slid down a steep embankment adjoining a thick forest. All of a sudden, something distracted the guards; in that instant Helen saw their chance to escape, telling Tola to quickly follow her.

They fled into the nearby forest, running until they dropped from exhaustion. There they remained still, sleeping on the damp ground with little protection from the night chill. The next morning they began to walk and by midday they saw a barn with a Red Cross painted on the roof. Cautiously, they approached. The hospital was for military personnel and was being administered by nuns. Even though they were wearing prison garb and thus were easily recognizable, their hunger was so great that they decided to take a chance on the nuns' humanity. Their gamble proved to be fortunate. The nuns welcomed them and gave them bread and hot chocolate, the first food they had had in several days. Suddenly a burst of artillery fire exploded nearby, causing panic in the hospital. As shells began to fall, Tola and Helen fled. Late that afternoon, they found a deserted lumber yard and hid in a small compartment formed by the boards. For the next two days, they remained in hiding, sleeping most of the time, and venturing out only to drink water from a nearby pump. For food, Helen stole some boiled potatoes from a farmhouse. On the third day, April 27, 1945, American tanks entered Buchloe. After the city surrendered, the girls emerged excitedly from their hiding place. They were escorted into town by American soldiers. A sympathetic German family offered to house them. Surprised but relieved, they accepted the offer. They were given their own room on the second floor of the family's home.

The summer of 1945 was a glorious time for Tola and Sol. They felt safe and secure and they finally began to enjoy their lost youth. They made new friends among the survivors in the area and Sol discovered other friends whom he had known at various slave labor camps where he had been imprisoned. It was a gathering of exiles, both Christian and Jewish. They spoke many Eastern and Central European languages. All had lost everything: their homes, their livelihoods, their possessions, and most of all, their families. All had suffered horribly. Thrown together, they formed a mutual support network. All were determined to put their lost worlds behind them; gradually, they began to build bridges to the future.

Days were carefree and unregulated. Sol once again took up soccer, a sport he had not played in years. By this time he had regained his strength and with his health restored, his prewar skills returned. He joined one of the leagues then springing up among the survivors in Landsberg and played almost daily. Back in Buchloe in the evenings, there were movies, good food, and relaxed conviviality. For the first time in years, he was at peace, no longer struggling just to survive. The sleep disorder that had caused him to awaken in terror in the middle of the night with hallucinatory nightmares gradually disappeared. In a few weeks, his hair had grown back , and his ruddy complexion had returned to normal. He was relieved and grateful.

Sol and Tola caught rides to Landsberg on U.S. Army vehicles. There they spent hours leisurely walking through the historic town or sitting by the river where they ate sandwiches and talked. Before long, Tola became Sol's best friend and confidant. They discussed their backgrounds, and talked about their families, their lives in the camps, and where they had been during the war. The more they were with each other, the more Sol realized how much they had in common. He felt very comfortable with Tola and very close to her; above all, he no longer felt alone. The beauty and peace of the town and their growing affection for one another helped them to adjust to a brand new life, even though it had not been the result of their own choosing.

The camp teemed with amorous couples, seemingly eager to make up for lost time. Each day seemed to bring a joyous new celebration of life—camp entertainments and outings, weddings, births, and circumcisions; it was like being part of a large extended family. For the short term, the festivities and camaraderie helped Sol blot out the haunting memories of the past. On days when there were no major events in the camp, Sol would hitch a ride on the camp bus into Munich. There he wandered aimlessly exploring the city, regaining the feeling of freedom which he had so long been denied.

One day in Munich, he encountered two priests, one a Pole, the other a Belgian. The Pole and Sol instantly recognized each other and embraced. The Polish priest was none other than Father Kaminski, the compassionate priest for whom Sol had stolen medications right out from under the noses of the SS while at Flossenburg. As they hugged, the priest noticed that Sol was carrying a package from the Joint Jewish Distribution Committee. He said to Sol: "I thought you might be Jewish because of your command of German. Most Polish boys, you know, don't speak German. I'm glad you made it. When we get back to Cracow, please look me up. I will always be grateful to you for getting the food and medicine we needed to survive in Flossenburg. You were and are a special friend."

There were encounters with others who reminded Sol of his recent past. One afternoon, while riding a bicycle between Landsberg and Munich, Sol recognized a man near the road. He turned the bicycle around and pedaled up to Rosensweig, his former camp commander at Czestochowa. Both men greeted each other enthusiastically; they began to ask each other questions about what had happened in their lives over the last few months since they had last seen each other at Weimar. Rosensweig, while a collaborator, had never been cruel or sadistic. He had been patient with the inmates, cautioned and counseled many of them including Sol, and tried to shield them from Nazi abuse. Sol, therefore, had a grudging respect for him. Toward the end of their conversation Sol reminded Rosensweig of the bread he was still owed: "You took my potatoes. I gave you what you wanted, but you never delivered your part of the bargain."

Rosensweig laughed. "You are right, you know, but it wasn't my fault. It would have been much easier on me if the Germans had not shipped me away." In lieu of the promised bread, Rosensweig removed his wristwatch, insisting Sol take it. Sol hesitated, but Rosensweig was firm. "This should be a fair exchange," he said. They visited a while longer. Rosensweig said that he and his wife were living nearby and invited Sol to their home. Sol thanked him, but said he had to be on his way. They wished each other well and parted with a promise to maintain contact in the future. Sol rode off, glad to know that Rosensweig too had survived.

During the summer of 1945, many of the survivors left the camps to try to rebuild their lives. Some set out for their prewar homes in eastern Europe, expecting to be allowed to return to their former houses, live in peace with their neighbors, and resume their lives as if nothing had ever happened. Several Polish Jews, preparing to return to Poland, asked Sol to join them. But Sol remembered all too well the bullying, humiliation, and discrimination inflicted by the Poles; he wanted no part of it. He chose to remain in Buchloe for the time being, hoping eventually to work out his destiny in the West. Much later Sol heard on the refugee grapevine of the anti-Jewish riots that had erupted in scores of Polish cities already virtually devoid of Jews. Hundreds of other Jews faced more immediate dangers when they returned to their hometowns and villages. They found strangers living in their homes and their possessions confiscated. In town after town, Jews who had survived the Holocaust were murdered by Poles for no other reason than the fact that they were Jewish. Sol realized that his premonitions had been correct; he would never go back.

That summer, too, Sol made the important decision not to face the future alone. He wanted to be with Tola always. Sol proposed, and Tola accepted; they set the date for their wedding on November 9, 1945. As Sol had no money, he went to the Mayor of Buchloe and told him he wanted to get married. He asked the Mayor and several Jewish soldiers he had become friendly with for assistance, inviting all of them to the wedding. All those he approached agreed enthusiastically to help; the Mayor gave Sol extra ration cards to obtain meat and eggs, and the G.I.'s promised barrels of beer, wine, and whiskey from the base Post Exchange. Sol then contacted some survivors at the Displaced Persons' Camp in Landsberg who had formed a band. They agreed to play at the wedding at no charge. Sol also prevailed upon a Romanian Rabbi from the camp to perform the marriage ceremony; in his case, Sol promised payment in the form of a fur coat which he had taken from a nearby warehouse holding plunder the Nazis had stolen from their victims. Sol's good friend, Henek, already married to Helen, promised to organize the cooks to prepare the donated food. Helen offered Tola her wedding dress, and a German restaurant in Buchloe volunteered its facilities. All arrangements for the wedding were concluded on little more than handshakes, with no money exchanged. Everything fell into place, and the wedding went off as planned. Only the weatherman refused to cooperate. The day of the wedding, a light snow began to fall; nevertheless, the ceremony took place outside the Gasthaus Kroner restaurant on Ludwigstrasse with the entire Jewish community of roughly two dozen people in attendance.

After the wedding, Sol and Tola moved into the second floor apartment of one of the most imposing homes in Buchloe. The two-story stucco building was in perfect condition and was located on the main street in the center of town at Banhoff Strasse 40. It was within walking distance of all the stores where they shopped. Indeed, the Rosenbergs couldn't have asked for a better location.

The apartment was tastefully furnished; it had a comfortable bedroom with a tall armoire, as well as a living room which contained a large pine table, four chairs, a sagging sofa, and two easy chairs. Large windows, which overlooked the street, allowed in the sunlight, giving the apartment a bright and cheery atmosphere. For Tola and Sol, starting their life together under such favorable circumstances was like a dream come true.

The apartment was owned by a former member of the Nazi party, who continued to live downstairs. Mr. Busch had been given explicit orders by the American military to provide rent-free housing to the Rosenbergs for as long as they wished to stay. The Busch family owned a profitable butter factory and thus was able to afford the spacious home. Given the circumstances of Sol's arrival and his background, it is surprising that Busch and the Rosenbergs learned to coexist. While their relationship was not warm, it was tolerable and open. Indeed, over the course of the next few years, they actually became friends.

The Army also provided Sol and Tola with used bicycles, which they used to run errands. Indeed, with means of transportation, both were able to find jobs quickly. Sol and Tola both obtained work with the Americans. Tola worked in the nearby base Military Exchange and Sol began the first of a variety of jobs with the army. Initially he worked as a cook on the army base in Buchloe, where he assisted in preparing and serving meals for the 702nd Tank Battalion of the Third Army. After this unit was shipped to Japan to join the occupation forces there, he worked with the constabulary units out of army headquarters in Augsburg. Then, he was recruited to help expose SS officers and former Nazis for their war crimes. Sol was issued nondescript civilian clothing and sent out to mix with the local populace in order to learn the identity of any Nazis who had gone underground. Operating under a security clearance, Sol obtained several leads which he reported to his supervisor, an Army Lieutenant in Augsburg. Indeed, he identified several former Nazis in the area who were immediately picked up for questioning. However, disillusionment quickly set in after all the former Nazis were released without explanation.

Sol soon realized that the Cold War had begun, and the former enemies, the United States and Germany, were being forced by circumstances to cooperate with each other. His work, however, although it was not acted upon, did impress American intelligence. They offered to send him to Czechoslovakia for further training in the Russian language and in espionage tactics. Sol refused as he did not want to leave his wife.

It was during this period that Sol realized a longtime dream. A Jewish soldier surreptitiously gave him a pistol, a 45 caliber, to carry with him for protection. Sol took lessons at the military firing range until he became proficient in its use. Sol's only regret was that he had not had a weapon like this with which to protect his family during the worst days of the occupation.

In 1946, in order to augment their income, Sol and Tola formed a business partnership with Henek and Helen and a German civilian in Buchloe. They opened a small fruit stand; they purchased produce from local farmers and sold it retail to the military commissaries and to civilians. Working two jobs was tiring for Tola and Sol, but they shared the hours with each other and with their associates, and the extra income, although small, compensated for the demanding work days.

That year, too, Sol registered with immigration to come to the United States. Living and working in the American sector of occupation, Sol had grown comfortable and familiar with Americans and their way of life. Moreover, America represented freedom, security, and opportunity, three qualities he had not known during the war and which were now important in his hopes for the future. While Sol was not fluent, his English was improving daily, and he could understand and communicate in the language. After filling out the papers and going through the interview process, he began the lengthy wait which he hoped would result in his leaving Europe forever.

In so doing, Sol made the conscious decision to cut himself off permanently from his native Poland. He had tried to repress the memories of his family's suffering, but he was still tormented by anger at his countrymen for their collaboration with the Nazis. He had no desire to reestablish links with his past. He wanted to get as far away from Europe with its haunting memories as possible. Thus, after much deliberation, he renounced his Polish citizenship, classifying himself as stateless. He now had no citizenship, no homeland. In repudiating his origins and trusting his fate to the future, Sol was strongly influenced by the fact that Tola was expecting their first child. Sol wanted to leave the blood-soaked fields of Europe behind in order to give his wife and future children the benefits of a fresh start in life. Only then could the psychological and emotional trauma he and Tola had endured begin to heal.

In the meantime, tensions were reaching the boiling point in the Middle East. The survivors in the Landsberg Camp and nearby Buchloe followed the unfolding events closely. Clandestinely, Jews began to leave the camp, taking a roundabout route to the

Promised Land in order to avoid the British blockade. Many of the survivors were smuggled into Palestine through an underground network. In fact, several of Sol's friends left.

One evening, Sol was approached by representatives of the Irgun, one of several resistance groups then operating in Palestine. Sol had followed the activities of this group closely, especially since it was headed by his old mentor, Menachim Begin. The agents told Sol that they needed a dynamite specialist and Sol's background in munitions made him an ideal candidate. Urging him to join the exodus, they outlined an evacuation route which would take him to Marseilles and then by ship to Haifa. Sol was interested and inquired whether Tola could accompany him. The Irgun representatives, however, answered that this would be impossible; the trip was too dangerous for a pregnant woman. She could join him later after the fighting was over. Sol emphatically turned the Irgun down unless his wife, now three months pregnant, could accompany him. He would not, he said, leave without her. He could not permit himself, however briefly, to be separated from his wife. He had no family now except for Tola and could not think of life without her. Subsequent requests were also firmly rebuffed. Sol remained in Buchloe, although with mixed emotions; yet, he never doubted that he had made the right decision. He desperately wanted to be part of the birth of the new state of Israel and knew every able-bodied man was needed. However, he could not leave at the expense of his wife and unborn child.

On May 30, 1947, Tola gave birth to their first child, a son they named Joe. Sol quickly filled out the additional paperwork on Joe and had his new son photographed. The forms and photos were sent to the United States Consulate to update and complete the application forms required for immigration. Following Joe's birth, the Irgun renewed their appeal, but Sol was now obsessed with going to America and did not want to jeopardize this opportunity.

Months passed with no word from the United States. Sol's life centered on his home and family; he continued working at two jobs and tried to wait patiently for confirmation that his papers were in order. As the months turned into years, he became impatient and concerned. Finally, three years after he had begun the process, in June 1949, Sol received word that his application for immigration had been approved; at long last he received the coveted visas for America.

That night they celebrated the good news. In spite of all the uncertainties he and Tola faced, Sol had no doubt they would have a better life in the New World. He quit his job and moved his family to Hamburg. There he was directed to an apartment for displaced persons in the downtown area near the port. The apartment was confining, consisting of only one room, with kitchen and bathroom facilities shared with another family. Sol had saved some money from his jobs and carefully budgeted his expenses to make his funds last as long as possible.

The wait for a military ship with space for refugees lasted far longer than they had expected. As weeks turned into months, their patience was soon exhausted. Adding to their frustration was the inadequate nature of their housing and lack of privacy. Sol checked the ship departures daily, but returned to the apartment disappointed. Just as his meager savings were almost depleted, Sol finally received word that the *General Samuel Sturgis*, a merchant marine ship, was departing for New Orleans in December 1949, and would take the Rosenbergs aboard. Joyfully, he ran back to the apartment to share the exciting news with Tola.

The ship left on schedule, but what was supposed to be a nine to ten day passage stretched into two weeks, as the ship had to circumvent several north Atlantic winter storms. The voyage itself was very difficult for the entire family. Joe came down with measles right before the trip. Fearing that if the ship's captain knew about this he would refuse them passage, Sol covered Joe's blotches with powder. Sol risked taking Joe aboard, although the baby was running a fever, had a serious ear infection, and cried constantly from the pain. However, Sol could not wait any longer. With his patience and savings virtually gone, he could not gamble on a later sailing date. Once the ship was underway, Sol took Joe to the ship's medical clinic for treatment. The ship's physician told Sol that Joe would have to remain in the dispensary until he recovered.

The women, including Tola, were given sleeping accommodations in the Officers' Quarters. By now Tola was pregnant with her second child; nausea associated with her pregnancy was compounded by sea sickness. Sol, together with the other displaced men, ate with the crew, and slept in a hammock in the hold. He also had to work to earn his passage; he was given a daily assignment scrubbing down the walls, decks, and pipes of the ship. When he finished his task, he always managed to find time to visit Tola and Joe.

Sol, too, had to fight seasickness, but he was invigorated by breathing the fresh air up on deck and eating the hearty meals. It was an exciting time for Sol. It was the first time he had been on a ship or even seen the ocean. Moreover, he knew that each day brought him closer to a new life and a new beginning in America; at the same time, each day distanced him from the trauma of his past. As he stood on the deck of the ship at night and gazed out at the moonlit sea, Sol reflected on his life, both past and future. His mood was joyful, but mixed with deep sadness. Life as he had known it had been annihilated and his family had been taken from him. But somehow, by some miracle, he had escaped death and now had begun a new family. Under the most adverse circumstances imaginable, he had won his struggle for survival by the narrowest of margins. Now he had to construct a new life. He pinned his hopes for his family's future on this new life in America. After a two week journey, the Rosenbergs arrived in New Orleans, their dreams finally realized.

Chapter X

Epilogue

Immediately after the war, Sol had no desire to return to Europe ever again. However, after over a quarter of a century, Sol felt the need to confront his past, no matter how painful. In August 1973, accompanied by his son Jackie, Sol traveled to the Dachau Concentration Camp, the last stop on his journey before liberation. In the years since the war, the huge complex, like so much else in postwar Germany, had undergone a thorough restoration; it had been converted into a historical site.

Sol and Jackie arrived early in the afternoon. As they approached the main entrance, Sol wondered whether his return had been a mistake. Crowded around the camp were newly built apartments. Children were playing and families were living out their everyday lives. After entering the camp through the gate, Sol and Jackie walked slowly to the *Apellplatz*, or roll call square, which was dominated by a huge metallic sculpture. The memorial, which seemed to embody prisoners entangled in barbed wire, stood as a silent tribute to the dead. To Sol it symbolized the suffering and misery of the camp. Once inside, Sol walked to what appeared to be the main center of interest, a long building, part of which was once used by the SS to store prisoners' belongings. Another section of the building which had once been used to torture, whip, and hang prisoners now housed photographs of life in the camp and an array of documents covering the camp's history from its beginning in 1933 through liberation by the U.S. Army in 1945. Sol made his way slowly through the various rooms of the museum, taking in all the pictures, stopping at many to relive the events in his mind.

The number of visitors to the camp that afternoon was in the hundreds, and all, like Sol, were deeply immersed in their own thoughts. As Sol walked through the museum, revisiting the scene of so much pain, his mind flashed back to the unbelievable sights he had witnessed there almost thirty years before. Although the setting around the camp had changed, much of the camp was as it had been. The railway sidings had been rebuilt, the crematorium itself was identified and marked, and the darkened gas chamber open to public viewing. However, all but two of the barracks had long since been torn down. Only the concrete foundations on either side of the camp road, or *Lagerstrasse*, remained. Numbered plaques in the ground identified the sites where the barracks once had stood. One barrack had been rebuilt to give visitors an idea of the living accommodations. Sol hardly recognized the simulated barrack, with its empty bunks now stretching row upon row. Visions of living skeletons, crammed one against the other, suffering a slow death from typhus or starvation, kept reappearing in his mind. The mounds of corpses littering the camp were replaced by well-kept landscaping. A stark silence enveloped the site. Other than the photographs in the museum, all vestiges of the violence and slaughter had disappeared. To Sol, the experience was surreal. It was almost as if the events of the past had never happened. The camp had been transformed into a sanitized mausoleum in memory of the countless dead. So many conflicting emotions swirled around Sol: unbearable sadness, desire for vengeance, dismay, and yet gratitude for the gift of life which had been denied so many others. Several hours later, emotionally drained, Sol quietly left the camp. He had come to the conclusion that it was too difficult to relive the past.

Over the years Sol has tried to discover the fate of his missing friends and relatives. He has contacted private agencies, government authorities, religious bodies engaged in refugee resettlement, and attended numerous meetings of Holocaust survivors. He has chased down every lead, pursued every rumor, and allowed his hopes to soar on news of even the slightest bit of information. However, every effort has resulted in a dead-end. Sol was one of the few to survive. Sol's father was one of ten children, and his mother one of four. All were married and most had children. Sol's family of aunts, uncles, and first cousins numbered over fifty people. Of this number, besides Sol, only two first cousins survived: his mother's sister's son, and his father's brother's daughter. In addition, almost all of Sol's friends perished in the Holocaust: his comrades in the Ghetto uprising, his friends at Majdanek, and his co-workers at Skarzysko. Of the many whom he encountered during the years 1939-1945, as far as Sol knows, only a few such as Sam Radoszewski, who befriended him at Majdanek, as well as the Kornhauser brothers and Henek who were with him on the death march to Dachau, managed to survive the catastrophe. Today, Sam lives in New Orleans and he and Sol remain friends. The Kornhausers and Henek also settled in the United States after the war and stayed in touch with Sol. All of the others, Moniek, Fawv, Julek, Schlomo, Moishe, Lolek, and Leon, just to name a few, disappeared without a trace. Although Moniek and Fawv successfully escaped from Treblinka with him, Sol never learned what happened to them after they separated.

Nor did Sol learn until many years after the war the unbelievable number of deaths associated with Treblinka. Of over 265,000 Jews deported to Treblinka from Warsaw, Sol, Moniek, and Fawv were among only a handful ever to successfully escape the death camp. Even more shocking, roughly 15,000 Jews were gassed each day, for a total of 840,000 by war's end.

Sol's tormentors had mixed fates. Moshe Tofee and Naftula Gazle, the sadistic Kapos at Majdanek, were shipped to Auschwitz in the closing days of the war; there they were killed by other prisoners after they learned the two were collaborators. Weinberg, the devious Kapo at Czectochowa, survived the war and emigrated to the United States; Dr. Arthur Rost, the director of Factory C at Skarsysko, was put on trial after the war by an East German Court operating under Soviet auspices and condemned to death for his crimes. Gustav, the "Butcher of Buchenwald," also survived the war. He too was put on trial for war crimes; however, he was acquitted because, in his defense, he argued that his actions and policies safeguarded the lives of many of the orphans in his charge. As for all the others, Germans and collaborators alike, including "Blondie," the notorious murderer who tormented Sol at Majdanek, Sol was unable to locate them or learn of their fates.

It took Sol many years to learn to cope with the haunting memories of six years of terror, oppression, and suffering. For years, he kept his innermost thoughts to himself. He did not reveal his true feelings to others, not because he did not want others to know of the Nazi brutality, but rather because he himself found the memories too painful to deal with. Nor did he think that people who lived routine lives in the United States could begin to comprehend the depths of barbarism resorted to by the Nazis.

Yanked from a civilized world, Sol was thrown into a six year maelstrom. He was given a number, reduced to living as an animal, and stripped of his humanity. He underwent whippings, isolation, deportations, suffering, hunger, forced labor, and the death of his family. Somehow he survived. A combination of factors—youth, physical stamina, fluency in German, luck, timing, and instinct—worked in his favor. But the miracle of his survival is still difficult for Sol to understand.

Mentally and emotionally, Sol refused to succumb. Although physically imprisoned, he refused to surrender his innermost being. There were times when he came perilously close to giving up, but he continued to believe that ultimately he would prevail. The beatings at Majdanek were the turning point.

While many dark days lay ahead, Sol would not let the Germans triumph by his death. It became a personal challenge; he had an overriding will to resist. He would defy the Germans and live to tell of their crimes. However, the crack of a whip, the smell of burning flesh, rifle shots, and hanging scenes are still vivid memories fifty years after the fact.

Sol's religious beliefs also fortified him. He spent countless hours on his bunk at various concentration camps trying to understand how this descent into hell had been possible. He questioned how God could have allowed this unimaginable horror to happen. But, he was afraid to admit he had lost faith, hesitant to blame God for the evil. For to do so would deprive himself of his only source of strength. Indeed, the murder of his family helped to fortify his resolve not to forget his faith. Nobody, he thought, could begin to imagine the suffering he had gone through. So Sol continued to cling to his beliefs. He had to have something to hold on to. The moments of prayer gave him relief and shut out the world. For a few minutes he was at peace and had hope. He never abandoned his faith. The Lord was his salvation, the emotional support that was always with him. Surrounded as he was by death, Sol firmly believed that God was helping him survive every minute, every hour, every day.

Nevertheless, Sol has continued to ask himself how the Holocaust could have happened. He has never been able to arrive at a satisfactory answer. Indeed, after all these years, he still cannot grasp the enormity of the tragedy, nor can he understand why so many were destroyed. Time has yet to heal his wounds. The seemingly senseless murders in cold blood of defenseless unarmed civilians is still incomprehensible to him. Nor can he ever forget his parents, sisters, relatives, and friends who were killed. He still misses them and is haunted by their memories. The pain never leaves him. He has refused to give up hope of locating other relatives or friends, but his hopes are dimming.

In January 1997, Sol's children honored him by hosting a lavish birthday party. His friends, including many community leaders, were invited. My wife and I were honored to be included among his friends. After all, if anybody's life deserves to be celebrated, it is Sol's. Sol and Tola could look back over their almost fifty years in America and be proud of their accomplishments. In a sense, they have fulfilled the American Dream.

They raised five children, three boys and two girls. Although they lost their families in Poland, they were able to transmit the values they learned from their families to their offspring. The boys live in Monroe and help Sol run his business, which continues to thrive. The girls are both registered nurses living in Houston. Sol and Tola also have twelve grandchildren and it is unlikely there are any prouder grandparents anywhere. Nevertheless, as time passes and crucial milestones in his family's life occur—births, graduations, and marriages—Sol cannot forget those who were taken from him.

Sol and Tola have rebuilt their lives in spite of the difficult challenges with which they were confronted in America: the struggle to adapt to a new culture, to learn a new language, and to earn a livelihood. By means of seven-day work weeks, they created a business from nothing, raised a family, and became respected and welcome members of their new community.

Nevertheless, Sol will always carry inside him the suffering he endured. The grief will never disappear even if no one can see the scars. But his very survival is an inspirational testament to human courage. For Sol, each day is a celebration of life. Indeed, merely to be able to tell his story is a triumph of the human spirit.

CPSIA information can be obtained at www.ICGtesting.com
Printed in the USA
BVOW08*0955130616

451211BV00011B/14/P